Additional Praise for *Cultures of Thinking in Action*

"*Cultures of Thinking in Action* is a wonderful book. Unlike too many books for teachers, Ron Ritchhart invites, inspires, and supports educators to think, to examine the why of teaching instead of imposing on them a set of good practices."

—**Yong Zhao, Ph.D.,** Foundation Distinguished Professor, School of Education, University of Kansas and Professor in Educational Leadership Melbourne Graduate School of Education

"Ritchhart's newest book gets to the heart of one of society's most pernicious problems—how to meaningfully improve education—by helping teachers and administrators understand the social and cultural 'why's' behind the procedural 'how's' of pedagogical practice. *Cultures of Thinking in Action* is essential reading for anyone genuinely interested in building schools that effectively support children's learning."

—**Mary Helen Immordino-Yang,** Director, Center for Affective Neuroscience, Development, Learning and Education and Professor of Education, Psychology & Neuroscience, University of Southern California

"No one has thought more about how to teach for good thinking than Ron Ritchhart. Drawing on decades of experience and multiple bodies of research, *Cultures of Thinking in Action* offers wisdom, guidance, and inspiration for any teacher grappling with the 'why' and 'how' of classroom teaching."

—**Jason Baehr,** Author of *Deep in Thought: A Practical Guide to Intellectual Virtues*, co-founder of Intellectual Virtues Academy of Long Beach

T0243407

Cultures of Thinking in Action

Cultures of Thinking in Action

10 MINDSETS TO TRANSFORM OUR TEACHING AND STUDENTS' LEARNING

Ron Ritchhart

JB JOSSEY-BASS™
A Wiley Brand

Published by John Wiley & Sons, Inc., Hoboken, New Jersey.
Published simultaneously in Canada.

For general information on our other products and services or for technical support, please contact our Customer Care Department within the United States at (800) 762-2974, outside the United States at (317) 572-3993 or fax (317) 572-4002.

Wiley also publishes its books in a variety of electronic formats. Some content that appears in print may not be available in electronic formats. For more information about Wiley products, visit our web site at www.wiley.com.

Library of Congress Cataloging-in-Publication Data is available:

ISBN 9781119901068 (Paperback)
ISBN 9781119901082 (ePDF)
ISBN 9781119901075 (ePUB)

Cover Design: Wiley
Cover Images: © naihei/Shutterstock; © Artos/Shutterstock
Author Photo by Max Woltman

SKY10082124_081624

To my father, who has always been my biggest supporter and who steadfastly reads all my books, not because he will necessarily use the ideas, but because he loves me.

CONTENTS

LIST OF FIGURES

LIST OF QR CODES

ACKNOWLEDGMENTS

This book has been years in the making. Although some of the ideas explored here were present at the very beginning of the cultures of thinking project in 2005, they have since grown, developed, transformed, expanded, and taken on new resonance over the years through my ongoing work with schools and teachers around the world. In these settings, I have had numerous informal conversations in which new ideas have been sparked and my thinking spurred. Sometimes it was a question a participant asked at a workshop; other times it was an issue a teacher was having that they wanted to explore, or a coaching conversation with a school principal. These moments have consistently fueled my curiosity, deepened my understanding, sometimes challenged me, and always enriched my thinking. These conversations have encouraged me to identify and explore the mindsets foundational to the creation of a culture of thinking. Without those conversations, as incidental, ad hoc, and fleeting as they might have been, this book would not have happened. We develop our ideas through dialogue within a community, not in isolation. So, to all those who have engaged with me in conversation around the joys and challenges of building a culture of thinking, I thank you.

In taking these ideas from merely floating around in my head or in conversation to an actual framework, I am greatly indebted to the generous support of the Melville Hankins Family Foundation, which has nurtured my research for many years. Its funding supported a team of researchers at Project Zero at the Harvard Graduate School of Education. This team spent years digging into the research behind each mindset, looking at case studies, and clarifying what each mindset might mean to students and teachers. A special thanks to the team of Christine Beltran, Natasha Blitz-Jones, Yudith Dian, Hazel Peh, Emily Piper-Vallillo, Catherine Mcconnell, Carolyn Ho, Ursula August, liana Gutierrez, Elyse Postlewaite, Richard Mannoia, and Sean Glazebrook for their dedication in this exploration. Our team was led with great skill by Terri Turner. Terri's curiosity about the world, about children, and about learning motivated and inspired us. Her willingness to ask questions, to puzzle, and look at ideas from new perspectives encouraged our exploration. In addition, her organizational skills, good humor, and sense of community held us together as a team.

The Melville Hankins Family Foundation funding has also facilitated a multiyear collaboration with Mandela International Magnet School (MIMS) in Santa Fe, New Mexico. In this setting, we have been able to explore these mindsets as they were just taking shape in my head and through our research. Most recently the Cultures of Thinking Fellows project (more on this in Mindset 1 and the Epilogue) has provided the forum for teachers' inquiries into how these mindsets can transform teaching and learning. I want to thank our pilot group of CoT Fellows for their willingness to jump into this uncharted space. With much appreciation to Nevada Benton, Dory Daniel, Erin Gaddis, Randy Grillo, John Hise, Virginia Hofferber, Lydia Hogan, Kristine Kamrath, Janssen King, Rachel Langone, Scott Larson, Susanna Mireles-Mankus, William Neuwirth, Ashlee Pagoda, Sairey Pickering, Matthew Rapaport, Christina Romero, Ahlum Scarola, and Terri Scullin.

For over 25 years, I have stood on the shoulders of giants at Project Zero at the Harvard Graduate School of Education, learning from my mentors David Perkins and Howard Gardner. I'm grateful for their guidance and generosity. I have also had the good fortune to work alongside inspirational colleagues Tina Blythe, Mara Krechevsky, and Ben Mardell. Their research in schools continues to inspire me. Throughout this book, I have drawn on examples from their work on the use of protocols, professional learning communities, documentation, play, and making learning visible. I know you will be as inspired by their work as I am.

A special partner in dialogue whom I wish to thank is my longtime friend, colleague, and co-author on two other books, Mark Church. This book would not have been possible without him and is certainly much better because of his involvement. No matter where in the world either of us were, I could always count on Mark to respond to a text, phone call, or email query if I had an idea I needed to talk through. He was, and continues to be, there with good questions, useful insights, and just the right amount of push back and humor to keep me in check. Growing these ideas with such a talented thought partner has been a true blessing. As an early reader of this manuscript, he offered invaluable feedback and editorial assistance that substantively shaped my writing. Joining Mark in offering great editorial assistance and suggestions were my dear colleagues Connie Weber and Julie Landvogt. Having this incredible triad of professional educators and deep readers who were steeped in the ideas of cultures of thinking to read and respond to my writing has been crucial in making this book what it is. Thank you for letting me know when I was hitting the right notes, when things were missing, when more clarity was needed, and when I should have used *effect* instead of *affect*.

Finally, I wish to thank all the teachers who have invited me into their classrooms and shared their teaching with me. Sometimes, I have been able to be physically present; other times, I observed via video, and still on other occasions I was invited into classrooms through our correspondence or the sharing of student work. Their generosity allowed me to write the case studies in each chapter that embody each mindset. Thanks to Susan Osgood, Trevor MacKenzie, Jeff Watson, Kristen Kullberg, Thalia Ormsby, Ravi Grewal, Heather Woodcock, Mean Gretzinger, Kate Mills, Mike Medvinksy, Adam Hellebuyck, Anna Ramirez, Doug McGlathery, and Cameron Paterson.

Finally, I must thank my husband for giving me the space, and at times distance, I needed to immerse myself in writing and put my thoughts into words. I know it's not always easy living with a writer, so thank you for your patience and encouragement. I couldn't do what I do without you.

ABOUT THE AUTHOR

Ron Ritchhart is a world-renowned educator, researcher, and author. For over 25 years, Ron served as a Senior Research Associate and Principal Investigator at Project Zero at the Harvard Graduate School of Education where his research focused on understanding how to develop, nurture, and sustain cultures of thinking for both students and teachers. A strong theme of learning from best practice runs throughout all of Ron's research and writing. Consequently, he spends extensive time in schools and classrooms. Ron's ability to seamlessly merge theory, research, practice, and application together in a highly accessible and engaging manner has made him a bestselling author of numerous books, including *Intellectual Character*, *Making Thinking Visible*, *Creating Cultures of Thinking*, and *The Power of Making Thinking Visible*. After leaving Harvard in 2021, Ron has continued his classroom and school-based research and writing to further the ideas of visible thinking and the creation of schools and classrooms as cultures of thinking.

Ron is a sought-after speaker for his ability to connect with and engage fellow educators in powerful, big-picture ideas, while simultaneously providing useful insights into and practical ideas for advancing the complex world of teaching and learning. This is no doubt, in part, due to Ron's diverse experience as a teacher, which includes teaching elementary school, art, secondary mathematics, undergraduates, and graduate students. Upon Ron's Harvard retirement from the Harvard Graduate School of Education, Howard Gardner commented, "Of all of us at Harvard Project Zero, you have had the most influence on what teachers around the world do in their classrooms and how to talk and think about it."

INTRODUCTION

It's not common for an author to introduce his new book with an apology, but perhaps one is in order on this occasion—for at least some readers. Given the title, *Cultures of Thinking in Action*, you may have picked up this book excited to learn how to "do" cultures of thinking. Perhaps you thought, "Finally, a practical how-to guide that spells it all out step-by-step!" Or maybe you were thinking, "Great, a resource book I can hand teachers to work through how to implement cultures of thinking." To be sure, this book is meant as a resource for all those eager to cultivate a culture of thinking in their schools and classrooms. You will also find that it offers many practical ideas, tools, and resources. However, first and foremost, it is about the "why?" of our teaching. Thus, it is a book meant to spark self-examination and collective reflection with both oneself and with colleagues. My goal is not merely to offer up a new collection of ideas, but to stir reflection that will spark transformation. Who are you as a teacher? What do you believe about teaching and learning? How do those beliefs reflect your stance toward teaching and play out in your classroom? How do these beliefs inform and propel your actions?

It is in those moments when we look critically at our practices and challenge our assumptions that we make the leap from informational learning, focused on learning about something, to transformational learning, the learning that allows us to challenge the status quo and embrace the complexity of the enterprise of teaching and learning (Mezirow 2000). For decades, policy makers, innovators, and administrators have often located professional learning in a set of practices. These folks often assume that if one changes teaching practices, revamps the curriculum, trains teachers in new instructional methods, then schools have been transformed. However, decades of failed efforts and unsustainable reforms have shown that this isn't the case. True transformation resides not at the surface level, the "what?" of teaching or even at the implementation or the "how?" No. True transformation resides in plumbing the depths of the "why?" of our teaching. What are we teaching for? What do we believe and hold true about teaching and learning?

In his writings and popular TED Talk, "How great leaders inspire action," Simon Sinek (2009) explains the relationship between the what, the how, and the why through a diagram he calls the Golden Circle (see Figure I.1). It is common, and perhaps even intuitive, for businesses, leaders, and even teachers to start with the outside of the circle, the practical, the "what" and then perhaps spend time thinking about the "how?" After all, the "what" is so tangible. It's clear to everyone what the group does, makes, or delivers. This can be put on a spreadsheet, shelf, or test. The "what" can easily be translated into a measurable "SMARTT" (specific, measurable, achievable, relevant, targeted, and time-framed) goal or "KPI" (key performance indicator). It also is easy for leaders to manage, track, and oversee.

However, Sinek explains that truly great companies and leaders operate from the inside out. They begin with the "why?' This grounds them in a vision that directs and guides both their current and future work. It provides a sense of mission, purpose, and inspiration. As Sinek explains, Apple

Figure I.1 The Golden Circle.

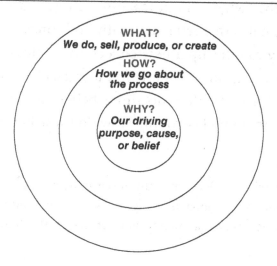

as a company doesn't just make computers (the what); they believe in challenging the status quo, in thinking differently by making beautifully designed products that are simple to use (the why) (Sinek 2009, #947). It is not the "what" that drives their success, extreme customer loyalty, and long lines outside their stores when new products are introduced, but the "why."

By focusing on the "why?" I am not just transporting a popular idea from the business world to schools. There has been a long line of research on the importance of teachers' beliefs, values, and sense of purpose (Calderhead 1996; Thompson 1992). Alan Schoenfeld, professor at UC Berkeley and past president of the American Educational Research Association, conducted a multiyear line of research focused on the beliefs of teachers as central to understanding what does and does not happen in the classroom. His research focused on developing cognitive models that explain and predict teacher behavior (Schoenfeld 2010, #938). When all is going as intended in the classroom, teachers rely on their plans or experience to deliver a lesson—but things rarely go to plan. Students ask questions, make unexpected observations, get confused, have misconceptions, and so on. In these instances, teachers must make decisions. They are no longer merely implementers. Teachers make decisions based on their beliefs and values combined with their repertoire of teaching practices and knowledge of the curriculum. Although the "why?" doesn't act in isolation, it is at the core of the decision-making process. And, of course, conflicts arise. What happens when one's beliefs don't align with one's pedagogical knowledge and skill? These can either represent moments of conflict, angst, and regression or great opportunities for growth and self-discovery.

As part of a study of effective pedagogy conducted by the South Australian government, researchers found that teachers' beliefs and the way they understood their role as teachers were a better predictor of their teaching actions and general pedagogical repertoire than were their age, gender, or years of experience (Atkin 2019, #2155). Furthermore, teachers' epistemic awareness—that is, their awareness of how they understand the enterprise of teaching and the assumptions they are making about their teaching practice and students' learning—was found to be an important factor in promoting teacher growth and change (Atkin 2019, #1866). Teachers who were more epistemically aware tended to reflect on both their practice *and their assumptions*. As a result, they tended to question and probe their beliefs and embrace the complexity of teaching: transformative learning. Such occasions provided them with the opportunity for growth and self-discovery. In contrast, teachers who were less self-aware tended to view teaching as being more about content coverage and control. Although these teachers did reflect upon their practice, they did not question their underlying assumptions about teaching and learning. Thus, they tended to view teaching practices as either working or not working and were more likely to abandon new practices that didn't fit well into their existing repertoire or weren't immediately effective for them.

Through her years of helping schools and teachers foster inquiry learning, my good friend and colleague Kath Murdoch has witnessed the importance of teacher beliefs firsthand. She points out,

"Our beliefs shape our practice. How we perceive our role as teachers has a profound influence on the language we use with students, the way we organize for learning, the design of learning tasks and what we look and listen for as we assess" (Murdoch 2022, p.47). Kath argues that while it is possible to mimic the practices of any particular approach, in her case inquiry learning, such actions tend to be just going through the motions and lack the dynamism that inspires students' learning. She says this approach "simply wallpapers over existing beliefs that are at odds with inquiry, those underlying beliefs will find all sorts of ways to manifest and even unconsciously undermine or sabotage the practice itself" (p. 47).

Others have written about the core beliefs and values people hold as representing their *stance*, thus connoting a physical as well as intellectual orienting. Cochran-Smith and Lytle use *stance* as a deliberate metaphor in order to "carry allusions to the physical placing of the body as well as to intellectual activities and perspectives over time. In this sense the metaphor is intended to capture the ways we stand, the ways we see, and the lenses we see through" (Cochran-Smith 1999, pp. 288–289). Mehta and Fine (2019) use the term to capture the way the teachers they studied for their book, *In Search of Deeper Learning*, viewed constructs key to teaching: the nature of learning, the role of failure, and the ability of their students. For instance, those effective at teaching for deeper learning viewed students as capable creators, failure as critical for learning, and the process of learning as a rich and engaging enterprise. Mehta and Fine also noted that one's stance is contextual. A teacher may engage her advanced students in deeper learning precisely because she saw them as capable creators, but then revert to traditional teaching practices with her lower track students.

My colleague Mark Church has been exploring the importance of a leader's stance in nurturing their school's progress toward a culture of thinking. In our discussions, the two of us have come to see *leadership stance* as being rooted in one's deeply held beliefs and values about how things work, what matters most, and the nature of the enterprise of leadership itself. A leader's stance will determine how they frame problems, see opportunities, and direct their energies. A leader's stance is what motivates and enlivens any set of practices, or conversely robs them of the oxygen needed to develop. The development of one's leadership stance, as with the stance of teachers, is an organic process, growing out of participation in multiple opportunities for conversation, practice, and reflection.

Recently, the term *mindset* has found a prominent place in education. The term is perhaps most familiar to educators from Carol Dweck's work on the way people view intelligence: as growing or fixed (Dweck 2006). Others have taken the term to suggest that our succeess at anything depends on how one views the enterprise: *Inquiry Mindset, Innovator's Mindset, Ultimate Maker Mindset, Creator Mindset, Super Achiever Mindset, Successful Mindset, The Richest Mindset, Alpha Mindset,*

The Inclusive Mindset, The Ballerina Mindset (yes, these are all actual books). Despite its ubiquitousness, I still find the term beneficial. It captures the idea that the way one views and thinks about things matters in terms of shaping our actions and directing our energies. And, as all these books suggest, our mindsets can be examined and thus changed. Furthermore, mindsets are directly tied to and grow out of our beliefs and values, and they position our stance. Thus, I have chosen to use the term *mindset* in this book to talk about the core ideas we as educators must seek to develop in ourselves.

Two experiences in my work with schools further drove home the importance of mindsets for me. At one school the school leaders were desperate to see some take up of these ideas (cultures of thinking and visible thinking) in the mathematics department. Every year they asked the research team to show videos and give examples of "how this can work in a mathematics classroom," and in fact we did just that for well over a decade, but it was all for naught. Our examples were rejected out of hand. They simply didn't fit into the teachers' ideas of what teaching was about or how one learned mathematics. Therefore, our examples were worthless to them. Perhaps even less than worthless as, according to them, they reflected the *wrong* way to teach math: "Where was the direct instruction? The clear explanation and concrete examples? Why wasn't the teacher in the video correcting them and telling them the answer? It's all too slow. I could get twice as much work done in a class period." Their students scored well on state tests through their current methods, so there was simply no need to change. They were focused on the "what," the content of the state exam, and saw no need to go deeper. They were unwilling to uncover, let alone challenge their underlying assumptions about teaching, learning, schooling, the nature of mathematics, or purpose of education. To them mathematics was mastering procedures for the test.

At another school, I was confronted by an experienced history teacher after a professional learning session. He was a bit frustrated and confused by our gathering and asked a simple and straightforward question, "What exactly is it you want me to do?" He was willing to give things a go, to try some new practices, but his experience of professional learning was that you were given things to implement in your classroom. He was unused to the reflection, questioning, and examination he was being asked to do and didn't see the point. How would understanding his students' thinking help him teach history? But at least there was some hope. If I could get a few practices happening in this teacher's classroom, I might be able to leverage them for an examination of his beliefs and assumptions. And in fact, when he visited another school and saw students engaging deeply in debate about history, he did begin to question some of his assumptions about how he was teaching and what students were capable of doing.

This kind of self- and collective examination, reflection, interrogation, and questioning lies at the heart of developing schools and classrooms as cultures of thinking. It cannot be achieved by merely adding on a set of new practices. One must also reflect upon those practices and one's assumptions about teaching and learning. Therefore, although you will find many practical ideas throughout this book, my hope is that they will be neither your starting nor ending place. In writing and structuring this book, I have done my best to ensure this is unlikely to be the case. Our mindsets orient our stance toward teaching, propel our decision making, and motivate our actions. For this reason, the 10 core mindsets of the Cultures of Thinking Project form the conceptual basis of this book. These 10 mindsets are:

1. For classrooms to be cultures of thinking for students, schools must be cultures of thinking for teachers.
2. We can't directly teach dispositions; we must enculturate them.
3. To create a new story of learning, we must change the role of the student and teacher.
4. Students learn best when they feel known, valued, and respected by both the adults in the school and their peers.
5. Learning is a consequence of thinking.
6. Learning and thinking are as much a collective enterprise as they are an individual endeavor.
7. Learning occurs at the point of challenge.
8. Questions drive thinking and learning.
9. The opportunities we create for our students matter to their engagement, empowerment, and learning.
10. We make thinking and learning visible to demystify, inform, and illuminate these processes.

The strength of these 10 mindsets is that all are drawn from our two decades of effort helping schools and teachers grow into cultures of thinking. Furthermore, each has a strong research base drawing from the literature on cognitive, developmental, and social psychology, as well as from studies connecting to sociology, leadership, and the field of philosophy. Although I do not present an exhaustive review of all the literature connected to each of the 10 mindsets, I strive to provide an overview of key points and accessible ideas that can ground one's thinking about them and provide a foundation for action.

No doubt these 10 mindsets won't strike you as wholly new or original. The convergence between the ideas presented here and the work being done by others (for instance, work on "Deeper Learning" done by the Hewlett Foundation, the work on "Questioning" done by The Right Question Institute, or the many efforts around social and emotional learning) is a key strength that can create synergy, connection, and coherence while attesting to the general salience of the ideas to our current time as educators. Another quality that makes these ideas powerful is their relevance and broad applicability across subject domains, cultural contexts, and institutional levels. They are as germane to a secondary science teacher in Santa Fe, New Mexico, as they are to a kindergarten teacher in Kobe, Japan. Because I hope that these mindsets will become more than just words on the page, that they become part of your professional stance, each chapter is structured to promote examination, reflection, and discussion as well as action. I encourage you to engage in such reflection and examination on your own as you read. In addition, if you have the opportunity to read and reflect with colleagues, this can be extremely fertile ground for promoting even deeper learning.

Reworking Simon Sinek's Golden Circle (see Figure I.2), I have conceptualized each chapter expanding from the center:

Figure I.2 The Golden Circle as an outline for this book.

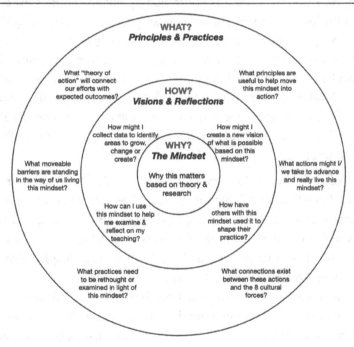

Each chapter begins with a statement of the mindset and an exploration of why it matters to us in the Worldwide Cultures of Thinking Project (Ritchhart 2022). **Why** should it constitute one of our core values as educators? What key ideas or concepts are embedded in or are an important aspect of this value? This is followed by an examination of what research has to say about how this mindset benefits teachers, students, and schools. This core provides us as educators with an anchoring place from which we can then survey the surrounding landscape of both what currently exists and what further actions we might want to try.

From this stance, I invite readers to look outward and consider **how** this mindset might orient and inform one's action. This orientation has three components: First, you are asked to *envision* this mindset as being realized and to capture images, stories, and metaphors that will ground your vision. Second, an examination of two *case studies* drawn from either my own experience or the research literature is presented to expand your view of how it might look when realized. Third, you are invited to orient the mindset with regards to your current practices by critically *reflecting* on your teaching and/or leadership.

Next, I turn your attention to an examination of the current state of things in your classroom and school. To accomplish this, you will need to collect some *street data* to inform your efforts. One might contrast street data with the satellite data often used in schools. Satellite data seeks to measure, compare, evaluate, score, and label, often in a hierarchical manner. Such data typically is removed from our lived experience and is controlled by outside entities. In contrast, street data seeks to understand the lived experience of teachers and students. It is often qualitative and experiential, though it can be quantitative. Street data resides not only in how or what one collects but in the way one draws meaning from it. As Shane Safir and Jamila Dugan explain, "Street data embodies both an ethos and a change methodology that will transform how we analyze, diagnose, and assess everything. . . . It offers us a new way to think about, gather, and make meaning of data" (Safir and Dugan 2021, p. 2). As educators, we make use of street data to make sure that any actions we take will fit our context and help us avoid mindless implementation or the "wallpapering over" that Kath Murdoch warns us about.

The final section of each chapter focuses on *what* we as educators can do in our classrooms to advance the mindset. Even though this section is focused on "the what" and aims to be practical, it will be important that one's actions not just be related to the mindset being examined but grounded in key *principles*. Identifying underlying principles helps one understand why an action may be useful as well as helps to identify other possible actions. With these principles identified, you are then ready to explore *actions* you might take. I connect these actions to the 8 cultural forces (see Figure I.3) so that readers can better understand how these actions work as culture builders. Before rushing to put these actions in place (remember this isn't your basic "how-to" book), it will be useful to identify what current actions are already happening in your school or classroom. Being thoughtful as educators requires us to attend to the coherence of our actions. Are there things one needs to stop doing? Are there practices that need to be abandoned, rethought, cultivated, or built upon? What barriers exist to moving forward on the actions and how might those be cleared away?

Our collective examination of each chapter's mindset concludes by formulating a *theory of action* (City, Elmore, Fiarman, and Teitel 2009). A theory of action sets a plan in place. It identifies what one aims to do, as well as how one will know when they are successful. Consider a fire chief deciding

Figure I.3 8 cultural forces.

The 8 Forces that Shape Group Culture

Language
Directs attention and action. Our words not only convey an explicit surface meaning, but also impart a set of deeper associations and connections that shape thought and influence behavior. Our words matter. **How can we use language to notice, name, highlight, and reinforce what is truly important?**

Opportunities
Serve either to constrain or enhance the activity of both individuals and the group as a whole. In a strong culture, rich opportunities for growth, advancement, and creativity are prominent. **What kinds of opportunities are we creating for our students?**

Expectations
Influence our efforts in relation to the achievement of goals and outcomes. In this way, expectations not only set our course, but also act as an internal compass that keeps us moving toward our goal. **What are our expectations for our students?**

Routines
Represent a set of shared practices that constitute a group's way of doing things. They are the classroom infrastructure, guiding much of the activity that happens there. Ultimately, routines become patterns of behavior for both individuals and the group. **What ways of thinking do we want to develop as a pattern of behavior in our classroom?**

Time
Allocations reflect our values. Our sequencing of events, construction of moments, and reflections on actions allow us to scaffold and draw a connecting thread through learning occasions to create unity. Time is an investment. What is worth investing time in?

Interactions
Form the basis for relationships. They knit together the social fabric that binds us together in community. The interactions among group members define the emotional climate, tone, or ethos. **How are we showing an interest in and respect for students' thinking?**

Modeling
Operates on both an explicit and implicit level. Explicitly, we demonstrate techniques, processes, and strategies in a way that makes our own thinking visible for students to learn from and appropriate. Implicitly, our actions are constantly on display for our students. **What do our students see of us as thinkers and learners?**

Environment
Is the "body language" of an organization, conveying its values and key messages. The physical environment will dictate how individuals interact, their behaviors, and performance. The physical space can inhibit or inspire the work of the group and the individual. **How are we using the environment as a third teacher?**

to deploy 200 firefighters to the northern edge of a wildfire. The chief is implicitly working from a theory of action: "If we deploy 200 firefighters to spray fire retardant and dig trenches on the northern edge of the wildfire, then we will be able to contain the fire and keep it from spreading northward." Success is not determined once the firefighters have been deployed as the chief commanded, but only after the result, containment, has been achieved. If the desired outcome is not achieved, then the situation is reviewed: Why didn't that work as expected? Perhaps the winds were too strong. Perhaps the firefighters were too tired due to long hours of work. Perhaps crews had problems with equipment or supplies. A new plan of action is then determined based upon what was learned to better achieve the desired result. So too, our theory of action around each mindset establishes what we will do and specifies the outcome by which we will measure our success.

Because some readers will dip in and out of this book and not necessarily read it chapter by chapter, I have tried to make this as easy to do as possible by keeping a common format for each chapter as previously described. This means you will notice some familiar language as I introduce various sections and try to orient the reader. I have highlighted such sections in shaded boxes to alert you that this is a common introduction you may have read before but may nonetheless find helpful to read again if you have stepped away from your reading for any length of time.

I have written this book to encourage you to work from the inside out. My hope is that you will use it to examine your assumptions and beliefs about teaching and learning as a means of setting your anchor as a teacher and to lean into your values even as you may feel yourself buffeted by change. To be sure, this journey is not for the faint of heart. As Carlina Rinaldi of Reggio Schools wrote: "Sometimes we move so quickly through our lives we lose the courage of meeting ourselves. What are you doing? Where are you going? This courage to listen, this attention to what is inside ourselves is a sort of interior listening and reflection." So, while you may be initially disappointed that the long-hoped-for, how-to-do-it handbook for implementing a culture of thinking isn't what you are holding (again my apologies), I hope it represents so much more: not merely the instructions for implementation but inspiring guidance for transformation.

For Classrooms to Be Cultures of Thinking for Students, Schools Must Be Cultures of Thinking for Teachers

It is no coincidence that I have chosen to give this mindset top billing on our list. It is the launching pad from which all substantive efforts to create cultures of thinking in schools must proceed. On a personal level, this mindset informs the stance I take in my initial conversations with schools and school leaders interested in taking on this work precisely because it lays the foundation for any program of professional learning that we might design. To understand this mindset, we need to first understand the concepts of *informational learning, transformational learning,* and *institutional mirroring.*

When speaking with school leaders for the first time, I always strive to convey that the work of developing a culture of thinking is not about "training" teachers in one-off workshops, but engaging them in ongoing, embedded learning over time. We must step out of the old, dominant paradigm of *informational learning*; that is, the learning that primarily focuses on increasing our knowledge and skill level in a merely additive way. Frequently the goal of such learning is to fix problems or weaknesses in short order by training up teachers in a set of new practices. In informational learning, the goal is to put these practices in place (often as quickly as possible) rather than seeing them as mere tools to help one achieve some greater vision and purpose. Indeed, too often the tool becomes the vision in such trainings. For instance, teachers in a workshop may learn how to implement new assessment practices without ever examining what one is trying to achieve through those practices, how they fit into the ecology of the school, are contextualized by one's teaching practices, or related to one's views of learning. However, when such underlying issues are not fully addressed, the practices being implemented will necessarily lack a strong footing. Consequently, they may be abandoned quickly if they ever take hold at all. Thus, the flurry of activity around the practices imparted in the training may not achieve any lasting change.

Working within the paradigm of informational learning, leaders often assume that more is better, creating a full plate of professional offerings to skill up teachers. Teachers may even respond positively to such efforts, speaking about a workshop as being useful, practical, giving them something they can use, focused on the nuts and bolts of teaching, and so on. Although such efforts can have their place and be of value, the problem is that informational learning rarely goes very deep and is often fleeting. Estimates are that the implementation rate for such programs is only around 10% (Knight 2007, p. 10). Furthermore, informational learning cannot produce the substantive change and rethinking of schooling we seek when we talk about creating cultures of thinking. This requires transformational learning.

Transformational learning calls on us to question the assumptions that undergird our practice through participation in constructive discourse with our colleagues (Mezirow 2000). It is about examining and revising our practice in fundamental ways as opposed to merely adding on to it. To be sure, transformation, deep learning, and substantive change are complex endeavors. Therefore, we must support educators in embracing this complexity by providing opportunities to inquire into their teaching practice within a rigorous, challenging, and nurturing community of professionals, professionals who are willing to take risks and question the status quo themselves. Such inquiry communities move beyond a soft collegiality "in which care is taken not to cause offense" and toward the tough collegiality that allows for hard questioning of our collective practice and is grounded in a willingness to explore other perspectives (Humes 2007).

To accomplish this shift from the purely informational to the transformational (see Figure 1.1), we must develop dialogic structures while providing ongoing, protected time for substantive interchange and reflection. As opposed to a discussion in which ideas and proposals

Figure 1.1 Informational versus transformational learning.

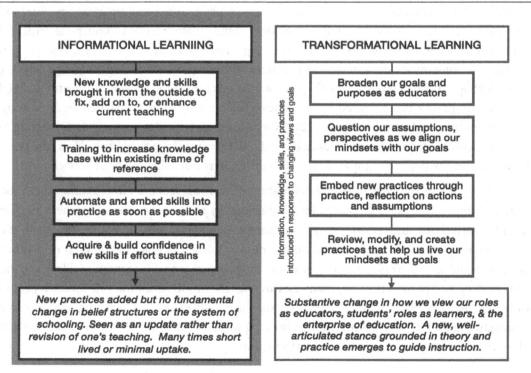

are bandied about with the goal of reaching an outcome, a dialogue brings us together in joint inquiry to build understanding. "In dialogue participants explore complex, difficult issues from many points of view. Individuals suspend their assumptions freely. The result is a free exploration that brings to the surface the full depth of people's experience and thought, and yet can move them beyond their individual views" (Interlead 2019). There is a fundamental shift in the way teachers approach such dialogue as well, moving from a stance of proving and justifying one's actions to improving one's practice (Nelson, Slavit, and Deuel 2012). The first is a defensive posture one might assume when feeling threatened or confronted. The second looks at dialogue as an opportunity for growth. The more we develop this capacity in teachers, the more a school will be capable of meaningful change and reinvention (Abernathy 1999; Senge 2006).

To promote and support such dialogue, schools must create a safe and open environment of trust, respect, vulnerability, and authenticity. This will often mean that rather than imposing top-down structures and expectations on the group, a more collaborative structure in which leaders become learners and learners become leaders emerges. Groups may be co-facilitated through informal leadership and a co-construction of agendas and goals, which brings in multiple voices and increases ownership. In such settings, efforts are made to de-privatize teaching so that educators come to view teaching as a collaborative rather than purely individual act (Campbell 2018). In addition, discussion protocols are often employed to focus and slow down conversations, create equity, and facilitate participants' embrace of complexity. Protocols change the free-flowing nature of conversations and may at first be rejected by some. However, their benefit in creating a safe environment for the examination of issues, asking of questions, and challenging of the status quo makes them invaluable tools.

A hallmark of a school culture, whether focused on thinking or focused on running the machine, is often revealed in what I call "institutional mirroring." The idea is that in any institution, people will generally mirror the practices, behaviors, and treatment they experience in their communities when they are interacting with those they supervise or lead. The way teachers get treated as learners and as professionals by their ministries of education, state-level education departments, district-level administrators, and school principals will be mirrored in their classrooms. If teachers are controlled and micro-managed, they will tend to control and micro-manage their students. By the same token, if teachers are encouraged to innovate, collaborate, and inquire, they will tend to promote these same processes in their classrooms. Thus, we need to support teachers in the ways we want them to support their students. For teachers to be able to create a classroom culture in which students think, inquire, collaborate, discuss, take risks, and learn from mistakes, teachers need to experience such learning for themselves.

WHAT THE RESEARCH SAYS: *WHY* DOES IT MATTER?

When we develop cultures of thinking for teachers, we create fertile ground for professional growth and change. In such cultures, teachers "feel safe to be vulnerable, to admit failings or mistakes and to trust that their colleagues are giving feedback in order for them to improve" (Schwartz 2020). When teachers are part of a culture of thinking, they are more likely to engage in rich conversations about learning, including the discussion of problems, strategies, and solutions. Learning then becomes an "ongoing, collective responsibility rather than an individual one" (Opfer and Pedder 2011). In this atmosphere, individuals can take risks and stretch themselves because there is mutual trust, support, and a shared vision (Keay, Carse, and Jess 2019; Piggot-Irvine 2012). What is more, the learning that occurs in such spaces has a much higher rate of implementation in the classroom, 85%, versus the 10% rate for informational learning (Knight 2007).

Transformative Power of Inquiry

Inquiry-based conversations in which teachers work toward making collective meaning of events, data, and experience through constructive dialogue with peers is a fundamental characteristic of a culture of thinking. In these spaces, teachers embrace wondering and grow comfortable with ambiguity and uncertainty. Conversations are alive with conditional language, such as: "I wonder," "maybe," "this might be," "one possibility could be," and so on. Conditional language allows one to remain open to other perspectives, invites a greater sharing of ideas, and avoids early closure and quick fixes (Langer 1997). In contrast, absolute language, such as, "we should," "it is," "we need to," "we can't," and so on, tends to constrict conversation, exclude other perspectives, and force early closure.

The presence of more inquiry-based talk in professional learning groups is linked to teacher's transformative learning, leading to substantive changes in teaching practice (Cochran-Smith and Lytle 2015; Nelson et al. 2012; Schon 2010). However, this kind of talk is not the norm in most schools. Nelson, Slavit, and Deuel (2012) found that teacher conversations in schools ranged from disconnected, connected, exploratory, to inquiry-based. The connected conversation was the most prevalent. In connected talk, "The presentation of ideas tends to be authoritative or as statements of fact, and questions are usually logistical, procedural, or technical. Differing perspectives, if recognized, are seldom questioned, tested against evidence, or contrasted with other ideas. Conversational turns may be related to each other in short sequences as teachers complete a task or report results of an activity" (Nelson et al. 2012, p. 27). Helping teachers move beyond connected talk to more exploratory and inquiry conversations by using conditional language and protocols is both a mechanism and a goal of creating a culture of thinking.

This kind of professional learning, centered on collaborative meaning-making, feels authentic rather than manufactured by outsiders and has been shown to have a positive effect on student achievement (Goddard et al. 2010; Hargreaves and O'Connor 2018; Lara-Alecio et al. 2012). Through such collaboration, teachers are better able to reflect on their teaching practice, allowing them to assess if what they are doing works or if changes are needed (Reeves, Pun, and Chung 2017). However, it is important that this reflection focuses not only on one's actions, but also on the assumptions and beliefs underpinning those actions. Teachers who do this are more likely to employ responsive teaching techniques that help students build understanding (Atkin 2019).

When a culture of thinking exists for teachers, morale improves, and teachers report higher job satisfaction, which contributes to increased gains in student achievement. Unfortunately, this kind of meaningful, sustained collaboration among teachers is too rarely found in schools (Sarisohn 2018; Schwartz, 2016). Without time and opportunities to learn together, discussions centered around student learning simply don't occur. This inevitably leads to less teacher learning and a decline in the quality of instruction (Burgess, Rawal, and Taylor 2021; Goddard, Goddard, and Tschannen-Moran 2007; Myers 2018).

Institutional Mirroring

In a culture of thinking, innovation, creativity, and experimentation are the norms. Risk-taking is necessary to drive innovation and transform schools (Le Fevre 2014). As Deborah Meier has said, "Taking on risk and being more daring is a real important part of creativity." To build a classroom culture that encourages student risk-taking, teachers need to demonstrate their own willingness to try new things. However, teachers tend to be risk-averse for various reasons, including the fear of being ostracized and the fear of public failure (Le Fevre 2014). Therefore, a supportive school culture that embraces teacher inquiry and innovation is important in helping teachers feel safe enough to take risks. When teachers explore and experiment with new ideas that may not always work, students observe how their teachers react and adapt. Thus, students learn the value of failure, understand that learning is a lifelong process, and accept that mistakes are a natural part of that process (Mizell 2010; Schwartz 2016).

The importance of teachers' own learning mirroring the type of instruction we want to see in classrooms has been well documented (Borko 2004; Wei, Darling-Hammond, Andree, Richardson, and Orphanos 2009). This is particularly true when the focus is on helping students to develop new and more powerful ways of thinking (Gadge 2018). If teachers are to engage their students in any thoughtful action—inquiry, deep learning, problem solving, close looking, complex analysis, or metacognition, for example—then they need to delve into these practices themselves. They need to experience these various approaches first as learners before they can attend to them as teachers. This allows them not only to see the power of these methods, but also to understand them from the inside out, developing empathy for their students as learners. This results in the kind of authentic implementation that can influence student learning (Greenleaf et al. 2011).

Mirroring extends beyond teachers' initial learning, however. The learned practices, approaches, and ways of thinking must also be sustained in the ongoing lives of teachers at a school if they are to make their way into the classroom in a sustained way. Researchers in Ontario, Canada, found that teachers who experienced rich professional learning around cooperative learning were, nonetheless, unable to sustain their efforts unless their school culture was one that employed these same practices among the teachers (Hargreaves and O'Connor 2018). Thus, if school leadership felt the new learning was just a "training" designed to add new skills to a teacher's repertoire and not also for the learning of adults in the school, the new practices languished. In our own work, we have seen that when school leaders view the practices related to creating a culture of thinking as important to them personally in their work with teachers, a culture of thinking is more likely to take hold in classrooms.

VISIONS AND REFLECTIONS: *HOW* MIGHT IT LOOK?

What might a culture of thinking for teachers at a school look like? What might it feel like? How can we imagine a new reality beyond what currently exists? To help us formulate such a vision, we first tap into our own experience, then we reflect on the current state of professional learning and collaboration at our schools.

Constructing Our Vision

We have all been members of cultures of thinking at one time or another. Perhaps, for you, this was when you were part of a study group, book club, professional organization, workshop, or graduate class. Think back to a time when you were a part of a group in which your individual thinking as well as the group's collective thinking was valued, visible, and actively promoted as part of your ongoing and regular experience. Identify one specific group that fits this description. Make sure it is a group you were a member of rather than its leader. Recall what it was like to participate in that group. Think about how that group felt when you were a part of it. *Write down at least five adjectives that capture your feelings of the group.* Feel free to use the pages at the end of this chapter, the margins, a sheet of paper, or your electronic device.

Having your responses recorded in some way will help you create a vision. Now, think about how that group functioned, the activities it engaged in, the way time was spent. *Identify and record at least five actions or verbs that characterize the way the group functioned and acted.* Finally, see if you can *come up with a metaphor, image, or symbol that captures something important about the group. Record that as well.* Guided imagery and reflection on our experience help us to construct a vision of what is possible. Elements and practices from our own experience can be used not only to reassure us that creating a culture of thinking is possible, but also to fuel our imagination and identify our wants and desires for the future we are working toward.

Group Discussion

If you are reading this book with others, bring your lists, writings, and perhaps drawings to share and discuss.

➤ What does your collective compilation reveal about important practices and features of a culture of thinking?

➤ What commonalities do you notice in people's reflections?

➤ What new ideas emerge from other's experience that you hadn't considered but are now intrigued by?

Contemplating Pictures of Practice

To further extend your vision of what a culture of thinking for teachers might look like, the forms it might take, and how it might feel, we now examine two pictures of practice that exemplify some key elements and important practices in developing a culture of thinking for teachers. Keep in mind these are not templates, but examples to inspire. How do these connect to your own professional experience? How do these connect to what is currently happening at your school?

Case One: A Workshop With Donald Graves. I remember a writing workshop I attended as a new 3rd-grade teacher led by Donald Graves. Don was not just a pioneer in literacy instruction; he was a revolutionary. Many credit him with transforming the way writing is taught throughout much of the Western world. His book, *Writing: Teachers and Children at Work* (1983), clearly located teachers as learners with their students. While I don't remember much of what Don actually "said" at the workshop, I do remember engaging in writing and reading. A lot. Every day. For sustained periods. I also remember conferencing about my writing and discussing my reading with colleagues. It was scary to do this the first time, and I felt very vulnerable. What would others say? What if my writing was just bland and banal? Throughout the week, everything we did mirrored what he was asking us to do in our classrooms. He created for us the conditions he wanted us to create for our students. He aimed to move us away from "instructing" students in writing to authentically engaging *with* our students in the act of reading and writing in a mutually joyous and supportive atmosphere. In the process, he helped us to notice and capitalize on the occasions for learning that would emerge from these conditions.

I recall, for some, this felt too slow. They were eager to plan out their year and wanted to be handed tools and structures rather than experience them. It took time for them to embrace the radical authenticity Don was providing us. For the more experienced teachers in the group, it was a radical departure from traditional trainings, but they leaned into it. During the week, I learned to support others and offer ideas to push them and move forward even as they did the same for me. We developed strong bonds of trust emerging from our mutual vulnerability and risk-taking. It's no surprise then that this week-long, summer workshop transformed my teaching. I didn't just learn how to teach writing, but also to think like a writer and support my students in doing the same.

My learning extended beyond my teaching of writing, however. As I engaged my students in the authentic work of readers and writers, sharing my thinking and experience, participating with them in the very processes, I recognized a disconnect with the way I was teaching mathematics. There, I was focused on teaching procedures and having students' practice them. Where was the connection to do the real work of mathematicians? Where was the modeling of thinking and not just the demonstration of algorithms? Surely, mathematics could be taught and learned in a better way. This led me to pursue a master's degree in mathematics education, which reshaped my teaching to revolve around problem solving and investigation. Donald Graves' workshop not only made me a better literacy teacher, but it also made me a better teacher, period. It did this by offering me the chance to challenge many of the assumptions I had about teaching and learning. Assumptions based mostly upon my own experience as a student in school. I would later go on to develop an immersive week of mathematics inquiry for teachers modeled after the Donald Graves' workshop. Once one has experienced a culture of thinking, it is hard not to want to share it.

Case Two: Cultures of Thinking Fellows. In the 2021–2022 school year, 22 teachers from Santa Fe, New Mexico, and Durango, Colorado, began a year-long collaboration as Cultures of Thinking (CoT) Fellows. Teachers joined as teams from their schools alongside a school leader. Fellows came together as inquirers into their own teaching and leading, drawing on the 8 cultural forces and the 10 mindsets for inspiration. The goal was to learn through dialogue, reflection, analysis, and action in a supportive context. Six meetings were held across the school year, hosted by the various schools in the network during the regular school day. Using a Design Cycle to guide inquiry (see Figure 1.2), the group immersed itself in developing both collective and individual understanding of a chosen cultural force the first semester and a mindset (from those discussed in this book) the second semester. Throughout the process, thinking routines and

Figure 1.2 Inquiry Design Cycle.

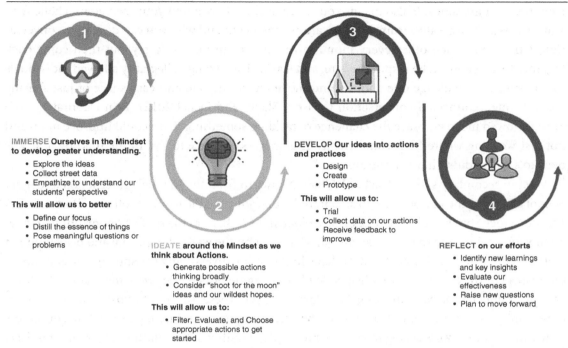

IMMERSE Ourselves in the Mindset to develop greater understanding.
- Explore the ideas
- Collect street data
- Empathize to understand our students' perspective

This will allow us to better
- Define our focus
- Distill the essence of things
- Pose meaningful questions or problems

IDEATE around the Mindset as we think about Actions.
- Generate possible actions thinking broadly
- Consider "shoot for the moon" ideas and our wildest hopes.

This will allow us to:
- Filter, Evaluate, and Choose appropriate actions to get started

DEVELOP Our ideas into actions and practices
- Design
- Create
- Prototype

This will allow us to:
- Trial
- Collect data on our actions
- Receive feedback to improve

REFLECT on our efforts
- Identify new learnings and key insights
- Evaluate our effectiveness
- Raise new questions
- Plan to move forward

Design Cycle for Exploring Culture *of* Thinking *in* Action Mindsets

protocols were used to guide thinking and prompt dialogue. A key aspect of the inquiry relied upon collecting street data, trialing practices, and sharing emerging insights and questions. This culminated in a community-wide sharing event.

Having school leaders join not only deepened the inquiry, but also the commitment. The presence of leaders sent the message that they valued the learning taking place. David Perkins refers to this as "symbolic conduct," that is, conduct that conveys a message beyond just the action itself (Perkins 2002). As one Fellow commented, "It was very helpful to learn alongside our principal because they could clearly see our interests, our attempts, and our goals. It gave us a common language and set the playing field a little more even. This helped us better understand and build empathy for each other." Leaders were also able to leverage the Fellows as teacher leaders at their school.

Working across schools, cities, grades, and subject areas meant that there was an opportunity to challenge perspectives and step outside one's experience. Erin Gaddis, an elementary science specialist from Rio Grande School, remarked, "Seeing the same people over a year is important.

You build up trust, safety, and relationships. You build an interest in other people's goals and learn from their progressions. It also means you are excited to share about your own goals, challenges, and successes. You create a team who you are engaged with and who you can develop a conversation with. Seeing each other every month gives time to think, work, try, but then come back together to get support, be inspired, share, and learn." This strong collegiality allowed individuals to question and challenge one another and move out of the safe and easy space of just sharing ideas through connected conversation (Nelson, Slavit, and Deuel 2012). Erin elaborates, "The group allowed me to embrace the challenge of tackling something that I could improve upon and not just working where I felt comfortable. This was a safe space to live in the unknown. It was okay to say you didn't have all the answers."

Veteran secondary science teacher William Neuwirth from the Mandela International Magnet School also used the opportunity to step into the unknown and learn from others. "Post-COVID I chose to focus on the cultural force of *environment*. I felt this was the perfect opportunity to thoroughly look at how the space was arranged, what went on the walls, the spacing and orientation of tables, where I stationed myself and students in the room, diversifying the sub-spaces, and more." One aspect of the Fellowship that helped William imagine possibilities were the Snapshot Observations conducted at each meeting (see Appendix A). These 10-minute observations were an opportunity to reflect on one's teaching. Rather than judging or evaluating the teaching, observers analyzed what they were seeing to gain a better understanding of the cultural forces and mindsets into which they were inquiring. As Erin put it, "The goal was not to judge, it was to see where we could be inspired and see concepts in practice in real-time, real-spaces, and real-people."

Through his observations, William came to an important realization: "Collaboration and interaction are fundamental to human nature, and when facilitated well, can multiply thinking products." As a result, he began to make changes by creating "a classroom with no straight passageways through, clustering of stations, no front, a center that is open and changeable, with walls showing their thinking." Subsequently he found, "Students took agency. They became more involved in class. Their questioning and ability to connect improved. Keeping the environment open allowed them to step in." You can read more and watch videos of these and other CoT Fellows by scanning the QR Code.

CoT Fellows Program Website QR Code

SCAN ME

Discussion. The preceding cases were well-designed and focused professional learning calculated to immerse teachers in new ways of thinking and to mirror the type of learning teachers were to promote in their classrooms. These opportunities did not occur in isolated PD sessions, however. Professional learning tends to be more effective when it sits within an embedded model of professional learning that allows teachers to inquire into their own teaching, supporting them in learning *through* their efforts (Coggshall, Rasmussen, Colton, Milton, and Jacques 2012; Croft,

Coggshall, Dolan, and Powers 2010; Pacchiano, Whalen, Horsley, and Parkinson 2016). Cohen and Ball assert that the knowledge and skill of teaching are most effectively learned in practice because "Teaching occurs in particulars—particular students interacting with particular teachers over particular ideas in particular circumstances" (2000, p. 10). It is no coincidence then that my week with Donald Graves was followed up with embedded learning facilitated by the Public Education Coalition of Denver and that the CoT Fellows program was conducted over the school year in an embedded way.

Such embedded learning opportunities are sometimes known as professional learning communities (PLCs). There is a wealth of evidence on the power of PLCs to promote teacher learning (Cochran-Smith and Lytle 1999; Stoll, Bolam, McMahon, Wallace, and Thomas 2006; Vescio, Ross, and Adams 2008). However, not all PLCs are created equal. Some are neither truly *professional* in nature, nor clearly focused on *learning*, nor true *communities* of practice. In some cases, they are just a way of grouping teachers for meetings, offering only a soft collegiality that rarely pushes the status quo. For a PLC to support teacher growth there needs to be robust debate, respectful challenging and probing of one's practice, collective responsibility for the learning of colleagues, and a general de-privatizing of teaching (Owen 2014; Owen 2015). In essence, effective PLCs depend upon them being cultures of thinking for the teachers involved. This means incorporating 8 elements into their design. (Ritchhart, Church, and Morrison 2011). All of these were key components in designing the CoT Fellows program. They are:

1. Adequate time for inquiry;
2. Facilitative structures that guide conversations;
3. Common language to talk about teaching and learning;
4. Diverse perspectives so we can break with our assumptions;
5. A bias toward action;
6. Visibility through documentation;
7. Grounding in student work or classroom observations; and
8. A desire to push and challenge ourselves and our beliefs.

Reflecting on Current Practice

While school leaders are often at the forefront of creating a culture of thinking in schools, teachers themselves take an active role by respecting their colleagues, being open to new ideas, and approaching the act of teaching as inquirers. When leaders and teachers have the mindset that creating a culture of thinking is a shared goal, they lay the foundation for the adults in a school to grow, innovate, question, take risks, reflect, examine, inquire, learn from, and learn with one another (Swanson 2014). Teachers are then able to create those same conditions for their students. Consequently, I offer the following two sets of reflection questions. The first set focuses on leaders (principals, coaches, directors of teaching and learning, team leaders, department heads, and others in any type of leadership position formally or informally), and the second set focuses on teachers.

Choosing Questions and Recording Responses

Different questions serve us at different times in our learning. Therefore, I suggest you read through the questions and:

➢ Identify one or two that speak to you now. Questions that might challenge you or take your thinking in new directions.
➢ Identify one or two you would most like to discuss with your colleagues.
➢ Circle and date the questions you select now so you can identify how your focus shifts with time and experience.
➢ Use the blank pages at the end of this chapter or your note-taking device to record your reflections.

Reflections for Leaders

- What are we currently doing to realize/create a culture of thinking for teachers? Be as specific as possible, avoiding generalities.
- What practices at our school are not congruent with this mindset or might be barriers to achieving it?
- How am I, and the school leadership team, modeling what it means to be a risk-taker, innovator, learner? When have I openly reflected on mistakes and new learnings? When have I solicited feedback to facilitate my growth?
- Create a vision of what a culture of thinking classroom would look like: engaged students, curiosity on display, lots of deep questioning, and so on. Now, where and how have you created conditions and opportunities like this for your teachers?

- Where, when, and how are teachers currently observing their colleagues? How much is structured and how much is informal? How might these opportunities be enhanced and supported to go deeper? If I can't answer this definitively, how can I find out?
- What does collaboration look like here? Is it deep, meaningful, and generative, or is it cursory and mostly focused on work alignment? What are my examples to support this assessment?
- Where are opportunities for teachers to drive, shape, and direct their professional learning? To what extent do teachers make meaningful choices in their professional learning? Where and how might we provide more?
- What norms, informal or formal, do we have for our interactions, discussions, and collaborations? If formally stated, how do we hold ourselves accountable? If informal, how is this working? How might we benefit from formally articulating our norms?
- As a leader, what am I spending teachers' time on? To what extent is this time generative and focused on exploring issues of teaching and learning?
- Which teachers at my school have grown the most over the last two years? What accounts for their growth?
- What might be blocking teachers at my school from being more innovative?
- Would teachers see their PLCs as supporting innovation, risk-taking, and growth, or would they say they are more work-focused?

Reflections for Teachers
- How am I currently helping and supporting my school to grow as a culture of thinking for teachers? What specific behaviors and actions can I point to as facilitating this process?
- What practices at our school are not congruent with this mindset or might be barriers to achieving it? How can I help call attention to these and work to change them?
- How am I tapping into the expertise of my colleagues to improve my teaching? Where and when do I seek out feedback, use colleagues as sounding boards, or observe others I want to learn from?
- When was the last time I took a real instructional risk in a desire to innovate, try something new, and disrupt the status quo? What did I learn? What supports do I need for that to happen more often?
- If I haven't taken a risk lately, why not? What is standing in my way? Is that a legitimate constraint or is it more my perception?
- How often am I reflecting on my own practice to better understand the effects of my teaching and the needs of my students? What structures have I found helpful in pushing my reflection deeper? What other structures, routines, or protocols might I try?

- In addition to reflecting on my practice, how am I examining the underlying assumptions directing my actions?

- Which teachers at my school could I talk to or observe who might challenge my preconceived notions of teaching and learning and inspire me to try new things?

- Where and when do I engage in conversations that cause me to question and explore my teaching? What supports me now or might encourage me in the future to be more exploratory and questioning of my teaching?

- How am I growing as a professional this year? What am I getting smarter about? If we expect students to achieve a year's growth in a school year, how am I achieving a year's growth as a teacher?

- How do I use documentation for my own reflection and to better understand my students' learning? Where and when do I share and discuss documentation from my classrooms with colleagues? What structures do or might we use to ensure a deep conversation?

DATA, PRINCIPLES, AND PRACTICES: *WHAT* ACTIONS CAN WE TAKE?

With a clear understanding of why it is important to create a culture of thinking for the teachers at a school that mirrors the culture we want to create with students, as well as a sense of how such a culture might look and feel, we are ready to move into action. Of course, we want our actions to be responsive to our context and help us to advance the culture of thinking beyond what is currently in place. The reflection questions in the previous section can be helpful in this regard. So, too, can the collection of "street data" that helps one understand the current state of things.

Collecting Street Data

Street Data

- ➤ Helps us understand our own context as well as students' perspectives.
- ➤ Is relatively easy and quick to collect.
- ➤ Can be immediately analyzed and acted upon straightaway.
- ➤ Is meant to inform and suggest action.
- ➤ Is NOT an evaluation or measure of success but a snapshot of practice.
- ➤ Can take many forms: observations, interviews, surveys, exit tickets, recordings, and so on.

In constructing any street data activity, consider: What might you learn from this data and how might you use it to inform your next actions? How will this data shed light on the status of things and help identify things that need to change or promising practices you can leverage? There is no limit to the amount of street data one might collect. The important thing is constantly taking stock of where you are both individually and as a school in promoting this mindset that schools must be cultures of thinking for teachers if they are to be cultures of thinking for students. This will allow you to continuously move forward.

Street Data Action One: A Survey of Professional Learning Opportunities. A method we have used in our ongoing work with schools is a survey designed to find out what kinds of opportunities teachers viewed as valuable, what they took away from each, how they might be improved, which have the most impact on teaching, and which had an impact on the culture of thinking being created at the school. You will need to create your own list of all the different types of professional learning opportunities both formal and informal at your school. Note: The key information is what opportunities were deemed most valuable to individuals and to the school culture and why. (See Table 1.1 for an example.)

In our case, we found that teachers greatly valued our opening session, an off-campus retreat, because it was an opportunity to informally reconnect and focus on our mission as opposed to the "work" of school. We also learned that the Snapshot Observations that teachers participated in were valuable because they allowed teachers to discuss real teaching and learn from one another (see Appendix A). These sessions were viewed as fostering reflection and allowing people to raise important questions about their teaching. Both activities were seen as contributing to the overall culture of the school. Coaching sessions, on the other hand, were seen as directly impacting teaching by those who participated in them. However, only a few did. We learned that structured and scheduled opportunities were seen as being more useful because they required people to commit to the learning.

No doubt, your list of professional learning opportunities will look quite different from ours, particularly if you are just starting this process. Perhaps your opportunities fall more into the informational learning realm. If this is the case, consider adding a few blank lines to let teachers identify other, perhaps more informal, professional learning they found beneficial. You might even create an open form in which you ask teachers to identify the five professional learning opportunities across their careers that most shaped them as teachers. In whatever way you frame this prompt, the goal is to gain information on teachers' perceptions of their professional learning to help you plan forward.

Street Data Action Two: Teacher Reflection on Change. We used this street data instrument as part of a large-scale study with hundreds of teachers across multiple districts. It focuses on identifying ways in which teachers' classrooms are changing because of their learning to create a

Table 1.1 Professional learning survey.

Please comment on each of this year's learning opportunities thus far. Name (optional): _____

Name of each professional learning opportunity (formal or informal) in which teachers engaged	What did you find valuable and useful about this experience/opportunity?	What suggestions would you make for further enhancing this as a rich learning opportunity?
Opening Faculty Meeting/ Retreat		
Optional Book Study Groups		
One-on-One Coaching Sessions		
Snapshot Observations		
Pineapple Chart Observations		
Inquiry Groups		
Sharing Carousel		
Guest Speaker		
Reflection Journals		

[1] Please place a star or asterisk * beside the two learning opportunities you feel had the most impact on your teaching.
[2] Please place a check mark ✓ beside the two learning opportunities that you feel contributed the most to creating a school-wide professional culture and common commitment to the goal of creating a culture of thinking.

culture of thinking. We asked a few simple questions and gave teachers 30 minutes to reflect in writing:

1. As a result of your focus on making your classroom a culture of thinking, how are your teaching, your classroom, and your students changing? What specific things might an outside observer notice?

2. What are some differences that might not be immediately obvious to an outsider, but are now evident to you?

We were interested not merely in what ideas and practices were implemented by teachers, but also in their long-term effects. Because we were working with hundreds of teachers, it wasn't possible to get into everyone's classroom. We also felt that teachers themselves were in the best position to identify how their teaching was changing. We decided to focus both on changes that were obvious, what an outsider might witness, as well as those that were less overt but still significant. Teachers identified such things as:

- *My students feel more comfortable sharing, their confidence levels are rising. Listening is another skill that is improving steadily.*
- *Children have a bigger sense of wonder about what is going on in the world around them. And this, in turn, increases their language skills, verbal communication, self-esteem, and confidence, and they are making better choices.*
- *An outside observer might notice that my students are allowed to maintain an engaged chatter in the classroom. There is a freedom for students to ask questions and discuss ideas that, as a less mature teacher, I might have been afraid of in the past.*
- *The children are stimulating each other on a different level. They are dialoguing more and sharing their thoughts about their work more.*
- *My questioning is different, in part, motivated by my interest in my students' thinking. I'm no longer just asking questions I know the answer to.*

Reviewed as a whole, major changes teachers noticed were in students' engagement, conversations, and increased curiosity. Teachers noticed their own movement toward deeper questioning. As a result of this data, we conducted further research into teacher questioning to better understand how it was changing in these classrooms.

Stating the Mindset as Principles for Action

Converting the mindset "For classrooms to be cultures of thinking for students, schools must be cultures of thinking for teachers" into principles for action is a way to further guide and direct one's efforts. Principles tell us what to do in a top-level, overarching way. Specific actions then connect to the principles to bring them to life. Based on a review of the research and drawing on our experience working with schools to create cultures of thinking for teachers, I offer the following guiding principles:

- De-privatize teaching so that teachers can learn from and with each other.
- Shift the types of professional conversations in which teachers engage from being primarily informational and work-focused to conversations that explore and inquire into teaching and learning.

- Prioritize time for teacher learning so that professional learning becomes part of the fabric of the school week and not a one-off event.
- Encourage innovation and risk-taking by normalizing mistakes, learning from practice, piloting new ideas, and designing prototype lessons.

You'll notice that each of these statements begins with a verb to help focus on actions that will set our direction. At the same time, the actions are not very fine grained. They don't spell exactly "what" we might do or the form each will take. We leave that for the next and final section of this chapter.

Possible Actions

There is no single way a culture of thinking for teachers at a school will look and sound. There is ample room for individuals to put their own creative stamp on things and bring in effective practices from other sources. The following actions are:

➤ Drawn from our work in schools as part of the Worldwide Cultures of Thinking Project.
➤ Placed under the related principle to help you focus on the driving motivation behind each action.
➤ Modifiable to fit your local context.
➤ Connected to the most relevant cultural forces to which each specific action is associated. Both frameworks, the 8 cultural forces and the 10 mindsets, are synergistic, and you can begin your journey either place.

De-privatizing Teaching. Teaching can be lonely. Despite being in the presence of students all day, we are generally the only adult in the room. This can make it hard to learn from colleagues and to develop a collective identity as teachers all committed to developing a culture of thinking for teachers and students. When we de-privatize teaching, we strengthen the bonds between teachers, prompt grounded reflection on the complexity of teaching and learning, and create support for risk taking and innovation. To de-privatize teaching, we need to make formal and informal observation in each other's classrooms a common occurrence. We must create space for reflection and questioning of teaching and learning. But how do we accomplish that within the business of schools? Some strategies we have used include Snapshot Observations, Learning Labs, and Open Doors.

Snapshot Observations. Whenever I talk about teachers observing in one another's class-rooms, it is generally received positively. Many mention how much they would like to see others teach. However, in practice, getting teachers into one another's classrooms rarely happens. The reason for this is that our typical model for peer observation is cumbersome and time-consuming. Furthermore, while most teachers want to observe others, only a few want to be observed. Many teachers fear the evaluation and judgment that might occur and so anticipate long hours of prep-aration to design perfect lessons. The Snapshot Observation seeks to upend these two impedi-ments (see Appendix A). As the name suggests, a Snapshot Observation is brief, just 10 minutes, though the follow-up discussion with colleagues can take up to 40 additional minutes. Second, the Snapshot Observation is not meant to evaluate or even provide feedback for the observed teacher. Rather, the Snapshot is an opportunity for the observers to use their observations to reflect on their own teaching and raise questions for examination. It is a mirror in which one can reflect on one's own teaching. The observed teacher is not a part of the conversation, but merely offers colleagues the gift of opening their classroom as the basis for reflective dialogue. Thus, the observation and discussion become easier to schedule. The Snapshot Observation itself focuses teacher attention on *routines*, *expectations*, and *opportunities*. Another cultural force may be cho-sen to add to the focus of the observation. In carrying out the Snapshot, teachers are using a protocol to structure their time and make the most of this opportunity for reflection. They also are developing a common language to talk about teaching and learning.

Learning Labs. Labs are designed to build a sense of collaborative planning, collective own-ership, and communal problem solving around new ideas. A Lab consists of three phases: design, observation, and discussion, which generally occur over three consecutive class peri-ods (see Appendix B). In the design phase, the group collectively plans a lesson focused on content from the host teacher. The idea is to try something new, often a thinking routine (Ritchhart and Church 2020; Ritchhart, Church, and Morrison 2011) as a prototype lesson that can be piloted. The observation is the heart of Lab experience. During this phase, the host teacher carries out the planned lesson. The facilitator of the Lab may also act as a coach during the lesson as needed. Observers act as documenters of the learning, collecting data that can then be discussed later. They are not evaluators, but co-learners with the teacher trying to bet-ter understand students' thinking and learning. In the discussion period, observers share their documentation and explore its implications. The focus is on understanding the lesson design and how it helped to promote students' thinking. All participants reflect on how they might adapt the thinking routine or techniques of the lesson to their own contexts. Relevant cultural forces connected to this action include *modeling* (done informally by the host teacher and by the facilitator acting as a model of reflection), *opportunities* (to plan and reflect with col-leagues), *time* (to engage in teacher planning at the lesson level), *routines* (as the Lab typically focuses on planning and trialing a new routine), and *language* (for talking about teaching and learning).

Open Doors. At the International Academy in Troy, Michigan, the development of a culture of thinking was led by a core group of teachers. They immediately recognized that one of their key goals was to get teachers talking about teaching and learning and the 8 cultural forces. They started an *Open Doors* initiative by hanging a cultures of thinking logo featuring the 8 cultural forces on it outside their doors, indicating that anyone was welcome to stop in and see what they were doing and perhaps have a chat with them later. It was informal and invitational. Others have used charts kept in the staff room to identify teachers who are trying something and are willing to have anyone observe informally. These are sometimes referred to as "pineapple charts" since the pineapple is a symbol of hospitality. Others have used the teacher-initiated #ObserveMe movement as a way of inviting colleagues into their classrooms and soliciting feedback (see Figure 1.3). All 8 cultural forces are connected to this action as the observation is an invitation to step in and observe how the cultural forces are being leveraged. It is an informal opportunity for learning through a naturally occurring model of teaching. There is also the opportunity for conversation and the development of a common language.

Shifting the Conversation. There is a lot of talk and conversation in schools, but is it productive, transformational talk? Is it discussion and debate in which ideas get pushed around, decisions made, and one viewpoint triumphs—or is it dialogue in which our collective meaning is enhanced? Is it nonthreatening sharing that preserves the status quo or does it invite challenging questions that move teachers into inquiry while building strong collegiality (Nelson et al. 2010)? Most importantly, if it is mainly superficial discussion, how do we move toward more of an

Figure 1.3 #ObserveMe.

Welcome

Please come observe.
I'd appreciate feedback on the following goals:

I'm working on the cultural forces of **Language** and **Interactions**
Specifically, I am trying to:

Ask more probing questions to encourage learners to think more deeply.

Please provide feedback on my goals through the QR code. #ObserveMe inquiry-focused dialogue? Tools like protocols from the School Reform Initiative (https://www.schoolreforminitiative.org/protocols) and other places (Allen and Blythe 2015) can be helpful, as can setting group norms or ways of being. However, beware of putting too much weight on the shoulders of facilitators alone. Everyone in a group has responsibility for enabling this shift in conversation.

It can be useful to share the continuum of teacher's dialogic interactions discussed earlier with teachers to raise awareness of different conversational patterns. Nelson, Slavit, and Deuel (2012) identify four types of teacher dialogue: 1) disconnected and distracted talk, 2) connected talk, 2) exploratory talk, and 4) inquiry-based talk (see Appendix C). Teachers recognize that they have been a party to all four types of dialogue at one time or another. Identify the reasons why one might be disconnected in our conversation or only focused on the soft collegiality that characterize the connected conversation. Examine the way such talk limits learning. From this vantage point, examine what exploratory and inquiry conversation can offer us both individually and collectively. Identify how teachers might support one another in getting to that place. It is important that everyone take responsibility for shifting the conversation, not just the facilitator. It is also useful to know what one wants to look for, as well as to avoid, in conversations. Only then can we notice and name those elements as they appear.

In shifting the conversation toward more complex, substantive inquiry, we also must attend to developing our listening skills. At the most basic level, it is important to remove distractions (phones, computers, that stack of ungraded papers) so that we can really be present for others. Although being quiet and creating the space for others is important, listening is much more than that. As poet Alice Duer Miller states, "Listening is not merely not talking," it is "taking a vigorous, human interest in what is being told to us." It is through our active listening that we open the door for others to make their thinking visible to us (Ritchhart and Church 2020). In a study conducted by the leadership consultancy of Zenger/Folkman, good listeners were those who ask questions to clarify points of confusion as well as pose probing questions that prompt the speaker to reflect and check their assumptions. When people are really listening, the conversation feels collaborative rather than one sided (Zenger and Folkman 2016). In addition, good listeners offer feedback and provide suggestions, often through such tools as the Ladder of Feedback routine (Ritchhart and Church 2020). The most relevant cultural forces connected to this action include *language*, *routines* (using protocols to structure conversation), and *interactions*.

Prioritizing Time for Teacher Learning. There is never enough time to accomplish all we want in schools. Therefore, we must protect the time for those things deemed most important and valuable. As the previous research reviewed makes clear, protecting time for teacher learning benefits morale, increases professionalism, supports innovation, and enhances student learning (Darling-Hammond et al. 2017). Practically, this means making sure most staff meetings are about learning rather than logistics. This will ensure that they are more authentic and engaging. When information needs to be delivered, consider using emails or videos. Ensure that learning is ongoing, sustained, and cumulative rather than episodic and disconnected. This means scheduling adequate time for teachers to engage in regular inquiry, in-depth discussion, and meaningful engagement at least every fortnight. Protect that time. Learning groups are most effective when they engage teachers across departments and grade levels. While it is not impossible for a learning group to consist of educators from the same department or team, the challenge is that such groups already have a "work agenda" and a set of tasks they must accomplish. When this is the case, too often, the work agenda will swamp and take over the learning agenda. As Steven Covey (1989) conveyed decades ago, the pressing needs of the immediate too often supersede the needs of the important. Thus, we shouldn't confuse "working groups" or committees with "learning groups." The former aims to complete a job or task, to implement something. The latter seeks to develop understanding of a question, problem, or issue through investigation, action, and reflection. Unsurprisingly, the most relevant cultural force here is *time*. In addition, we are thinking about how we will spend that time and what kinds of *opportunities* we want to create for our colleagues and ourselves.

Encouraging Innovation and Risk-Taking. When we focus on growth and improvement rather than implementation, we naturally move toward piloting, risk-taking, and learning through first attempts. On a practical level, this means a shift in language. Leaders, facilitators, and teachers should use the language of prototyping rather than implementing. A prototype is a first attempt carried out for the purpose of gathering feedback and learning from one's efforts. Implementation implies that something is to be fully realized. Recognize failure as a learning moment, and regularly engage teachers in conversation about productive failures or First Attempts In Learning. Get in the habit of asking yourself and others: What is something new that you tried this week, and what did you learn from that first attempt? How will you use that learning to reshape or modify your next attempt? These questions set *expectations* for innovation. Relevant cultural forces connected to this action include *language, modeling, opportunities, environment*.

Fitting New Actions with Current Realities

I hope some of the preceding actions sparked curiosity, excitement, and felt like a call to action. We all need new ideas and possibilities to spur us on. In addition, powerful actions often beget other actions. Once the first thing happens, the second is not so hard, and, over time, new actions come to feel like the natural next step. At the same time, we want to avoid a superficial implementation that simply wallpapers over existing problems or issues. There-fore, before you rush to implement the actions you are anxious to try, step back and think about what you are currently doing (see Figure 1.4):

➢ What practices need to be rethought considering this mindset?
➢ What actions, already in place, can be amplified and grown by applying some of the pre-ceding principles identified?
➢ What do you need to stop doing altogether and why? Does it run counter to this mindset? Is it ineffective?
➢ What "moveable barriers" are standing in the way of truly living this mindset?

I use the term *moveable barriers* because it is often not worth our time moaning about mandates and policies that we have no control over. However, many of the barriers we face are of our own creation or are simply a part of the grammar of school that we have grown so accustomed to that we only assume they are immoveable.

Figure 1.4 Amplify-Modify-Remove-Create.

Review of Current Practice: What do we need to...

AMPLIFY	MODIFY	REMOVE	CREATE

Conclusion: Our Theory of Action

We conclude our examination of this mindset "For classrooms to be cultures of thinking for students, schools must be cultures of thinking for teachers" by formulating a "theory of action" in which we hypothesize the likely effects of our actions. What are we likely to see as a result of acting on the principles we have laid out? This is not merely a hoped-for outcome, however. It is based on the research and experience upon which we have drawn. A theory of action can be useful because it clarifies both what we are doing and why we are doing it. As such, it identifies particulars we might look for to know when and to what extent we have been successful. One shouldn't be too quick to claim success based upon mere implementation of any set of actions. It is only if those actions have the desired effects that we can declare some measure of success. In this spirit of tying together our actions with anticipated outcomes, I offer the following theory of action for Mindset 1. Use it if it captures the actions you plan to take and the outcomes you expect. If it doesn't, feel free to craft your own theory of action that will better fit your context.

> *If* we support and empower the adults in the school to continually grow, innovate, question, take risks, reflect, examine, inquire, and learn from and with one another, *then* teachers will create those same conditions for the students in their classrooms.

Notes

We Can't Directly Teach Dispositions; We Must Enculturate Them

Throughout my time as an educator, two questions have guided me in my work creating cultures of thinking:

1. Who are our students becoming as thinkers and learners as a result of their time with us?
2. What do we want the students we teach to be like as adults?

These are questions we should all be asking ourselves as educators, parents, and community members as they speak directly to our purpose, to our "why?" These questions capture the central goal and reason why we seek to create cultures of thinking in our schools and classrooms (Ritchhart 2015). A quality education not only fosters rich understanding of content, but also develops the thinking dispositions one will need for a lifetime (Katz and Raths 1985; Schulz 2008). This is not an either-or proposition. Our research has shown schools can both achieve high academic standards (even when measured by standardized tests) and develop students as thinkers (Claxton, Chambers, Powell, and Lucas 2011; Ritchhart and Church 2020).

Dispositions go by many names: traits, qualities, character, virtues, makeup, nature, soft skills, and habits. By whatever name, psychologists, philosophers, sociologists, and educators have long been intrigued by their development.[1] Dispositions constitute a person's character—both who they are and who they are becoming. For instance, when we call someone reflective, it is because we have observed that behavior in the past and predict it will likely be the case in the future. Dispositions matter because they tie together observed abilities and skills with future potential and action. As teachers, we seek to develop students who not only can read, but who also do read. We want students who are not just capable of asking questions, but who also regularly do so because they are curious. We desire students who not only stop and reflect on their learning when required to do so, but who engage in this action spontaneously as they see the need for it (Tishman 1994). Thus, dispositions bridge the ability-action gap, serving as a motivating force that propels action. If we have a disposition toward open-mindedness, we are more likely to spot occasions to be open-minded and to act upon those occasions by deploying our skills in this area (Perkins, Jay, and Tishman 1993). This motivation toward action is precisely what makes the construct of thinking dispositions so compelling.

The problem, though, is that dispositions cannot be directly taught. Transmission-style teaching, where students passively receive information about a valued trait and its associated behaviors, is insufficient to develop dispositions (Sparks 2010). We can't merely teach a unit on "curiosity," have a month devoted to "risk-taking," and then next move on to "balance"—though

I have seen schools try this approach. Simply filling the walls with posters extolling the virtues of a serial list or profile of "habits of mind" is unlikely to have much effect either. As Alfie Kohn (1997) notes, "This seriatim approach is unlikely to result in a lasting commitment to any of these values, much less a feeling for how they may be related." Furthermore, it is not enough for teachers merely to state what they want to see happen in the classroom. Students need to experience dispositions in action. If dispositions cannot be directly taught, what do we do? The short answer, not the easy answer, is that we must enculturate them. That is, we must allow students to develop dispositions through the culture we create.

WHAT THE RESEARCH SAYS: *WHY* DOES IT MATTER?

Which dispositions should we prioritize and promote in schools? Lists abound: Habits of Mind (Costa and Kallick 2002), Intellectual Virtues (Baehr 2011; King 2020), 21st-Century Skills (Magner, Soule, and Wesolowski 2011), the IB Learner Profile (Bullock 2011), and various lists of Thinking Dispositions (Facione, Facione, and Sanchez 1992; Tishman, Perkins, and Jay 1995). As positive and useful as these lists are, they tend to be lengthy and can seem like a grab-bag of broad, nebulous, and at times, overlapping items. In the book *Intellectual Character* (Ritchhart 2002), I analyzed these proposed lists to identify six dispositions that seemed to appear on almost everyone's list and were well supported by psychological research. The six include the disposition to be open-minded, curious, metacognitive, a seeker of truth and understanding, strategic, and skeptical. All of these contribute to being a more independent and effective learner and thinker. However, two have emerged as what we might call "master dispositions" when it comes to learning and thinking: curiosity and metacognition.

The Case for Curiosity

Susan Engel (2015b) has called curiosity the engine of learning. It initiates exploration and inquiry, stimulates deep thinking and reasoning, increases motivation, and encourages questioning. Curiosity helps students make new knowledge and information meaningful (Pluck and Johnson 2011). But how? Neuroscientist Dr. Matthias Gruber used fMRI scans to better understand the effects of curiosity on learning. He found that curiosity puts the brain in a state that allows it to learn and retain almost any kind of information and makes the process more rewarding to the learner (Kaufman 2017). Research at the Motivated Memory Lab at Duke's Center for Cognitive Neuroscience Duke University further illuminates the link between curiosity and motivation. Dr. Alison Adcock, who runs the lab, elaborates, "Our work suggests that the motivational systems prime the hippocampus [the part of the brain responsible for memory] to record what's important. And it's a powerful explanation for why we remember what we do. It's a brain state that makes us more receptive." At the same time, the lab's work suggests what might stand in the way of promoting this motivated brain state, "From what we understand about the brain systems for motivation, you can't be afraid, you can't be anxious—because anxiety systems really clamp down on curiosity and produce stereotyped, rapid, simple responses that short circuit the kind of playful curiosity we're so interested in facilitating in education and in therapy, too" (Briggs 2017).

It is not surprising, then, that curiosity, what some researchers call "motivational giftedness," has been linked to academic success in schools (Kaufman 2017; Shah, Weeks, Richards, and Kaciroti 2018; Tough 2012; Weikart and Schweinhart 1997). Furthermore, promoting curiosity may be particularly valuable for traditionally under-served students (Shah et al. 2018; Weikart and Schweinhart 1997). While curiosity's link to learning and inquiry (Murdoch 2022) is well established, recent studies have shown a strong link to other outcomes, such as happiness, creativity, satisfying intimate relationships, increased personal growth after traumatic experiences, and enhanced perception that one's life has meaning (Kaufman 2017).

Despite all the research on the importance and power of curiosity, its presence is not very robust in schools. Engel (2015b) notes that children's questioning naturally drives learning outside the classroom, but this drops off dramatically in the classroom. The frequency of *episodes of curiosity* (through questions, direct gazing, and manipulating objects) diminishes as students progress through school. Her research concluded that pressure on teachers to cover content leads to discouraging curiosity (Engel 2015a). Seth Goldenberg, author of *Radical Curiosity* (2022), goes a step further, arguing that our world today has been designed to eradicate curiosity not just in schools, but also in our adult lives. Why does society diminish curiosity when it is such a potent force for learning, motivation, invention, and discovery? Goldenberg argues that we move too quickly toward solutions without giving adequate time to develop our questions. Businesses prioritize action and decisiveness, and leaders emphasize management of old knowledge over the creation of new—sounds a bit like schools. If curiosity is linked to our need to explain the unexpected (Piaget 2003) and grapple with uncertainty (Lamnina and Chase 2019), where do students have opportunities for this in schools?

The Case for Metacognition

Teachers often associate metacognition with reflection or thinking about one's thinking and actions. However, metacognition actually involves three key dimensions: 1) effectively planning and directing one's thinking, 2) actively monitoring and controlling one's thinking processes as they unfold, and 3) reflecting on one's thinking afterward (Scott and Levy 2013). Metacognitive processes aid retention and transfer while promoting deeper learning (Saaris 2017). They also have been shown to be a key factor in reading comprehension (Haller, Child, and Walberg 1988), the development of conceptual understanding in science (Hennessey 1999), and enhanced mathematical fluency and reasoning (Kramarski and Mevarech 2003). Through metacognition, students also become self-aware as learners. They recognize how they are learning, their learning pitfalls, how they might grow in their learning, and when to ask for help. This self-awareness leads to self-regulated learning, adaptation of strategies as needed, and increased student motivation (Deci 1995). Students' metacognitive abilities are also associated with the use of more effective study strategies (Vrugt and Oort 2008). Dewey's extensive writing on experience, thinking, understanding, and reflection are often boiled down to the widely shared aphorism, "We don't learn from experience. We learn from reflecting on experience."

Teaching metacognitive strategies, modeling them, and actively encouraging their use has been shown to greatly aid learning and academic performance. A wealth of evidence shows teaching metacognitive strategies can substantially improve student learning outcomes (Donker, De Boer, Kostons, Van Ewijk, and van der Werf 2014). John Hattie's seminal meta-analysis of educational interventions measured the average effect size of metacognitive strategies at 0.69, putting it near the top of influential teaching practices (Hattie 2009).[2] *The Australian Teaching and Learning Toolkit* states that classrooms where metacognitive strategies are regularly taught, demonstrated, encouraged, and supported can be expected to make, on average, eight months more progress over the course of a year compared to students not receiving such learning opportunities (Department of Education 2017).

Developing Dispositions

What does the research say about how best to develop dispositions? Both sociocultural perspectives on learning as well as research on effective practices for character education help answer this question. As the psychologist Lev Vygotsky famously stated, "Children grow into the intellectual life of those around them" (Vygotsky 1978, p. 88). When students are a part of a culture that sends messages about the value of thinking and that supports its development, then students are more likely to take on these values. Likewise, when beliefs about knowledge and the processes used to build understanding are regularly modeled, supported, and expected, then students come to take on and internalize these beliefs (Muis and Duffy 2013). We can think of this kind of learning as a sort of "cognitive apprenticeship," in which we learn in and through our company with experts who are regularly making their thinking visible to us (Collins, Brown, and Holum 1991; Rogoff 1990).

Although all 8 cultural forces must be leveraged to send the message that the use and development of thinking dispositions are central at a school, a few specific cultural forces emerge as particularly relevant based upon the research into effective character education. Schools inspire and encourage dispositional development by providing *models* of the dispositions valued, rich *opportunities* to put dispositions into action and experience their power, regular occasions to *interact* with peers in discussion and problem solving in which everyone's dispositions are in play, and an *expectation* that dispositional development is a central part of a well-rounded education (Berkowitz and Bier 2005; Berkowitz Bier, and McCauley 2016).

Is there a place for teacher instruction in the development of dispositions? Yes. Dispositions have a skill component to them that must be developed (Perkins et al. 1993). To that end, it is necessary to unpack the nature of a particular disposition, identify the skills and practices implicated in it, and provide opportunities to practice those skills in *meaningful* contexts with support and feedback. Furthermore, one shouldn't confuse enculturation with simple osmosis. One does not merely soak up a disposition. Teachers must bring dispositions to the fore so that they can be an object of study and reflection. This may mean students regularly self-assess, and teachers comment and give feedback on students' development of dispositions (Baehr 2013). However, we recognize that direct instruction is only one part of dispositional development and is most effective in the broader context of building a culture of thinking.

VISIONS AND REFLECTIONS: *HOW* MIGHT IT LOOK?

What might it look like to leverage the culture of a classroom to support and nurture students' thinking dispositions? How might we recognize that these dispositions are indeed developing? What practices should we attend to in our classrooms and what behaviors should we look for in our students? To help us formulate this vision, we can use a modified version of Scott Murphy's "Back to the Future" protocol (Murphy 2008), which first asks us to imagine a future vision concretely and then work backward to identify ways we can get there.

Constructing Our Vision

Imagine it's the last month of school and you take your students on a field trip to a museum, gallery, business, outdoor center, or another venue appropriate to your students and subject area. At the end of your visit, the museum docent/educator comments on how much she enjoyed working with your students. "They were so curious and reflective," she says. "So different from most of the groups that come through." What did the docent observe from your students? How were they different? Be as specific as possible in naming the behaviors. Instead of simply "they asked questions," identify the characteristics of the types of questions they asked, perhaps even writing down sample questions. *Record your responses on the pages at the end of this chapter, the margins of this page, a sheet of paper, or your electronic device.*

Now imagine that this docent's response is almost 180 degrees from what you received when you took your students on a field trip earlier in the school year. The kids didn't embarrass you, their behavior was okay, but, frankly, you were disappointed that not much learning seemed to happen. It wasn't that you prepared differently for these two excursions; it was that the students changed. What did you do in the intervening months that changed their ability to engage with and reflect on new learning? What kinds of moments became important for you to either create or capitalize on in the classroom? What behaviors did you notice, name, and acknowledge because you wanted to see more of them? What did you do more of and less of to cultivate this curiosity and reflection? Keep in mind that this is a *visioning* exercise and not a reflection on your actual practices. You are imagining the types of things that would be likely to lead to the result you envisioned. This kind of projective imagination helps develop our vision and think about possibilities. Consider it a first step. These become future actions to consider taking. *Record your new responses beneath your previous ones.*

Group Discussion

If you are reading this book with others, schedule a time to bring your ideas to share and discuss.

➢ What does your compilation reveal about your collective vision of what curiosity and meta-cognitive reflection might look like?
➢ What practices do people identify as supporting these dispositions that go beyond what you are currently doing?
➢ Use your collective ideas to push further. What more could you be doing either individually or collectively?

Contemplating Pictures of Practice

To further extend your vision of what is involved in enculturating dispositions and how we might know that dispositions are developing, we now examine two case studies that further flesh out both important dispositional behaviors and teaching practices that support them. The first looks at the assessment of dispositions as a holistic, naturally occurring process. The second is drawn from one of the most well-researched interventions that sought to develop students as powerful thinkers and learners, The Perry Preschool Project.

Case One: School Council Member. After a decade of developing cultures of thinking at a preschool through grade 12 school, I had an opportunity to meet and debrief with a member of the school council. Over dinner, my host, Oliver, explained how he and his wife had made the decision to send their students to this school. Their first inclination had been to send them to the same school they had themselves attended. However, they decided not to do that, and he told me why. He explained that at his business, he regularly interviewed and hired new applicants. Over time, he had noticed a pattern. A significant number of his new hires had gone to this school. Yes, they all had degrees from various universities, but this seemed not to be much of a factor in distinguishing one applicant from another. It was their earlier schooling that was a common denominator. He found these interviewees to be curious, thoughtful, independent, and exciting people. In short, he noticed their dispositions. Far from being amorphous, intangible, and soft, he was assessing their character the way all of us do, through their behavior and the way they interacted with others. To verify his assessment, he checked references and talked to others. What he didn't do was ask to see their grade transcript or admission test scores.

As a result of this assessment, Oliver told his wife that they needed to check out this school for their preschool-aged children to see what was making it different. What they saw impressed them, not just in the early childhood program, but at all grade levels. Students spent time exploring ideas and projects in depth. They revisited and modified their work. They had conversations with both their teachers and each other about their learning. When he talked to students, he was impressed by how they talked about their learning and thinking, not just the work they were doing. Students were encouraged to have and pursue their passions. Classes were active. Teachers pushed students to think and engage deeply. He was assessing the culture. What messages was the school sending about learning? What was being valued and promoted? What did it feel like to be a learner at this school? What Oliver and his wife didn't do was ask to see the curriculum documents and test score data.

Case Two: Perry Preschool. It was 1963 and Louise Derman-Sparks (2016) began her first job as a teacher at the Perry Preschool as part of a project developed by educators from the University of Michigan and Eastern Michigan University. She, along with other teachers at the school, was involved in an ambitious undertaking: trying to raise the IQ of the African-American children living in poverty with whom they were working in Ypsilanti, Michigan. The "lessons" she was to teach appeared simple to outsiders, but were full of intention, focusing on experience and creative engagement. For instance, kids might dress up and perform, creating their own imaginative script. And Louise would interact with them, asking them questions, posing problems for them to solve, adding complexity to their play. Louise shares, "Planning skills, expanding their awareness of the world. We felt that communication and developing and expanding language was really important for the kids because it's important in society, and it's very important in order to be successful in school" (Vedantam, Cohen, and Boyle 2019).

Significantly, teachers also took the learning outside the classroom, taking students to a bakery, an orchard, the airport. "We wanted to expand their world experience because the families were very poor, and most of them didn't even have their own cars," Louise explained. "What we wanted to do was for them to be able to have the concrete experiences in the world that children from middle-class homes had and to learn to be comfortable in these larger arenas of the world" (Vedantam, Cohen, and Boyle 2019). In addition to the in-school experience, teachers also spent 90 minutes each week visiting students' homes, playing with them in the presence of their mothers, modeling ways of interacting with and engaging children in imaginative play and authentic language development.

The Perry Preschool Project was, at first, considered a failure. Students' IQ were raised, but only in the short term. Gains faded. By the time children were 10, there wasn't much of a difference in how children in the experimental and control groups performed on tests of cognitive ability. However, because the study was conducted in the 1960s, researchers have been able to follow students over the past six decades, and the results are dramatic. Over time, the children involved in the experiment were found to be more likely to be cooperative, engaged in school, graduate high school, earn more in their jobs, attend university, have stable marriages, and far less likely to commit crime than their counterparts in the control group. Not only that, but findings released in 2019 show that the children of the children in the original Perry project, are now reaping the same benefits (Mongeau 2019).

Discussion. In both of the preceding cases there is an important lesson for us about results and outcomes. As Nobel prize winner James Heckman observes, "If you start doing interventions and then evaluate them within a few years and [you do] not recognize that these programs have multiple effects, and you don't allow those effects to kind of generate and express themselves, we can reach very premature negative conclusions" (Vedantam, Cohen, and Boyle 2019). I argue that while we must make dispositional development one of the primary goals of a quality education, while we must offer opportunities to "expand students' world" and provide formative feedback on development along the way, it is important to take the long view. Dispositional development takes time. We shouldn't be too quick to try to evaluate and measure students' progress.

Reflecting on Current Practice

The following questions provide an opportunity for reflecting upon what gets valued, shared, and celebrated in your classroom. These questions focus both on the process of enculturation as well as on the dispositions we want to see in our students. Although the questions are focused on teachers, school leaders can replace the word *classroom* with *school* and the word *student* with *learners* to reflect on how they are supporting teachers' dispositional development through enculturation.

Choosing Questions and Recording Responses

Different questions serve us at different times in our learning. Therefore, I suggest you read through the questions and identify:

➤ One or two that speak to you now. Questions that might challenge you or take your thinking in new directions.

➤ One or two you would most like to discuss with your colleagues.

➤ Circle and date the questions you select now so you can identify how your focus shifts with time and experience.

➤ Use the blank pages at the end of this chapter or your note-taking device to record your reflections.

- What kind of thinking do I wish were routine in my classroom? Why isn't it already? What can I do to make it more of a regular and necessary part of learning in my classroom?

- Where, when, and how do my students get an image of me as a thinker and a learner? What is that image?

- Which dispositions do I wish my students came to my class already possessing? Why are these important to me? Which dispositions do students leave my class possessing?

- Who are my students becoming as thinkers and learners as a result of their time with me? What types of data might I need to collect to better answer this question?

- Where in the curriculum are there opportunities for students to develop their thinking dispositions?

- When was the last time I noticed, named, and highlighted students' thinking and dispositional behavior? How can I help myself to do this more often?

- How would I describe the ideal graduate of our school? What would I like for them to be like as a person and as a learner?

- If children grow into the life around them, what dispositions am I fostering my students to grow into?

- Culture is about messages. What messages about learning, how it happens, and what counts am I sending? Is our school sending?

DATA, PRINCIPLES, AND PRACTICES: *WHAT* ACTIONS CAN WE TAKE?

With a clear understanding of why dispositions are a worthwhile and important aim of education, on which dispositions we might initially focus to impact student learning, and how dispositions develop through enculturation rather than direct teaching, we are ready to take action to move this mindset forward. Of course, we want our actions to be responsive to our context. The reflection questions in the previous section can be helpful in this regard. So too can the collection of "street data" that helps one understand the current state of things. Before considering "what" you might do to move this mindset forward, step back and assess the current state of things in your classroom and at your school. What data might you collect to best inform your future efforts?

Collecting Street Data

Street Data

> Helps us understand our own context as well as students' perspectives.
> Is relatively easy and quick to collect.
> Can be immediately analyzed and acted upon straightaway.
> Is meant to inform and suggest action.
> Is NOT an evaluation or measure of success but a snapshot of practice.
> Can take many forms: observations, interviews, surveys, exit tickets, recordings, and so on.

As you construct your "street data" actions (or use the following suggestions), consider: What can I learn from this data? How might this data be useful to me in informing my next actions? How will this data illuminate the status of things, help identify what needs to change, or point to promising practices we can leverage? Select collection methods that will work well for you and your students. Consider collecting data over time (with the same or different instruments) so that you continually take stock of where you are in promoting this mindset.

Street Data Action One: Messaging Ghost Walk. Carolyn Taylor says, "Culture is about messages sent. These messages demonstrate what is valued, what is important, what people do around here to fit in, to be accepted, and to be rewarded" (2005, p.7). These messages are mostly nonverbal in nature, living in the symbols, behaviors, and systems of a group or organization. The culture of a school then, might have very little to do with its goals or mission statement, which are largely aspirational. To understand the culture of a place, we need to look at what messages are sent. One way to do this is to conduct a "Ghost Walk" to identify what messages your school is sending about what the school community values, cares about, and thinks is important (see Appendix D). After your Ghost Walk, consider: What interesting or surprising details did you notice? What questions or reflections did the ghost walk provoke? What do you think students would say your school values, tries to promote, and celebrates based on the overall messaging you noticed? What kinds of personal as well as school-wide changes can be made to enhance the message that your school is focused on who students are becoming as thinkers and learners?

Street Data Action Two: Success Dispositions. The next street data action is designed to capture the dispositions students view as valuable. Do they agree with you and the research? When, from their perspective, do they feel they have occasions to further develop and use those dispositions in school. The following prompts could be done as a short reflection by students or even as an "exit ticket" as they are leaving class:

- As a person, not just a student, what three attributes or qualities do you think you need to be successful both now as well as in the future?
- Where and when in school have you had a chance to use and further develop these qualities recently?

It can be useful to categorize students' responses. You might even ask students to do this. It is possible that students' responses will be nondispositional. For instance, some students might say "being smart," "athleticism," "a good personality," or even "wealth." This is okay as it opens the door to talk about qualities we can develop in ourselves and have control over. Whatever students' responses, it is interesting to see what they think contributes to success. A key component of any disposition is our inclination to act. That is, are we inclined to see a particular skill or behavior as valuable, useful, or important to us in this moment? When we value a certain behavior—considering other perspectives, for example—we are more likely to engage that behavior. Students' responses also open the door to talk about dispositional development as an explicit goal of your school as well as providing an opportunity to share the research on metacognition and curiosity and how they contribute to our lives and learning. This can enhance intrinsic motivation (Berkowitz and Bier 2005).

The second prompt, related to occasions to develop qualities, can inform you if students see the school as actively nurturing their dispositional development. While inclination is important, we also need to spot occasions for using those skills. Are students able to spot occasions? Our research at Project Zero has shown this "awareness of occasions for use" is one of the key bottlenecks in developing dispositions (Perkins and Ritchhart 2004; Perkins, Tishman, Ritchhart, Donis, and Andrade 2000). People often have the skill, but simply miss occasions for deploying it. Consequently, teachers need to both create opportunities for dispositions to be used and help students to spot these occasions for what they offer. This doesn't mean that teachers merely do the spotting and direction, but instead prompt through questioning such as, "What might be important to pay attention to here?"

Stating the Mindset as Principles for Action

Turning a mindset into principles for action helps to guide and direct your efforts. Principles tell us what to do broadly in a top-level, overarching way. From our basic principles, we can then build specific actions that exemplify them and put them into play. In constructing these principles, we build the bridge between the "how" and the "what." For our mindset, "We can't directly teach dispositions; we must enculturate them," we might say that in principle we need to prioritize it, externalize it, attend to it, celebrate it, and make it routine. What exactly does that mean?

- Prioritize students' dispositional development as a major goal and priority in our schools and classrooms.
- Externalize the process of metacognition and other types of thinking so that students can learn from expert models in a cognitive apprenticeship.
- Attend to the four-part nature of dispositions by paying attention to developing: 1) skills, 2) inclination, 3) awareness of occasions for use, and 4) motivation in the moment.
- Celebrate the dispositions we want to reinforce whenever, wherever, and however they appear.
- Make thinking and the associated dispositions routine so that they are part of the fabric of the school and classroom.

Possible Actions

There is no single way to enculturate dispositions. There is ample room for individuals to put their own creative stamp on things and bring in effective practices from other sources. Keep in mind immersive, multifaceted, long-term approaches are best. The following actions are:

➤ Drawn from our work in schools as part of the Worldwide Cultures of Thinking Project.
➤ Placed under the related principle to help you focus on the driving motivation behind each action.

> ➤ Modifiable to fit your local context.
> ➤ Connected to the most relevant cultural forces to which each specific action is associated. Both frameworks, the 8 cultural forces and the 10 mindsets, are synergistic and you can begin your journey either place.

Prioritize It. Identify a few core dispositions of learning and thinking that you want your students to acquire. While you may use lists from various sources, try to identify just a few (no more than five) that you really care about and think are important. Looking at a list of 16 habits of mind, you may well see that all are worthwhile and important. However, how does a teacher actively attend to the development of 16 different characteristics in a deep and meaningful way? If you choose just a few from that list that you are passionate about, you will have more success. Use any list to spark your thinking about which dispositions on which to focus. Once you have selected a few, share and discuss with colleagues:

- Why do these matter to you?
- Why should they matter to your students?
- How are you a model of these dispositions?
- Where do you need to grow?

Consider these dispositions as a student entitlement. Something central to their education and not just an add-on. Establish where, when, and how students will have opportunities to practice and acquire these dispositions. The relevant cultural forces here are *expectations*, *modeling*, and *opportunities*.

Externalize It. The principle of externalization applies to any disposition you have selected. It is important that we are models of the dispositions so that students can learn from our example. Think of a disposition as being learned from the outside in. This is particularly important when it comes to the development of metacognition. Students first experience metacognitive processes externally, through their conversations and interactions with others. Gradually, these external conversations become internalized. Three specific practices that can be useful in supporting metacognitive development are: using thinking alouds, inviting students to talk about their actions, and scaffolding.

Think Alouds. Think alouds are used to model cognitive processes around such things as scheme activation, visualization, and comprehension monitoring in reading. In mathematics, the technique is useful to model approaches to problem solving by highlighting what an expert does when they don't immediately know what to do. The goal of a think aloud is to demystify the process of constructing meaning or solving problems by showing students all the active thinking involved in these activities. Thus, it is important that we choose material that is both novel and complex so that we can engage our own thinking authentically. When we do so, think alouds can humanize us by showing that we are learners too. By taking such interpretive risks in front of students, the think aloud approach can help build a community of learners.

Often the use of think alouds are a deliberate form of modeling in which the source material is pre-selected, and the modeling is done explicitly with the goal for students to later practice the modeled techniques independently. A useful intermediate step in this process is to have students identify and name the processes they witnessed. Teachers can document these steps and post them for later reference and direct students' attention to them as needed. Such documentation can also be helpful in guiding reflection on the metacognitive process itself. Which processes did you use? Which did you forget? Which were most helpful? However, not all occasions for this technique need to be pre-planned. We must be sensitive to occasions where the modeling of our thinking can invite students into a cognitive apprenticeship with us and where we can model our thinking one-on-one in the moment. Relevant cultural forces connected to this action include *modeling*, *opportunities*, and the *environment*.

"Talk to Me about What You Are Doing." This is a simple metacognitive prompt you can use every day with students. When students explain their actions and plans, they have a chance to review and clarify those plans. Often, students will adjust or identify problems just through the process of talking out their actions. This simple question takes the metacognitive process, which is crucial to independent learning, and makes it overt, apparent, and visible. In talking aloud, students are given the opportunity to develop the self-dialogue we want them to internalize and use regularly as independent learners. For teachers, students' responses can provide valuable formative assessment information. Talking with others, particularly an adult, about what you are doing and that person showing interest has also been shown to boost curiosity and engagement (Moore and Bulbulian 1976). The relevant cultural forces connected to this action are our *interactions* with students and the *language* we use.

Scaffolding. There are two main types of scaffolds teachers use to support students both in their thinking generally and in their metacognitive processes specifically: soft and hard. Soft scaffolds provide dynamic support in the moment, as needed, based on the learner's responses. These may take the form of prompts and questions teachers ask. Hard scaffolds are more static and are often planned in anticipation of students' needs and expected difficulties. These may take the form of guides, sequences, or steps to follow. Such scaffolds provide a template from which learners can work. The two types are not mutually exclusive. In practice, they often complement each other. For instance, thinking routines are hard scaffolds, providing a short sequence of steps to guide learners' thinking. In choosing a particular thinking routine, a teacher has made the decision that this structure will support students in engaging with the source material. In practice though, teachers still prompt and question students to further support their thinking, adding a soft scaffold to the hard as needed.

"Metacognitive scaffolding scripts" (Pozuelos et al. 2019) represent a hybrid of hard and soft scaffolding. Such scripts may be identified in advance or emerge from a teacher's ongoing interactions with students. They can be written down and formalized or held as part of the teachers' tacit knowledge of how to interact in a supportive way with students. Instructional coaches and teachers who model lessons often seek to share such scripts and make them known to teachers eager to support their students' thinking. Consequently, for teachers who are novices with this kind of scaffolding, the scripts may first be written down and used as somewhat hard scaffolds. However, over time such scripts are designed to foster a dynamic, reflective dialog between the teacher and student, softening over time and being used more responsively. Such scripts can also be written down for use by students to guide their own learning. Again, this makes external that which we want to eventually become internal. This might include questions such as:

- Am I on the right track with this project/task/assignment?
- How do my efforts so far help me to achieve the goal of the project and include all the required elements?
- What other options or actions might I consider?
- Who should I look to for help or to get feedback from?
- Am I making good progress thus far?
- Is there any part of this assignment that is confusing or might present a problem for me in the future?
- Am I making good use of my time?
- Am I using effective strategies for this assignment?

The cultural forces most strongly connected to this action are *routines* (scaffolds are many times a type of routine), *language* (since we are focused on developing students' internal voice our language is important), and *interactions* (recognizing that soft scaffolds are meant to be responsive and interactive in nature and depend on good listening).

Attend to It. As you will recall, a disposition can be understood as consisting of four components: 1) ability, 2) broad inclination or valuing, 3) awareness of occasions to apply one's abilities, and 4) motivation to act in the moment (Ritchhart 2002). In seeking to develop dispositions, it is necessary to attend to all four components. To develop the ability component of any disposition, begin by identifying the underlying skills needed to carry out that disposition. For instance, one necessary skill associated with curiosity is the ability to question. Thus, spending time helping students learn to question, perhaps by using a routine like "Question Sorts" is worthwhile (Ritchhart and Church 2020). In fact, teachers have found that the regular use of routines provides an opportunity for students to develop the skill component toward the broad disposition to build understanding.

Unfortunately, many efforts to cultivate dispositional traits in school stop with the ability component. It is also necessary to help students realize how these abilities are valuable. This involves helping them not only to see, but also to experience the benefits and payoffs of the dispositional behavior. Although it can be useful to share the research on the benefits of curiosity, for example, it is better for students to experience these benefits firsthand, to feel what is sometimes referred to as cognitive emotions (Scheffler 1991). These emotions, such as surprise, joy of discovery, or deep engagement in learning flood the reward center of the brain with dopamine that, in turn, enhances motivation (Gruber and Ranganath, 2019; Kort, Reilly, and Picard 2001; Lepper and Henderlong 2000). Thus, providing students with regular opportunities to experience this rush is more likely to advance their inclination toward being curious than simply telling them. With any disposition ask yourself how students can experience the value of it.

Research conducted with my colleagues David Perkins and Shari Tishman at Harvard University showed that even with ability and inclination, many individuals still do not act (Perkins et al. 2000). The bottleneck seems to be their adeptness at spotting occasions for applying one's skills. Not only is this awareness seldom developed in schools; often it is directly inhibited. Teachers know that the easiest way to provoke a skill is to directly ask for it. Consequently, telling students exactly what to do by handing out "success criteria" or clearly stating learning outcomes— for instance, "After reading the passage, write down three questions you have about the topic"— is one of the easiest ways of ensuring we get the performance we seek. However, when we wish to focus on the learning experience and on dispositional development, stating the learning goal or handing out success criteria may inhibit students' learning (Maine Department of Education 2015). At other times, teachers may over-scaffold a task so that students only need to march through steps (Meyer 2010). Often these practices can, indeed, be beneficial. They can, in fact, develop abilities. Therefore, I am not saying to never use these practices, but only to make sure you *also* provide students with the opportunity to develop their awareness. This may mean that rather than over-structure a task, have scaffolds ready for those students who might need support. It might also mean rather than handing students success criteria, you use anchor papers and exemplars to allow students to spot and identify the elements that are important, perhaps by using the "Be-Sure-To" routine (Ritchhart and Church 2020). Mindset 7 offers more on the issue of over-structuring tasks.

Finally, there is motivation in the moment. Sometimes individuals don't engage a disposition because there are counter indications and de-motivators happening. The research on what happens to curiosity as students progress through school calls out these factors (Engel 2021). For instance, with the pressure to memorize and score well on tests in high school, students might not find the time to engage their curiosity. They may spot the occasion to be curious, but due to time and pressure they put their abilities on hold. If there is a disposition we want to see in the classroom, we need to be asking ourselves why we aren't seeing it. Are there things we are doing to de-motivate or de-legitimize that behavior, and how can we stop doing those things?

The key cultural forces implicated with these actions are the construction of *opportunities* to develop the four elements of the disposition and the use of *routines* to foster abilities. *Language* can also come into play. For instance, when we use absolute language, "What *is* the answer?" we signal a closing of options. In contrast, when we ask, "What *might* the answer be?" we indicate that the intent is to explore possibilities and then use reason to determine an answer at a later point.

Celebrate It. When students engage in the dispositional behavior we are trying to cultivate, we need to notice, name, and celebrate it. By doing so, we call attention to the behavior and demonstrate that we care so much about that behavior we notice when it is happening. Such noticing and naming is reinforcing, causing students to engage in the behavior more often. We can also celebrate a disposition like curiosity by creating a "wonder wall" or "parking lot" for questions as they come up. This signals that, although we might not have time to explore the question right then, we value questions enough to capture them and keep that documentation on our walls because we expect to come back to them.

We can also help students to celebrate dispositional behavior and spot occasions for it, by doing a weekly, or even daily, celebration of moments. For instance, you might ask students to identify a curiosity moment they had this week, either at school or at home. What was something they saw, heard, or experienced that just sparked their curiosity? Analyze these moments to see what they might tell you about your students and about curiosity in general. Researchers have often identified a degree of unexpectedness or discrepancy in an event as sparking curiosity (Arnstine 1995). Students might also identify when they witnessed other people being curious, kind, helpful, reflective, and so on. Teachers can focus this within their science, mathematics, sports, or other subject-specific classes to help draw attention to what these behaviors look like in a particular context. Such techniques could be documented and displayed. This kind of documentation and sharing can help create community and connection with each other as well. Who doesn't like to be recognized for their positive behavior? These celebrations are an *opportunity* to be sure, but they also make use of the *environment* and the *language* of noticing and naming (Johnston 2004).

Make It Routine. Dispositions are routine behavior. We say that someone has a disposition, be it friendliness, curiosity, or open-mindedness, because we witness them regularly engaging in that behavior. In fact, they do it all the time! So often, in fact, that we begin to associate that disposition with the individual. What do you wish was routine in your classroom? What patterns of behavior would you like to see? Once you've identified a few, create *opportunities* and use *routines*. Do it so much that this becomes part of your class's "ways of being." A colleague of mine at Project Zero shared a conversation she had with her son after he had changed schools. The new school was one with whom I had worked for well over a decade to develop a culture of thinking and make thinking visible. She asked her son, Max, what he had noticed about the new school. How was it different from his last one? He responded that at this new school the kids, "just see more." She asked him to explain. He said, "It doesn't matter what we are looking at. It can be a poem in English or an experiment we are doing in science or even in PE. When we go to talk about it, the kids just see so much. They notice things. And not just the easy things you would expect." What Max was noticing was dispositional behavior. The students had become so accustomed to looking closely and going deeply in every subject area through routines such as See-Think-Wonder that this was their default behavior. It had become routine.

Fitting New Actions with Current Realities

Before you rush to implement the actions you are eager to try, step back and think about what you are currently doing at your school (see Figure 2.1):

➤ What actions, already in place, can be *amplified* and grown by applying some of the preceding identified principles ?

➤ What practices need to be rethought or *modified* considering this mindset?

➤ What do you need to stop doing altogether and *remove* from your repertoire? Why? Does it run counter to this mindset? Is it ineffective? What "moveable barriers" are standing in the way of truly living this mindset?

➤ Finally, are there things that you need to *create*, totally new processes, structures, or actions to begin to put in place?

Figure 2.1 Amplify-Modify-Remove-Create.

Review of Current Practice: What do we need to...

AMPLIFY	MODIFY	REMOVE	CREATE

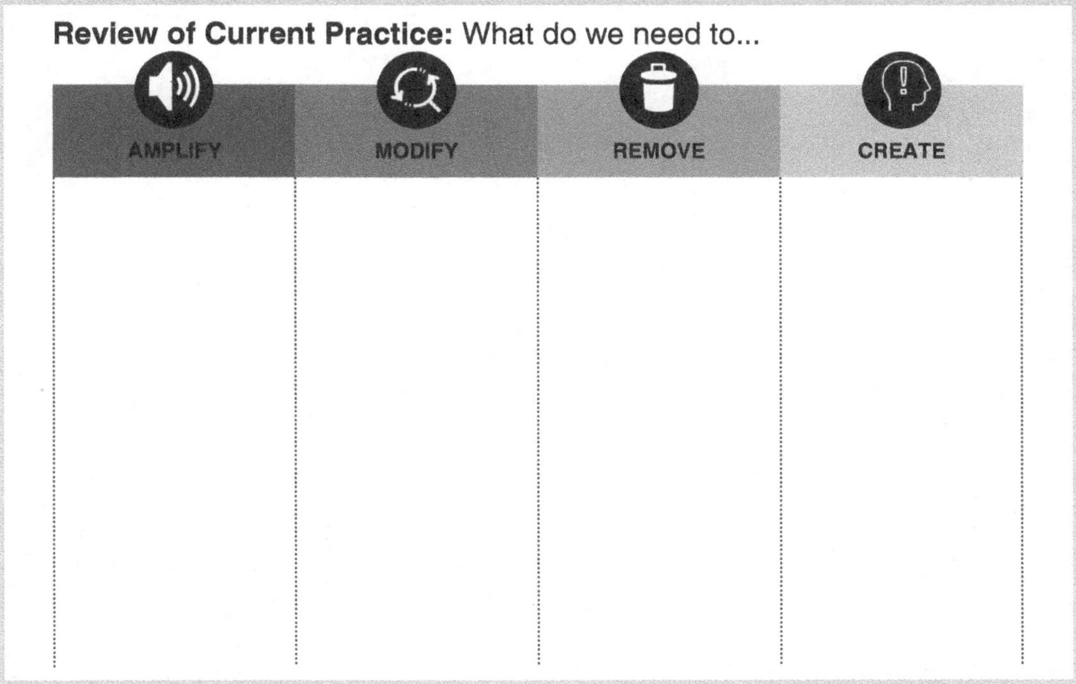

Conclusion: Our Theory of Action

What are we likely to see as a result of acting on this mindset and embodying the principles we have laid out? What do we expect to see as a result? This is our *theory of action*, a joining of our actions and outcomes. It exists as a goal, a guide, and assessment instrument. Not that we are assessing in the evaluative sense, but in the sense of trying to understand. If we have taken action but not seen the outcomes we expected, we then need to ask ourselves why not? Perhaps it is too soon to expect to see these results. If so, where do we see glimmers? Perhaps, the actions work in some contexts and for some learners but not others? Why might this be so and how can we adapt? Perhaps something was off in our implementation. How can we understand this? In this spirit of tying together our actions with anticipated outcomes, I offer the following theory of action for Mindset 2.

> *If* **we consistently model, promote, live, reference, honor, and demand the dispositions of a learner and thinker,** *then* **students will develop the intellectual character that supports a lifetime of learning and thinking.**

Notes

To Create a New Story of Learning, We Must Change the Role of the Student and the Teacher

Every school, every classroom transmits messages about learning: what it looks like, how it happens, what is worth learning, what it takes to be good in school, what it means to be smart, and so on. A culture lives in the messages it sends. Thus, culture management is message management (Taylor 2005). These messages get transmitted not through what we say or what is written down in a mission statement, but through what we *model*, the *opportunities* we create, the *routines* we establish, the way we set up the physical *environment*, the nuances found in our *language*, our *interactions* with students, our allocation of *time*, and the *expectations* we hold for our students. That is, through the way we leverage and deploy the 8 cultural forces (Ritchhart 2015). These messages taken together constitute the *story of learning* we enact with and for our students. To understand a culture, we need to understand the messages being sent. What story is being told? To change a culture, we must change the messages we are sending to write a new story of learning.

As in a written narrative, the story of learning being told in schools relies on an underlying structure or grammar. This grammar may be invisible to us even though we effortlessly work within it and our actions reinforce its existence. Consider, for example, a "rule" in English for the order in which adjectives are placed before a noun. The order is opinion, size, age, shape, color, origin, material, and then purpose. Adjectives go before the noun in that order. Thus, we might speak of purchasing a beautiful, big, blue, designer sofa. However, if you mess with that order, you'll sound a bit off in your description. Most native English speakers use this rule flawlessly without even being aware of it. It has become internalized through our lived experience. So, too, the "grammar of schools" shapes the way we organize schools, design the curriculum, and importantly, conceive of the roles students and teachers are expected to play (Cuban 2019). "The grammar of schooling operates at such a deep level that its rules become invisible, just part of the way things are. If a person uses bad grammar in speech, it just doesn't sound right; and when a school violates the grammar of schooling, it doesn't feel like a real school" to some people (Labaree 2021).

The grammar of schools is a hidden force that often makes transformation challenging (Cohen and Mehta 2017). Schools remain the way they are partly because students, teachers, and parents have become socialized in the established ways of doing things and have come to see established practices as "necessary features of a 'real school'" (Tyack and Cuban 1995). It is difficult to dislodge ways of operation that are decades, if not centuries, old. We have grown so accustomed to end-of-year exams, a six- or seven-period schedule, 45- to 60-minute instructional blocks, students grouped by age, social promotion, student lockers, teachers at the front of the room, textbooks, standardized curriculum, and so many other engrained structures that we simply take them for granted. Importantly, these grammars survive because they serve a function. They strike a balance between the generally accepted aims of schooling, what we view as goals worth working toward, and the organizational needs of the system and its stakeholders. The system will always gravitate toward what is doable, can reasonably be accomplished with available resources (personal and financial), and requires the least disruption to the status quo (Labaree 2021). This dynamic tension often accounts for why reforms fail. For instance, biological research shows adolescents would benefit in terms of health, grades, attendance, and engagement from a later school start (Dunster et al. 2018). And yet, few school districts can manage this change due to organizational needs (scheduling buses and after-school programs) and parental demands. When this is the case, the organizational needs win out over the worthwhile goal unless stakeholders make the goal a priority and are willing to spend both real and political capital to realize it.

One of the most deeply entrenched of school practices is teacher-centered instruction. For much of history, this has meant teachers at the front of the room as authority and control figures delivering information to students as receptive vessels expected to follow directions and comply (Forum 2020; Freire 2021; McGregor 2004b; Resnick, Asterhan, and Clarke 2018). This traditional view of teacher and student roles has proven remarkably difficult to change despite calls for more child-centered approaches being found in the teachings of Socrates, the works of Freire and Malaguzzi, as well as the theoretical writings of Mann, Dewey, and Foucault. The reasons for the resistance to these efforts to transform are multiple, but chief among them is that there were few resources, models, or supports to help teachers design new ways of teaching in the days of reformers like Mann or Dewey. Thankfully, today, we have more examples and resources to draw upon, creating more pockets of change. Nonetheless, the gap between vision and the constraining grammar remains. Take, for example, Yong Zhao's call for schools to foster an "entrepreneurial spirit" (Zhao 2012) or Sugata Mitra's vision of "self-organized learning environments" or SOLEs (Mitra, Kulkarni, and Stanfield 2016). Both these visionaries suggest not just new teaching practices, but also a fundamental rethinking of the grammar of schools in terms of scheduling, curriculum, student grouping, and teacher-student roles. Consequently, only a few schools are willing to embrace their vision.

The challenge of change exists even with less radical proposals. Consider a study of mathematics reform undertaken in urban schools based on the National Council of Teachers of

Mathematics' call to make mathematics more meaning centered (Hill, Litke, and Lynch 2018). Heather Hill and her colleagues observed that while teachers using new materials and resources did focus *content* more on meaning and explanation, the format of instruction remained the same teacher-centered approach as before. Class discussion requiring students to comment on one another's mathematical ideas occurred in only 5% of observed lessons. Thus, the curriculum changed due to extensive professional learning and provision of new resources, but the instruction didn't. The teachers maintained their roles as instillers of prescribed, albeit new, content. It was the teachers rather than the students who were making the meaning of the mathematics. To create change, we need to change the role of the teacher, the role of the student, and the opportunities provided (City et al. 2009).

It might be easy to assume that the preceding discussion is merely about teacher versus child-centered instruction. However, the reality is that most teachers rely on a combination of teacher and child-centered practices. Direct instruction has its place and so does inquiry. Furthermore, both approaches are ill-defined and include a wide variety of practices (Cuban 2022). To help us move forward, it is useful to re-center our discussion more clearly on the roles of the teacher and student. As the Canadian researchers Berierter and Scardamalia (1989) so eloquently note: "The [cognitive] skills a student will *acquire* in an instructional interaction are those that *are required by the student's role* in the interaction." Thus, we must be constantly aware of the roles we are putting our students in both explicitly and implicitly. This allows us to cut across any instructional approach—be it experiential, inquiry, or direct— to carefully consider the roles we allow students to assume, explore, and adopt as their own. Figure 3.1 provides guidance on how we might re-conceptualize student and teacher roles.

Yong Zhao (2012) characterizes this rethinking of roles as moving away from teachers as imparters of the prescribed curriculum to compliant students, and toward passionate adults working with students as community members. This conceptualization embeds the idea that both the image and the vision we hold of our students is the grounding force from which we can re-conceptualize our joint roles. When our vision is one of empowered students able to take their place in the world, educating becomes both transformative and liberating. We are then more readily able to embrace A.S. Neill's belief that "the function of the child is to live his own life—not the life that his anxious parents think he should live, nor a life according to the purpose of the educator who thinks he knows best" (Neill and Lamb 1992).

Take another look at Figure 3.1. What do the descriptors in each category reveal about how students and teachers are perceived? What vison of education is being advocated? You may notice that on the left side of the graphic, the student's role is largely to comply and conform. The guiding metaphor is one of school as work, which means students are workers and teachers are

Figure 3.1 Creating a new story of learning.

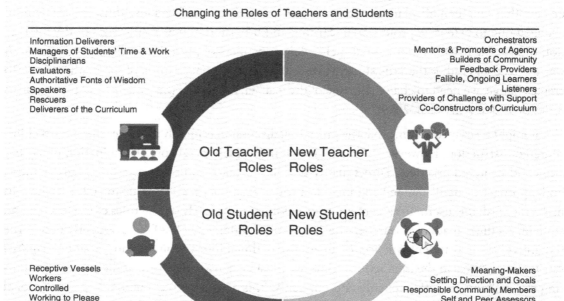

Creating a new story of learning.

Changing the Roles of Teachers and Students

Information Deliverers
Managers of Students' Time & Work
Disciplinarians
Evaluators
Authoritative Fonts of Wisdom
Speakers
Rescuers
Deliverers of the Curriculum

Orchestrators
Mentors & Promoters of Agency
Builders of Community
Feedback Providers
Fallible, Ongoing Learners
Listeners
Providers of Challenge with Support
Co-Constructors of Curriculum

Old Teacher Roles   New Teacher Roles

Old Student Roles   New Student Roles

Receptive Vessels
Workers
Controlled
Working to Please
Unquestioning
Listeners
Avoiding Mistakes
Confined & Defined by the Curriculum

Meaning-Makers
Setting Direction and Goals
Responsible Community Members
Self and Peer Assessors
Questioners
Active Communicators
Learning from Mistakes
Co-Constructors of Curriculum

managers and evaluative bosses. On the right side, there is a sense of students as more active and engaged in the learning, and teachers working with students in a responsive way. There is a sense of community and a metaphor of school as about learning and personal development. These shifts are further elaborated on in Figure 3.2.

I want to emphasize that these three types of learners—conforming, engaged, and empowered—are not a sequential progression. In fact, many students over-learn the message of school as work, and students as compliant, conforming workers, and then it becomes very difficult to engage them. They constantly look to authority to provide them with direction because they so want to please and conform (Deresiewicz 2015). It is also worth noting that conforming, or obedience, are not necessarily the foundation of respect, caring, good manners, and socialization— things we all care about. These practices are better understood as being rooted in community

Figure 3.2 What type of learner are we promoting?

What type of learner are we promoting?

	Guiding Metaphor	Key Student Actions	Key Teacher Actions	Define Success
CONFORMING	School as work set forth and defined by someone else.	Follows rules & directions, obeys, completes task as defined. Or, rebels by doing nothing (non-conforming).	Defines & explains task (which may be given by curriculum guides) along with associated rewards & punishments. Supports & monitors completion. Focuses on the "what" of teaching.	Grades, scores, completion, grade level expectations and standards
ENGAGED	School as learning done for a purpose.	Shows interest, sees relevance, extends task	Situates task in meaningful context, sets understanding goals and purpose, remains open to extensions, coaches individual growth, presses for thinking. Focuses on the "how" of teaching and begins to bring in the "why."	Depth, understanding, participation extension, excitement
EMPOWERED	School as growth and development of whole person.	Sets direction and goals, displays agency, makes choices, pursues passions, defines task, creates and innovates.	Looks for ways to help students develop confidence in their abilities, see the power of their contributions, and connect to the world. Helps students set goals for learning and focus on their own "why." Pushes and presses students' thinking.	Innovation, creation, agency, self-efficacy, passion, joy, individual growth

building and empathy toward others. Children who follow the rules out of obedience to authority and compliance are more likely to transgress when that authority is absent than those that adhere out of a sense of responsibility to their community. It is also important to acknowledge that we are not talking about a wholesale handing over of authority as we focus on engagement and empowerment, but rather a shift in how that authority is used. That shift is from the focus on control and obedience toward "liberation, empowerment, and supporting students in seeing and thinking for themselves" (Peterson 1992).

WHAT THE RESEARCH SAYS: *WHY* DOES IT MATTER?

Many factors are at play as we consider teacher and student roles and what is necessary to craft a new story of learning in our schools. Reviewing the research, I've identified four well-supported elements on which to focus: 1) supporting student agency, empowerment, and leadership; 2) attending to the balance of who's talking and who's listening; 3) encouraging behaviors that support initiative and resilience; and 4) celebrating powerful and productive identities. Each provides a good starting point for re-conceptualizing teacher and student roles.

On Supporting Agency

Schools have traditionally focused on producing compliant and conforming learners within a power dynamic where teachers exert control. However, in a culture of thinking, we envision students as more engaged and empowered learners (see Figure 3.2). To accomplish this, teachers must share power. When teachers hold all the power and make all the decisions in the classroom, students' levels of engagement decrease significantly (Wolpert-Gawron 2018). In addition, such environments don't provide students the opportunities they need to develop as independent, self-regulating learners, capable of decision making, critical thinking, or creativity (Flynn and Colby 2017; Stefanou, Perencevich, DiCintio, and Turner 2004; Tomlinson 2001; Zhao, 2012). What we are after is students becoming partners in their educational experiences so that we can build a robust community of learners inclusive of both teachers and students (Peterson 1992).

Teachers don't simply relinquish power, however. Teachers must gradually build students' capabilities and provide them with opportunities to exert greater control and choice over the direction and form of their learning (Broom 2015). Gradually releasing control to permit greater agency and choice to students helps students develop as responsible, independent learners (Garcia 2003). Thus, sharing power is not a zero-sum game. The teacher does not need to lose power for students to gain it. It is more a matter of developing students' capacity for self-direction, trusting them, and allowing them to take responsibility for their learning. In his book *World Class Learners*, Yong Zhao makes clear that this is not merely a question of providing students with more freedom, but requires creating "an infrastructure designed to assist children to personalize their learning experiences" (Zhao 2012, p. 181). When students have more autonomy over their learning processes, they develop a strong sense of "personal meaningfulness in the process and content," resulting in increased engagement (Furtak and Kunter 2012). Furthermore, having choice and being able to set one's direction is associated with positive feelings of "autonomy, motivation, and healthy functioning," which enhances one's intrinsic motivation (Ryan and Deci 2000) as well as increasing "effort, task performance, and perceived competence" (Patall, Cooper, and Wynn 2010).

On Teacher and Student Talk

On average, teacher talk constitutes 70% to 80% of all the talk done in classrooms (Hattie 2009). Teachers may dominate classrooms with their own talk for fear that a lack of sufficient explanation on their part could lead to misconceptions among students, while others talk to ensure that students have all the information needed to complete a task (DeWitt 2017). When teacher talk dominates, students are "swiftly disenfranchised by hierarchical models of education," which "inhibits their curiosity and initiative" (Ostroff 2020). Without opportunities to talk, not only are students unable to clarify their understanding, but also teachers lose the chance to monitor students' learning and intervene appropriately (Fisher and Frey 2014). This is why the preceding study of trying to teach mathematics more meaningfully was problematic when teachers dominated the discourse (Hill, Litke, and Lynch 2018).

Through classroom discussions, students learn the norms of discourse and develop the skills to explain their reasoning, provide evidence for their claims, and respectfully critique arguments, all of which are part of democratic discourse in civic life (McGregor 2004a). The amount of academic discourse in mathematics classrooms has been shown to improve learning outcomes even for English language learners and low-income students (Imbertson 2017). When the learning environment promotes classroom talk, students are consistently explaining and justifying their thinking, encouraging deep learning that mere didactic instruction cannot achieve (Gillies 2014). The process of articulating one's thoughts facilitates the learning process. However, if teachers, rather than the students, are doing most of the talking, then they are the ones doing most of the thinking (Fisher and Frey 2014).

When teachers stop talking and really listen to their students, students feel heard, cared for, and valued as individuals (Sadowski 2013). Listening allows us to better understand who our learners are, their passions, and what they are curious about. This information can be useful and important for designing and delivering deeper learning experiences (Pandolpho 2018). "Listening is the zone in which inquiry happens, in which questions arise and tug at us and the seeds of ideas germinate" (Steen 2017). When teachers listen, they are modeling "dialogue, collaboration, creativity, and compassion" (Steen 2017). By taking the role of listener, teachers shift the ownership of learning to students, allowing them to engage in deeper learning and develop the skills needed to become active members in the community (Michaels, O'Connor, Hall, and Resnick 2010; Rebora 2020). Trevor MacKenzie explains the transformative power of listening in his own classroom, "I asked them about their learning and their strengths and their stretches. I asked, and then I listened to what they had to say and ultimately, I learned from them. The more I listened and learned the more I realized I was changing" (MacKenzie 2021, p. xix).

On Initiative and Reliance

For students to develop a sense of initiative, self-efficacy, and resilience, they must be given roles that require those skills. At the same time, we must be careful of assuming the role of rescuer in which we rob students of the opportunity to develop these attributes. Too many students today find themselves ill-prepared for the rigors of university and professional life as they have grown up in a culture of "safetyism," which leads to more fragility and less resilience (Deresiewicz 2015; Lukianoff and Haidt 2019). Very often, when teachers notice a student stuck midway through a task or assignment, they are quick to dive in to "rescue" them (Thompson 2010). This may be due to a fear that students will perceive the "struggle" as a lack of support, and the frustration could push them to become completely disengaged (Fisher and Frey 2014). While it is true that teachers should create a supportive environment where learning is scaffolded within a zone of proximal development, overly protective practices or "helicopter teaching" is "counterproductive to building independent, confident, and creative students" (Kittle and Gallagher 2020) and may produce *learned helplessness* in which students lose their sense of agency and competence (Seifert 2004). While students may perceive that they learn more from "hand-holding" or "spoon feeding" by their teachers, this is not necessarily true. Students often misperceive that they are learning more from didactic instruction, when in reality, they develop a deeper understanding of the material when they are active participants in the classroom (Deslauriers, McCarty, Miller, Callaghan, and Kestin 2019).

On Identity

What it means to be "a good student" or considered "smart" in a particular subject or classroom are socially developed constructs. They are part of the story of learning we are telling. Not surprisingly, the dominant constructions of the "ideal student" tend to be raced, classed, and gendered (Archer 2012). Thus, not all students have equal opportunities to step into the identities being celebrated and reinforced in the classroom or within a subject field. When students' actions challenge or subvert these dominant identities, they will be viewed as out of place, subversive, or not worthy of a teacher's time (Butler 1999). Their actions will be perceived the way "bad grammar" is. Consider a classroom in which a good student is seen as someone who is quick with the right answer and completes all their work. In such a setting, asking "what if" questions may attract disapproval if not scorn from both the teacher and other students. Curiosity, which should be seen as a strength, gets characterized as disruptive, annoying, and off-task because it interferes with the teacher getting through the lesson.

At its core, learning is not merely the acquisition of new knowledge, but an ongoing process of identity development (Lave and Wenger 1991). Our identities are always in process, constantly under construction (Hall 1990). Furthermore, our identities are not singular in nature. In performing their classroom identities, students draw on the various identities they are forming within their culture, family, community, employment, friendship group, and more. All these worlds are constantly in play. As teachers, we must ask ourselves how we are leveraging these various identities in service of engagement in meaningful learning in our classrooms. In their longitudinal study of elementary science students' identities, Heidi Carlone and her colleagues (2015) found that the more overlap there was between students' identity development outside school and the classroom's celebrated roles and identities, the easier and less threatening it was for students to step into the role of being a "good student" or "smart scientist." For instance, when collaboration and helpfulness were promoted as part of being a good student, students could draw on their experience as family members with younger siblings to help realize that identity. Likewise, when questioning and a playful approach was encouraged, students drew on their natural identities as children to bring these qualities into the classroom. In contrast when being smart was "knowing the answers to the teacher's questions," many students came to view themselves as just not good students.

The opportunity to try on, assume, and feel comfortable in certain roles is important for students' identity formation. If students are to become writers, scientists, artists, geographers, entrepreneurs, designers, or mathematicians, they must have the opportunity to try on these roles and envision them as possibilities for their lives. "Even with overwhelming constraints of structures shaping daily interactions, practices, and meanings [in schools], youth exert some intentionality, making choices and creating meanings and narratives about themselves, marking some identities 'thinkable' and others 'unthinkable'" (Carlone et al. 2015). To assist our students' future happiness and success, we must make the broadest range of future identities "thinkable" for our students, allowing them to construct rich narratives of possibilities. We must constantly ask ourselves: How can we help our students to see themselves as competent, self-directed learners and thinkers in our subject area?

VISIONS AND REFLECTIONS: *HOW* MIGHT IT LOOK?

What might a classroom look like when the roles of students and teachers shift in a way that leads to greater engagement and empowerment? And, importantly, how is it that teachers might support this process over time?

Constructing Our Vision

The words *empowered* and *engaged* are thrown around a lot in education today, and I've used them quite a bit in discussing student and teacher roles. Take some time now to consider them more fully. Imagine stepping into a classroom where you immediately have the sense that students in the class are both engaged and empowered as learners. What do you see and hear them doing that causes you to make this assessment? See if you can come up with at least 10 actions. *You might want to jot these down.*

Review your list (either what you did mentally or wrote down) and select the three actions from your list that you feel have the most power, potential, or influence. You're prioritizing to identify high-leverage practices. Write these in the center of the page or document on which you are recording (your own paper, pages at the end of this chapter, or your device). Leave space on both sides of your list to make additional notes (see Table 3.1). For each of your "powerful

Table 3.1 Recording template: Engaged and empowered learners.

Teacher Scaffolding and Supports	Student Actions/High-Leverage Practices	Contribution of Student Actions
	1.	
	2.	
	3.	

actions" consider: What did the teacher need to do to scaffold and support this action to make it a comfortable and routine behavior for students? Write your responses to the left of that action. On the right-hand side, record how this action contributes to students' deeper learning and development as a thinker. What's the payoff?

It can be both exciting and frustrating to look at engaged and empowered students in a classroom (real or imagined) and realize that that image doesn't look like our own classroom. However, when this is the case, we shouldn't chalk it up to "Well that teacher just has a good class." Instead, we should consider what it takes to get students to that point. What are the scaffolds and supports, steps and processes along the way that enabled this? This helps us to see that teaching is always a process and that we cannot expect behaviors from our students that we have not developed and supported.

Group Discussion

If you are reading this book with others, bring your lists, writings, and perhaps drawings to share and discuss.

➤ Do you share a similar top-level list of behaviors you would expect to see in an engaged and empowered classroom?
➤ If not, how did individuals make and justify their choices?
➤ Discuss how you might further scaffold and support the development of these behaviors in your collective classrooms.

Contemplating Pictures of Practice

To further extend your vision of what it means to create a new story of learning in classrooms by shifting the roles of students and teachers, we now look at two pictures of practice that can be useful in drawing out some particulars and context. In both cases, the teachers embraced the idea of greater student independence and deeper learning through engagement and empowerment as an important shift they wanted to make in their teaching. Their efforts represent an organic shift they made in their teaching over time as they challenged some old assumptions and the traditional grammar of schools.

Case One: A Throughline of Empowerment. I had the opportunity to be in Susan Osgood's 1st-grade classroom in Denver, Colorado, frequently as we collaborated on various initiatives. One thing that has stayed with me from our association was how Susan empowered her students. Like every teacher, Susan wanted her students to behave and be respectful. This is especially important for 1st graders who are still new to school and working in groups. However, she didn't merely want students to behave out of a sense of compliance and obedience. Susan recognized that if her students were to learn from and with one another and to develop independence as learners, these behaviors must come from within. Thus, Susan chose to use her authority as a teacher to develop self-awareness and regulation in her students and cultivate empowerment.

Susan accomplished these by establishing two "throughline questions" in her classroom: 1) What is my responsibility to myself? 2) What are my responsibilities to our community? Susan began the year by discussing these questions with students, getting their ideas about what it means to take responsibility for oneself as well as in a community, and why each was important. The class talked through various scenarios to understand how responsibility can manifest into specific actions. For example, students named that when other people are concentrating it is distracting to talk loudly. You have a responsibility to them to be quiet. Or, when you are working on something you have a responsibility to try your best. Throughout the year, when problems, difficulties, and misbehaviors occurred, Susan did not simply reprimand students and use her authority to coerce them into behaving. Instead, she employed her authority to nurture self-awareness of the situation and what was happening and to promote self-regulation. It wasn't magic, and there were plenty of bumps in the road, but over time, Susan's class became not only more of a community, but also more empowered as individuals.

Case Two: Partners in Assessment.[1] There is perhaps no area of schooling in which teachers hold a tighter rein and exert more authority than grading and reporting. Assessment, and in particular, evaluative grading, is often something done *to* students rather than *with* them. However, if we truly want to empower our students and develop their sense of independence, efficacy, and agency, then it is important that we invite them into the process. There are many avenues by which this might occur, from self- and peer assessment to conferencing with students about their work, from co-constructing rubrics to student-led conferences. Trevor MacKenzie makes use of all these opportunities to bring students into the assessment conversation, but extends it one step further by co-constructing report cards with his secondary English and technology students at Oak Bay High School in Victoria, British Columbia, Canada.

Trevor initiates this collaborative process by creating a Google Form where students can reflect on the course learning objectives. He makes sure these are written in student-friendly language so that they are accessible. For example: "I can access information for diverse purposes and from a variety of sources to inform my writing," "I can recognize the complexities of digital citizenship," and so on. Students get ready for a conference with Trevor by self-assessing their abilities regarding the learning objectives and preparing for a discussion of questions such as: Who are you becoming as a learner? What are you noticing about yourself as a learner and thinker? What and how do you want to grow over time? What are your future learning goals for next term? Students also develop an actionable strategy for achieving their goals, reflect on their body of work, and use the routine "I used to think. . . . Now I think. . . ."

While others prepare, gather documents, or rehearse with peers, Trevor meets with students one-on-one for 10 minutes. As students share their reflections and observations, Trevor types directly into the school's online assessment portal. He works with students to shape the report so that it feels authentic, meaningful, and helpful. Once complete, Trevor reads the comment to the student for approval. For example:

> *A strong collaborator who does well in small groups, Jackson perfectly shares the workload with others and specifically enjoys working with a friend. A self-identified strength is his communication with others. Jackson always seeks out clarification from Mr. MacKenzie and his peers. He enjoys receiving and giving feedback to improve and broaden his perspective. Work ethic is another area of strength for Jackson. He is on task and does his work in a timely manner. A future learning goal is to improve his essay writing. A strategy to help in this area is to use a peer edit to revise his work.*

Grades are then determined together by reviewing the student's work. Emphasis is on the growth and current performance rather than a mere average of grades. Student's self-assessment is factored in as part of their grade so that the conference is not seen as a mere formality. Trevor finds that students tend to be much harsher graders then he is and only a few overestimate their abilities. If either an under or over estimation happens, a fresh and candid conversation based on students' actual work to identify a realistic grade together ensues.

Choosing Questions and Recording Responses

Different questions serve us at different times in our learning. Therefore, I suggest you read through the questions and identify:

➤ One or two that speak to you now. Questions that might challenge you or take your thinking in new directions.
➤ One or two you would most like to discuss with your colleagues.
➤ Circle and date the questions you select now so you can identify how your focus shifts with time and experience.
➤ Use the blank pages at the end of this chapter or your note-taking device to record your reflections.

- What am I doing for my students that they could be doing for themselves?
- Where do students have a voice in meaningfully shaping their experience, lives, and learning in my classroom? To what extent are students allowed to be decision makers in this process or are all ideas and suggestions subject to my approval?
- When was the last time a discussion in my class was mostly student-led? How did that go?
- Where do students need more supports, structures, language, or tools to assume a greater role in leading discussions? How might I do that?
- How effective is the seating arrangement in my classroom in terms of facilitating both productive learning and student self-direction? Do I use seating charts to control students? If so, how might I develop guidelines that permit effective and organized flexible seating as an option for students?
- Where, when, and how am I co-constructing curriculum and assessments with my students?
- How do I engage students in creating classroom procedures, policies, norms and/or ways of being in the classroom? How do these have a meaningful and ongoing life in our classroom? How are these guidelines evaluated, reviewed, and discussed regarding their effectiveness?
- How am I explicitly helping students to prioritize, organize, and manage their own learning?
- How am I helping students to improve in their self- and peer assessments? How can I create more opportunities to practice these skills?

- Where and when was the last time I found myself just listening to students without intervening? Where was a time I wish I could have a "do over" so that I could be a listener rather than an interjector?
- At the end of my last class, who was working harder during the lesson, me or my students?
- How might I bring in the positive identities students have outside of school into the classroom?
- How is my school bound by "the grammar of schools"? Are there things we simply assume must be the way they are but can in fact be changed?

DATA, PRINCIPLES, AND PRACTICES: *WHAT* ACTIONS CAN WE TAKE?

Having examined the research, looked at pictures of practice, and reflected on the story of learning being told in our classrooms, we now have a better understanding of why it is important to shift that story in a way that engages and empowers students. Furthermore, our exploration of the force exerted by the grammar of schools helps us to understand how the story of learning in schools is too often constrained and limited. As we seek to write a new story of learning, it is useful to keep in mind the adage: you need to go slow to go fast. Before we jump in to make changes, it is useful to collect some street data that can inform our actions and ground them to our context.

Collecting Street Data

Street Data

➤ Helps us understand our own context as well as students' perspectives.
➤ Is relatively easy and quick to collect.
➤ Can be immediately analyzed and acted upon straightaway.
➤ Is meant to inform and suggest action.
➤ Is NOT an evaluation or measure of success but a snapshot of practice.
➤ Can take many forms: observations, interviews, surveys, exit tickets, recordings, and so on.

As you ready yourself to take action, consider what data might inform your efforts and allow you to build on and address issues related to where you are currently. The following two street data actions can be a useful starting place. The first focuses on better understanding who is talking in class conversations and the second on helping to shape students' roles. It can also be helpful to construct your own "street data" actions that help you understand issues and events you are curious about. In doing so, consider: What might I learn from this data and how might I use it to inform my next actions? How will this data shed light on the status of things and help identify things that need to change or promising practices we can leverage? Use street data continuously, as opposed to only at the beginning, to take stock of where you are both individually and as a school in crafting a new story of learning and to identify ways in which you can continue to move forward.

Street Data Action One: Conversation Mapping. Create a visual snapshot of the flow of conversation in a discussion through a conversation map that captures who participates, when, and how often. Begin by creating a diagram with all students' names as they appear in the seating arrangement (a table, circle, or rectangular arrangement is likely to work best and facilitate mapping). Be sure to include yourself on the map. When the discussion begins, you, a colleague, or even a student will draw a line inside the circle from the first speaker to the second speaker. Next, draw a line linking the second speaker and the third speaker, and so on. Gradually, you will create a continuous web of lines that show the flow of the conversation. If possible, you may want to number each contribution to show you the order in which people spoke. This process can also be done using Equity Maps for the iPad. Other tech tools include: Talk Time, a Chrome extension for Google Meets that detects each speaker's voice automatically and records the time they speak. Time to Talk is an iOS app that detects and monitors male and female speakers' talk time, best for older students or adults. Unblah is an iOS app that monitors your own voice and issues a red warning if you go on for too long. You might also want to consider making note of different conversation moves (connecting on, respectful disagreement, raising questions, bringing in new perspectives, and so on) that students use. Some questions to consider from the data are:

- What interesting or surprising details, moments, or events from the conversation do you recall? Why were they interesting?

- What is interesting, surprising, or confirming about looking at the conversation in this way?

- What patterns, trends, or flows do you notice?

- Was this a balanced conversation? An equitable conversation? A lopsided conversation? A rich conversation? A fruitful conversation? What makes you say that?

- Did students listen to each other in the conversation as evidenced by how they built on, connected to, or recognized the contributions of others?

- Who didn't speak? Why might this have happened? How might you help this student to find their voice and contribute a bit more?

- Who dominated? Do you think these individuals were aware of their dominating the conversation? How can you help them to share the air?

- Where were there productive moments of silence for individuals to reflect, compose, and organize their thoughts?
- Where and when will you return this to your students for their examination and reflection?

Street Data Action Two: What makes a good student? Engage your students in an exploration of what makes a good student. This can be focused on a particular subject area, if you like, such as: "What makes a good science/math/art student?" This could be done through a whole-class or small-group discussion or simply having students write a paragraph explaining their thoughts. If you have time for individual interviews (of even some students), you might consider doing a card sort activity. On each card, write a behavior that someone might identify as being important to being a good student. For instance, "knowing the right answers," "listening to others," "keeping an open mind," "paying attention to the teacher," "doing your homework," "being curious," and so on. Aim for a variety of practices and try to identify at least 10. Working with an individual student, ask them to sort the cards into "yes," "no," or "maybe" categories to indicate the importance of that behavior to being a good student. Ask the student to explain the various practices to you as they sort and provide an example of it from their experience if they can. Next, have them select the three most important practices for succeeding in your class or at your school and explain why. Finally, ask them to identify the three practices that would be important in their "ideal" school or class. It is useful to work through this process yourself or with colleagues before doing it with students so that you will have a basis for comparison. It is not necessary to do this with every student to get a good sense of things. In addition, you could have students do this in small groups to spark discussion. Examining the data from both individuals and the group, reflect on:

- What is surprising to you?
- What practices did students pick that you expected? That you didn't?
- Do their responses indicate that they view good students as being compliant or engaged?
- Do their responses reflect a fixed or a growth mindset?
- Are there trends or patterns in the data?
- How different were students' picks on what is important in their current school/class from what would be important in their ideal school/class?
- How different are their responses from your own?
- Are there qualities and practices you would like to emphasize more in your class so students understand their importance?

Stating the Mindset as Principles for Action

Turning a mindset into principles for action helps to guide and direct our efforts. Principles tell us what to do broadly in a top-level, overarching way. From our basic principles, we construct specific actions that embody the principles and put them into play. Principles are the bridge we build between the "how" and the "what." For our mindset, "To create a new story of learning, we must change the role of the student and the teacher," we might say that in principle we need to share power, support independence and identity formation, and listen to our students. What exactly does that mean?

- Bring students into processes (such as, assessment, leading discussions, or the choice of curricular topics) that teachers typically control so that they are co-constructors who experience ownership of these processes.
- Scaffold and support students in developing the skills they need to engage in their learning more independently. Avoid stepping in to rescue them.
- Develop students' identity as learners and thinkers by pinpointing the cognitive skills students will be acquiring through each instructional interaction based on their role. Make sure these are the skills needed for successful deep learning in the subject area.
- Practice listening more and talking less. Be explicit about why you are doing this and what you are learning when you listen, and they talk.

Possible Actions

Crafting a new story of learning and changing student and teacher roles will likely look and sound quite different across various classrooms and disciplines. There is ample room for individuals to put their own creative stamp on things and bring in effective practices from other sources. The following actions described are:

➤ Drawn from our work in schools as part of the Worldwide Cultures of Thinking Project.
➤ Placed under the related principle to help you focus on the driving motivation behind each action.
➤ Modifiable to fit your local context.
➤ Connected to the most relevant cultural forces to which each specific action is associated. Both frameworks, the 8 cultural forces and the 10 mindsets, are synergistic and you can begin your journey either place.

Bring Students into the Process. Curriculum and assessment are two areas in which students—and sometimes even teachers—can feel disenfranchised by mandates and controls from outside the classroom. Often, these are viewed as an immutable aspect of the *grammar* of schools put in place to perpetuate the status quo. Indeed, they can be quite effective at doing so. A different perspective is to view curriculum and assessments as flexible structures to which students can add their voice rather than as immutable scripts to which both teachers and students must adhere (Greene 2000; Ketsman 2013). Treat the curriculum not as a contract but as a guide. Look for opportunities to connect the curriculum to students' lives and interest while still achieving prescribed objectives. Similarly, look for ways to expand your notions of assessment and reporting to bring students into the process through such practices as peer and self-assessment or student-led conferences as a reporting mechanism to parents and families (Edutopia 2015).

The idea of *co-construction* implies that both students and teachers contribute their ideas and evaluations to both the form and content of curriculum and assessments in a dynamic, creative interaction (May 1993). Although some might refer to this as providing *voice and choice*, co-construction involves entering into a true collaboration with our students. By placing students in this new role of co-constructors, they develop imagination, creativity, originality, and ownership. While the roles of students and teachers in co-creation are similar in that both bring ideas and meanings to the enterprise, they are different in that students' ideas may not always be directly contributed. Instead, they may come in the form of clues about the kinds of learning students are ready for. Pay attention to the clues students provide about their interests, passions, and questions. These do not always directly announce themselves, particularly with young children. The "clues received from students help a teacher to be a mediator, an agent between curriculum and students" (Ketsman 2013). Thus, teachers are still in charge of major decisions about the curriculum but are doing so based on clues they receive from students. Co-construction can extend to the environment as well. Enlist students in helping you curate, design, and organize the learning space of your classroom so it belongs to them as well as to you. The relevant cultural forces here are *expectations*, *interactions*, *environment*, and *opportunities*.

Scaffold and Support Students' Independence. Actively build the foundation of skills students will need to direct, monitor, and control their own learning, and then look for occasions when you can step back so that students can step forward. You can begin by identifying a process in which you would like to see more student independence and then identify the subskills and processes needed for that independence. Start small. Rather than turning over a whole discussion or major assignment, identify a small opportunity that can set the stage for grander performances later. In many instances, students' skills can be supported and grown through routines and protocols that outline specific steps and moves. For instance, structures such as "Leaderless Discussion" (Ritchhart and Church 2020), "Reciprocal Teaching" (Carter 1997), the "Micro Lab Protocol" (Ritchhart et al. 2011) or "the Harkness Method" (Sevigny 2012) can help students learn to lead discussions on their own.

Teach students what good discussions and productive group learning looks like by using techniques such as "the fishbowl" where students gather around to watch a small group engage in the process being learned. Students analyze the features, structure, and language of the small group so that they will be more effective at carrying out the process on their own. This learning can also be done by sharing videos of productive group work or discussions from previous years. By doing this repeatedly over time and with practice, students will start to incorporate these behaviors. Teach students to use "accountable talk" that focuses on listening and connecting one's own ideas to others. This can be introduced and reinforced by posting sentence stems for students' use such as, "I agree with . . . ," "Building on what _____ said," "I have another perspective on this," and so on. The relevant cultural forces here are *expectations*, *modeling*, *language*, *interactions*, and *routines*.

Practice listening more and talking less. When we are constantly in "teacher mode," it can be hard to listen because we are focused on opportunities to jump in and re-direct or provide information. It's not that those practices aren't needed, but they will be more useful and better informed if based upon our effective listening. When students are working in groups, or even individually, announce that you are in listening mode. You might even tell students what you are listening for—connections, confusions, questions, or whatever is relevant to that piece of learning. Take a pad of paper to record what you are hearing. If students try to pull you in or get you to rescue them, re-direct their efforts back to the learning while acknowledging you have made note of their issue or question, and it will be addressed. As you and your students get used to this process, the listening time is likely to grow longer. At the appropriate time, share with the class what you are hearing: "Many people seem confused by . . . ," "I'm noticing lots of connections being made related to . . . ," "Lots of great questions are surfacing." Offer the re-directs, support, and information to the whole group as needed, first inviting students themselves to address the issues, questions, and challenges. If an important question needs to be addressed or conversation had immediately, rather than only engage in it with the one student or group, invite the entire class to listen in to the conversation.

If you tend to over-explain or offer too many directions at once, look for ways you might rein yourself in. You might set a timer for 8 to 10 minutes and inform students that you are limiting your initial talk to just that amount of time. Review your directions and look for how you might chunk them and deliver them in stages instead of all at once. People need to know the purpose behind what they are doing, however, they will easily get overwhelmed if there are more than two steps to which they must attend. You can tell students there are several steps to the process, but at this stage you want them to only focus on one or two, and you will provide the other steps later. If students can provide some explanation to each other, call on them to do so. Keep in mind the WAIT principle by asking yourself: Why Am I Talking? The relevant cultural forces here are *expectations*, *language*, *interactions*, and *time*.

Develop Students' Identity as Learners. Due to the grammar of schools, students come to our classrooms with preconceived notions of what it means to be a good student, a mathematician, a scientist, an artist, and so on. To change that grammar, we must explicitly teach a new one. Identify the skills you want to nurture in your students. With students, discuss why these are important and identify specific grade-appropriate behaviors associated with the skills, perhaps even creating a poster for reference. Where possible, link these learning behaviors to behaviors and practices students already engage in. For instance, in playing a sport you need to notice a lot of things at once and pay attention to details and small moves. These same skills will be important in engineering. Then, create opportunities for students to practice those behaviors in authentic learning situations. Name, notice, and celebrate when you see students engaged in these behaviors. Make these behaviors part of your assessment conversations with students. Emphasize that development of these skills takes time and attention. Create opportunities for at least some of these skills to be used every lesson. The relevant cultural forces here are *expectations*, *language*, *opportunities*, *interactions*, and *time*.

Fitting New Actions with Current Realities

Before you rush to implement the actions you are eager to try, step back and think about what you are currently doing at your school (see Figure 3.3):

➤ What actions, already in place, can be *amplified* and grown by applying some of the principles previously identified?

➤ What practices need to be rethought or *modified* considering this mindset?

➤ What do you need to stop doing altogether and *remove* from our repertoire? Why? Does it run counter to this mindset? Is it ineffective? What "moveable barriers" are standing in the way of truly living this mindset?

➤ Finally, are there things that you need to *create*, totally new processes, structures, or actions to begin to put in place?

Figure 3.3 Amplify-Modify-Remove-Create.

Review of Current Practice: What do we need to...

AMPLIFY	MODIFY	REMOVE	CREATE

Conclusion: Our Theory of Action

We conclude our examination of this mindset "To create a new story of learning, we must change the role of the student and the teacher" by formulating a "theory of action" in which we hypothesize the likely effects of our actions based on the research and experience upon which we have drawn. I offer the following theory of action for Mindset 3. Use it if it captures the actions you plan to take and the outcomes you expect. If it doesn't, feel free to craft your own theory of action that will better fit your context. To do this, first clarify both what you will be doing and why we are doing it. Then, identify particulars you might look for to know when and to what extent you have been successful.

> *If* we support students in becoming active creators, initiators, problem finders and community members while we as teachers focus on coaching, mentoring, and being community navigators, *then* students' understanding, engagement, curiosity, and self-direction will increase.

Notes

Students Learn Best When They Feel Known, Valued, and Respected by Both the Adults in the School and Their Peers

A while back, a colleague shared the complaint of a secondary humanities teacher who recently had given up on using visible thinking routines. She made quite a public display of her frustration with them as teaching tools. This teacher stated that students (her own and others more generally) just didn't know enough to be able to use the routines effectively. She claimed that only a savant could engage in the cognitive demands of a thinking routine such as See-Think-Wonder at anything but a superficial level. Consequently, most students' responses were trite and didn't show any real grasp of the material she was teaching. Thus, she reasoned, one must rely on direct instruction as the only approach that can really be effective in producing learning.

The thing that struck me about her assessment was how little regard she seemed to have for her students as thinkers and learners. While they might not yet know the particulars she was teaching (why would she expect them to?), she completely dismissed all the skills, understandings, expertise, and various other types of capital her students did have. When teachers don't value what students bring with them into the classroom, we diminish students as individuals and dismiss their already substantive accomplishments as learners and thinkers. We also make it harder for them to integrate new ideas with their own existing understandings, which, in turn, impedes their application and retention of the new information we want them to understand. In doing so, we impart a message that teaching is transactional in nature, employing what Paulo Freire (2018) refers to as the "banking model" of education in which students are seen as empty vessels to be filled. This approach views students from a deficit perspective, focusing on what they lack and cannot do. In such a context, the only way for students to acquire worth is through the acquisition of the knowledge we impart to them. Since the way others see us, treat us, and respond to us shapes how we come to see ourselves, how then will these students ever come to see themselves as capable thinkers and learners?

Of course, one need not view teaching as transactional. Another stance is to view teaching as relational in which the goal is not the mere acquisition of knowledge but the transformation of who students are as people coming to understand and engage with the world. From such a stance, we focus not merely on imparting information, but also on understanding our students. This kind of teaching is rooted in curiosity. In the words of Vivian Paley, one of the all-time great teacher researchers, "The key is curiosity, and it is curiosity, not answers, that we model. As we seek to learn more about a child, we demonstrate the acts of observing, listening, questioning, and wondering. When we are curious about a child's words and our responses to those words, the child feels respected. The child is respected" (Paley 1986, p. 127). As a result of this curiosity, our image of the child is always evolving. The image we hold of our students is important because it directs our behavior. As Loris Malaguzzi, the founder of Reggio Emilia preschools, states, the image one holds "orients you as you talk to the child, listen to the child, observe the child. . . . All of this pushes us to produce a higher level of observation. We must move beyond just looking at the child to become better observers, able to penetrate into the child to understand each child's resources and potential and present state of mind" (Malaguzzi 1994, pp. 1–2).

In Mindset 3, I discussed the grammar of school, that is, the underlying structures we take for granted about how schools operate and are supposed to be. This grammar often keeps us locked in the status quo, making it difficult to see another way of doing things. In this chapter we rethink the role of teacher and students. The mindset we explore in this chapter represents a significant shift in the traditional grammar of schools as well. Here, the shift is from the transactional view of teaching to a relational and transformative model. We strive to move away from the empty vessel model of teaching in which we fill up students with our knowledge and toward a model that builds an inclusive community that respects what students bring with them. This view is rooted in our understanding that we are naturally social beings who strive for connection, inclusion, recognition, and a sense of belonging. These qualities are what make us feel safe and allow us to be more adventuresome in our learning, take risks, and make mistakes.

WHAT THE RESEARCH SAYS: *WHY* DOES IT MATTER?

In his 2013 book *Social: Why Our Brains Are Wired to Connect,* neuroscientist Matthew Lieberman makes the case that we are hard-wired to be social and that one of our deepest motivations is to stay connected with others and build community. He argues that Abraham Maslow had it wrong in terms of our hierarchy of needs beginning with basics like food, shelter, and warmth. What really drives us and has led our species to be dominant Lieberman argues is our desire and ability to think socially. Lieberman's studies have shown that the default resting state of our minds in those moments when we are not actively engaged in doing something else is to focus on social cognition, that is, thinking about other people, ourselves, or our relationship to others. In fact, specific regions of the brain become active in this resting set, which he refers to as the "default network." Lieberman and colleagues theorize that this keeps us primed to always be prepared for effective social thinking (Meyer, Davachi, Ochsner, and Lieberman 2019).

However, schools often view the tendency of students to be preoccupied with social concerns as a distraction, something we want them to stop doing so they can concentrate on the task at hand. Today, in some uninformed sectors, any attempt by educators to attend to social and emotional learning of students is viewed with suspicion (Anderson 2022; Atkin 2019). Lieberman argues that this is the wrong approach, that "almost everything in life can be better when we get more social. If we retune our institutions and our own goals just a bit, we can be smarter, happier, and more productive" (Lieberman 2013, p. 242). Furthermore, the interconnectedness of social, emotional, and academic development as central to the learning process has been well researched (Drulak, Domitrovitch, Weissberg, and Gullotta 2015; Jones and Kahn 2017). Thus, we need to use our students' natural social nature to our advantage, capitalizing on the motivational mechanisms that predispose us all to respond positively to signs we are connected to and appreciated by the group. In the process, we help students develop their understanding of themselves and others. We can do this by fostering a sense of belonging, building nurturing relationships with students, cultivating a climate of fairness and respect, and valuing our students.

Belonging

Feelings of relatedness and a sense of belonging are basic psychological needs (Baumeister and Leary 2017; Lieberman 2013; Ryan and Deci 2000). When these needs are met, people tend to be more personally motivated, leading to better performance and increased well-being (Wentzel and Caldwell 1997). An intervention by the Child Development Project in Oakland, California, found that fostering students' connectedness to school by developing caring communities of learners had both short- and long-term positive effects on elementary school students' attitudes, motivation, and positive behavior (Battistich, Schaps, and Wilson 2004). These effects continued as students entered middle school. In addition, students in the project had higher grades and test scores in middle school than those not involved. At the university level, Gregory Walton and Geoffrey Cohen (2007) found that "belonging uncertainty," most felt by underrepresented and marginalized groups, undermined students' motivation and achievement. This echoes findings from other studies that have shown social exclusion impairs performance on cognitive tasks with regard to both speed and accuracy (Baumeister, Twenge, and Nuss 2002). In contrast, when Walton and Cohen mitigated students' doubts about belonging, in this case, by simply sharing a letter written by an older student who had initial worries about fitting in but then successfully did so, students showed better academic achievement. What is most astounding is that this single, small manipulation endured over all of students' years at university. Study participants had a 0.2 GPA improvement over their peers each semester for three years.

One of the greatest threats to students' sense of belonging is bullying. Matthew Lieberman's work has shown that the emotional pain from bullying is felt as acutely as physical pain, perhaps even more so, as it is a threat to our connection to the group. He states, "Bullying hurts so much not because one individual is rejecting us but because we tend to believe that the bully speaks for others—that if we are being singled out by the bully, then we are probably unliked and unwanted by most" (Lieberman 2013, p. 69). Therefore, it is not surprising that attention, cognition, and motivation are affected similarly to how physical pain affects performance. The perceived prevalence of bullying at a school is negatively correlated with performance on achievement tests (Lacey and Cornell 2013). A recent large-scale study across 51 countries found that bullying victimization is associated with poorer academic achievement in all countries (Yu and Zhao 2021). At the same time, bullying is widespread and experienced by one out of every five students (Seldin and Yanez 2019). Early adolescents (ages 9–12) experience the most bullying at a rate of 49.8% (Patchin and Hinduja 2020).

Relationships

Strong teacher-student relationships provide the support students need to thrive, learn, and grow. They have a strong effect on student outcomes (Hamre and Pianta 2001; Hattie 2009). However, relationships must go beyond merely caring about students. It is important that these relationships provide challenge and stretch students while opening up new possibilities as well (Scales, Van Boekel, Pekel, Syvertsen, and Roehlkepartain 2020). Effective relationships are characterized by agency, efficacy, respecting what students bring to the classroom, and recognition of contributions (Hattie 2009). Studies of engaging classrooms find that these environments are both challenging and supportive. They are led by a "warm demander," that is, someone who cares deeply but also has high expectations (Ross, Bondy, Bondy, and Hambacher 2008; Shernoff 2013). Furthermore, the number of strong relationships reported by youth are positively related to academic motivation, socio-emotional skills, and responsibility, and inversely related with high-risk behaviors (Roehlkepartain et al. 2017).

As academic challenge increases, the greater the need for relational supports. Children are more motivated and willing to take learning risks when they feel supported by and positively related to others (Christenson, Reschly, and Wylie 2012). While research suggests positive relationships are important to all students, they appear to matter particularly in adolescence. Middle school students with high levels of teacher support are almost three times more likely to have high levels of engagement (Shernoff 2013). Middle school students who reported better student-teacher relationships were eight times more likely to stick with a challenging task, enjoy hard work, and accept mistakes when learning (Roehlkepartain et al. 2017). Unfortunately, quality student-teacher relationships are important but too rare. In a survey of 25,000 U.S. middle and high school students, the percentage of students reporting that teachers care *and* push them to be their best decreased from about a third of students in 6th grade to only 16% in 12th grade (Roehlkepartain et al. 2017).

Value, Fairness, and Respect

We all crave acknowledgment and a sense that we are valued. We want to be recognized not only for our accomplishments and hard work, but also for who we are as people. Of course, we want this from those closest to us, but studies show that even receiving positive affirmations from complete strangers activates the reward center of our brain and provides a dopamine boost (Davey, Allen, Harrison, Dwyer, and Yücel 2010; Izuma, Saito, and Sadato 2010), lifting our mood and engagement. Such recognition has been shown to be more of an incentive to workers than increased pay in some cases (Larkin 2011). The positive effects of such recognition can lead to improved thinking and decision making as well (Ashby and Isen 1999; Carpenter, Peters, Västfjäll, and Isen 2013).

Fairness and respect are two other important mechanisms that reinforce our connection to others and the group (Lieberman 2013). They have been shown to be important motivators of our actions and drivers of performance (Cornelius-White 2007; Rock 2009). Furthermore, data from workers in Western countries found being treated with fairness and respect is one of the strongest predictors of happiness at work (Friday Pulse 2022). Perceived fairness activates the reward center of the brain and makes us happier with the outcome, even in situations where we personally might benefit less (Tabibnia, Satpute, and Lieberman 2008). It draws us together and helps us to bond with others. Similarly, respect is a reciprocal concept that is grown and developed in a relationship, versus a hierarchical and forced form of respect, also connects us with others. As Sarah Lawrence Lightfoot states in her well-researched portrait of the concept of respect, "Respect creates symmetry, empathy, and connection in all kinds of relationships, even those, such as teacher and student, doctor and patient, commonly seen as unequal" (Lawrence-Lightfoot 1999).

VISIONS AND REFLECTIONS: *HOW* MIGHT IT LOOK?

What does significant learning in relationship look, sound, and feel like? What does it take to feel known, valued, and respected? How can we imagine a new reality beyond what currently exists? To help us formulate such a vision, we tap into our own experience. We then reflect on how we are helping our students to belong, grounding our teaching in fairness and respect, and building strong relationships with our students.

Constructing Our Vision

Take a moment to consider James Comer's oft-repeated maxim, "No significant learning can occur without a significant relationship" (Comer 1993). Think of your own moments of significant learning, times when you felt you had some real breakthroughs of understanding and development.

These might not be single moments, but a project or even a course. Try to identify two or three. Use the pages at the end of this chapter, the margins, a sheet of paper, or your electronic device to list these. See Table 4.1 for an example of how you might record your moments. Do this on the left side of your recording space in brief shorthand. For each of these, think about whom you were in relationship with. It might be colleagues, a mentor, or a friend. List these individuals in the center next to the associated significant learning example. Finally, on the right-hand side, identify how each individual supported and contributed to your learning. What did they do that made you able to engage deeply, take risks, try new things, and operate at your highest level?

Table 4.1 Recording template: Significant learning and significant relationships.

Significant Learning	In Relationship with . . .	They Supported and Contributed to My Learning by . . .
1.		
2.		
3.		

Group Discussion

If you are reading this book with others, bring your lists, writings, and perhaps drawings to share and discuss.

➤ What commonalities do you notice in your colleagues' identification of significant learning?
➤ What commonalities do you notice in your colleagues' identification of the supports and contributions individuals made to learning?
➤ How did each of the individuals you identified actualize the concepts of belonging, acknowledgment of value, fairness, and respect in their interactions with you?

Contemplating Pictures of Practice

To further extend your vision of what is involved in building strong relationships in which students feel valued, known, and respected that promote deep learning, we examine two case studies. Both teachers are colleagues I have worked with for many years in developing cultures of thinking at their respective schools. I've had the pleasure of visiting their classrooms to see their teaching in action. The teaching itself is masterful and incorporates many of the mindsets being explored in this book. However, in these two cases, I highlight the ways they help their students to feel valued, known, and respected.

Case One: Mathematics with Feeling. Jeff Watson has always worked hard to meet students where they are with the math content he teaches by scaffolding and supporting their thinking. As important as that was, over time, Jeff came to feel that he needed to meet students where they are emotionally as well, "How could I possibly jump into quadradic equations without checking in to see how students were feeling?" To accomplish this, Jeff created an emotions chart on his whiteboard next to the door.

The chart consisted of nine rows. The top row was labeled "Cloud 9" and then descended to "happy," "content," "meh," "sad," "angry," "emotionally lost," "stressed," and "not feeling it." He then purchased two dozen small, round magnets that students could randomly select and place anonymously in the row that matched their mood as they entered the class. In introducing the chart, Jeff explained that everyone (including teachers!) comes into class with emotions based on events throughout the day. Some students may be coming from a big test, some might have had a frustrating situation happen in the hallway, or some may have had something great just occur. These feelings, collectively and individually, provide the context for his teaching and their learning. For him to be a better teacher, Jeff tells them, he needs to know that information. In addition, as a community, if someone is hurting, we want to know so we can help. If someone is celebrating, we want to join in. The key to figuring this out is checking in with them through the emotion chart.

On a typical day, students walk in, choose a magnet, place it on the emotion chart, and then start doing a warmup activity. During this time, Jeff glances at the board to determine the general mood. If all magnets are "meh" or higher, he usually moves forward with the lesson. However, if magnets are scattered in "meh" and lower, he asks if anyone wants to share what they are feeling and why. Through this process Jeff often finds out things he didn't know about students. For example, one day a student said they were "tired" because they have swimming at 5:30 every morning. Until then, Jeff didn't even know they were on the swim team. Other students have shared frustrating events or celebrations, like the arrival of a new sibling.

Over time, Jeff feels this process has led to greater understanding and compassion for what students are going through. It makes it easier for him to connect with students, and for the students at this large high school to get to know each other. Each year, Jeff asks students what they want him to keep and what they want him to stop doing. Every single year the unanimous answer is to "Keep the emotion chart!"

Case Two: Together at a Distance. During the COVID-19 pandemic, all teachers struggled to connect with and get to know their students. Kristen Kullberg was no different. To build relationships and create community, Kristen leaned into her long-held values and prioritized listening to her students, promoting interactive dialogue, supporting creative engagement, and using thinking routines as scaffolding structures to support students' thinking and interaction. In a lesson over Zoom in which students explored the concept of *bravery* using the Making-Meaning routine (Ritchhart and Church 2020), these practices were in full display (scan the QR code to watch this video).

Making-Meaning video QR code.

As Kristen recaps the class's actions from the previous lesson, she continually mentions what "we" did, thus locating herself within the group and signaling the collective enterprise in which all were engaged. She then begins to display each student's questions about bravery on the screen one at a time, inviting them to read their response "loud and proud." This ensures all students' voices are heard early in the lesson and visually everyone can see their contribution to the class's burgeoning exploration of "bravery." With a sense of anticipation and excitement in her voice, Kristen instructs students to get the tin foil she asked them to bring, waving her box in the air to show she is ready as a learner with them. After explaining that they will each use the foil to make a representation of what bravery means to them over the next five minutes, Kristen instructs students to point their computer screens down so that their workspaces but not their faces are visible. This simple move allows students to take a break from having to look at themselves on screen as well as the excessive eye contact of Zoom, two documented causes of Zoom fatigue (Ramachandran 2021).

After a dramatic and exaggerated countdown, Kristen calls time and asks students to raise their hands and point their cameras back up. She explains that they will go into breakout rooms to discuss their creations. As Kristen sends students to their rooms, she notices one student still on the main screen who appears to have fallen asleep. After several attempts to arouse Marisa by calling her name in various intonations, she finally succeeds. Rather than criticize Marisa, Kristen empathizes with her about how all this online learning can get tiring. She then makes sure she is okay and reviews directions before sending her to her breakout room.

Instead of using this time to complete other tasks she might have, Kristen joins a breakout room herself and listens as three students share. After the sharing, she asks questions that help students go deeper: "What are some new ideas that you have about bravery that you wouldn't have had before?" As students share, Kristen listens intently and offers, "I totally connect with that as well." When one student responds, "I thought that bravery meant you were fearless, but now I know bravery means putting yourself in front of others in the case of fear," Kristen leans into her camera and engages with the student's thinking. "Yeah, I wonder: Can you be brave without first having fear? It's like you have to hold space for both." The authenticity and genuine interest she shows transcends the screen. Her curiosity is palpable. Before closing the breakout room, she thanks students for allowing her to join their conversation. Once again, a simple but powerful gesture. By thanking them, Kristen has indicated that she has received something of value from them.

As Kristen closes the lesson and sends students to their lunch, each says goodbye before exiting—all except Hector, who stays behind, eager to share his creation. Kristen listens as he explains what he has made, insisting it is not very good. Kristen interjects, "No I can see it. It's right there. That's awesome." At this point, Hector's mother enters the screen. Kristen inquires, "Is that your mother, Hector?" When he responds that it is, his mother approaches the screen and waves, "Hello." Kristen waves back and begins to tell her that Hector has been exploring "bravery." The mother then asks in Spanish how Hector is doing in class. Hector translates into English. Kristen responds to the question in her limited Spanish, adding in English when she doesn't have the words. Kristen's efforts, though not perfect, signal her desire to connect and her understanding of the challenges of navigating another language. She shows respect for Hector's home language and his linguistic skills.

Reflecting on Current Practice

As teachers, we like to assume that we have positive relationships with all our students. However, what is our evidence of this? What can we point to as specific practices to indicate we know our students as individuals? Have we changed our teaching in response to learning from and with our students? In addition to the academic growth we seek, are our students also growing socially and emotionally as individuals over their time with us? I offer the following questions for your reflections to help you probe a bit deeper into your building of community, support belonging, increase equity, and nurturing respect, fairness, and value. Some of the questions are adapted from the excellent book by Jalell Howard, Tanya Milner-McCall, and Tyrone Howard, *No More Teaching Without Positive Relationships* (2020).

Choosing Questions and Recording Responses

Different questions serve us at different times in our learning. Therefore, I suggest you read through the questions and identify:

- ➤ One or two that speak to you now. Questions that might challenge you or take your thinking in new directions.
- ➤ One or two you would most like to discuss with your colleagues.
- ➤ Circle and date the questions you select now so you can identify how your focus shifts with time and experience.
- ➤ Use the blank pages at the end of this chapter or your note-taking device to record your reflections.

- What does the seating arrangement of my classroom communicate? Does it reflect a community or individual orientation?
- When, where, and how are ALL my students' backgrounds, cultures, genders, neighborhoods, and sexualities represented in the visuals, literature, and examples in my classroom?
- How have/might I create an environment that honors and invites families to participate?
- How do/might I help students stay connected to their community and peers?
- Who might not feel included in my classroom or have a sense of "belonging uncertainty"? What can I do to mitigate those feelings?
- How do/might I deal with bullying behaviors, gossip, and micro-aggressions?
- What structures, routines, processes, protocols do/might I use to help students listen to one another and have meaningful conversations?
- Where is there humor, playfulness, or joy in my classroom? Where is there possibility for more?
- What does my language convey about inclusiveness, respect, community, and value?
- Where and how is my curiosity about my students as individuals demonstrated?
- How would my students know that I care about, value, and respect them?
- What do I know about each of my students as individuals beyond the classroom in terms of their strengths, passions, and interests in and out of school?
- What do students know about me beyond the classroom? What might it be helpful and appropriate for them to know?
- When was the last time I discussed nonacademic topics of interest to my students? What was it about and how did it help me to get to know my students?
- What do I know about my students' aspirations? How am/might I support the maintenance and growth of students' aspirations? When do I have conversations about students' future goals?
- What gets celebrated, acknowledged, or raised up in my classroom? For example, is it grades, progress, personal growth, kindness, collaboration, or . . . ? Who gets celebrated? Who doesn't?
- What does my approach to misbehavior and transgression say about my desire to build community and be empathetic, forgiving, fair, and supportive?
- How is my decision making transparent to my students? How might I do a better job of seeking out solutions that are fair and equitable for individuals and the class?
- Where and how do my students contribute positively to our community?
- When and how do I collect and use data or feedback to help me monitor and advance the relationships I am building with students?

DATA, PRINCIPLES, AND PRACTICES: *WHAT* ACTIONS CAN WE TAKE?

Having gained a better understanding of the facets of building relationships with your students and the importance of doing so, you are likely ready to take action to advance this mindset at your school and in your classroom. To lay the groundwork for your effective action, it is useful to collect some street data. By now, you are getting accustomed to collecting and using street data to inform your efforts. Whether you create your own actions or use those offered here, the important thing is to constantly take stock of where you are both individually and as a school in promoting this mindset.

Collecting Street Data

Street Data

➤ Helps us understand our own context as well as students' perspectives.
➤ Is relatively easy and quick to collect.
➤ Can be immediately analyzed and acted upon straightaway.
➤ Is meant to inform and suggest action.
➤ Is NOT an evaluation or measure of success but a snapshot of practice.
➤ Can take many forms: observations, interviews, surveys, exit tickets, recordings, and so on.

Street Data Action One: Relational Mapping. Carla Shalaby invites us to look at the unseen students, the disrupters, the disengaged, and even the troublemakers as the canaries in the coal mine (Shalaby 2017). These individuals can be an indicator that our classrooms and our teaching behaviors do not always make all students feel safe, known, respected, and supported. Use "Relational Mapping" to create a visual snapshot of students who are well supported and those most in need of additional support. The main steps of the process are presented here. More information and a video can be accessed by scanning the QR code.

QR Code for Relational Mapping video.

SCAN ME

1. List the names of all students (in a grade, department, class, or school) by first and last initial on chart paper or a whiteboard in a predesignated private meeting room. Alternatively, this could be done on a shared electronic document. However, the visual aspect of seeing all the data easily at once can be useful. Consider this information confidential, and only the teachers involved in the process should see the mapping and list.

2. Using circular red and yellow stickers (an "X" mark could also be used), each teacher involved with these students will place a yellow dot to the left of the name of any student

Figure 4.1 Relational mapping.

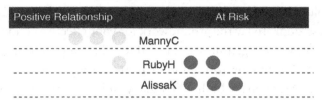

with whom they have a positive, trusting relationship and whom they believe *would come to see me if they had a personal problem*. Teachers place a red dot to the right of the name of any student they believe may be at risk for academic, personal, or other reasons. It is okay to place both red and yellow dots next to the same individual. While teachers will focus on students in their class, they should consider other students they know as well. Note: This step could be done individually before the group meets to discuss the data. See Figure 4.1.

3. Questions to consider from the quick data:
   - What's interesting or surprising?
   - What questions or reflections does the map evoke?
   - What possible factors contribute to some students having more yellow dots than others? More red dots?
   - Are there any students with no dots? Why might this be so? How can you get to know these students better?
   - What kinds of school-wide changes can be made to increase the number of yellow dots for students? Decrease the number of red dots?

Street Data Action Two: Interaction Analysis. Relationships are built in moments of small interactions accumulated over time. Consequently, attending to these small interactions, language moves, body language, posture, and micro-moments is important. This process begins with noticing these in ourselves and others. This analysis can be done in several ways to raise your awareness level:

1. Watch a video of a teacher you do not know (by yourself or with colleagues). The more unedited the video the better. You can search for these on the internet. One source is the

Massachusetts Department of Elementary and Secondary Education. Scan the QR code to access. While this analysis won't yield data, it can be useful in developing your analytical skills.

Massachusetts Department of Education videos QR code.

SCAN ME

2. Observe a colleague teach and take notes. This can be somewhat intimidating for the observed teacher, so it is important to have a trusting relationship. In addition, observation can be more challenging than using a video as interactions and language go by so quickly. This will yield some data.

3. The most useful data will come from videotaping yourself. Many schools have tech departments that can assist with this process, or you can simply use an electronic tablet or smart phone in a stand or on a tripod. You can either analyze the video yourself or do it with a colleague.

In your analysis, focus on examining the following interaction and language moves:

- Were there any language choices that seem to create space and opportunity for students to enter classroom conversation/dialogue? Conversely, was there language that shut students down or cut off the conversation/dialogue?

- How were students invited to communicate with each other or did all talk go through the teacher? Where were opportunities that might have been leveraged differently?

- Where and when did the teacher use inclusive language (we, our, us)? How and where else might the teacher have communicated that the class was a community of learners working together to build understanding?

- What does the teacher's body language, positioning in the classroom, and movement communicate?

- How were students acknowledged and valued? Did the teacher's comments focus on students pleasing them and being correct or on their contributions to the group's learning?

- Did the teacher use micro-affirmations (e.g., "I'm glad you're back with us today") that quickly and subtly communicated care, inclusion, or kindness?

- Was the feedback meaningful, specific, and true?

- Where and how did the teacher push students in a way that communicated they had high expectations and knew they were capable learners?

- How did the teacher show curiosity and interest in students' thinking beyond just being correct?

- Were there any micro-aggressions that diminished an individual or group? For instance, discounting someone's lived experience as not being the norm, using examples (or names) that only feature one group, jokes at other's expense, not using a person's preferred pronouns, not correctly pronouncing names, and so on.

Stating the Mindset as Principles for Action

Turning the mindset, "Students learn best when they feel known, valued, and respected by both the adults in the school and their peers," into principles for action can help guide and direct our efforts and shape our actions. We base these guiding principles on the research previously detailed:

- Nurture a sense of belonging so that all students feel welcome and included.
- Build relationships with all students by getting to know them as people and expressing curiosity about their lives and activities. Show you believe in them as learners and expect great things from them.
- Cultivate a climate of fairness, respect, and value across all interactions with students.

Possible Actions

There are many ways for us to connect with and build relationships with our students. These will naturally take on an individual flavor since it is important that these efforts be authentic to who you are. The following actions can jump-start your thinking:

➤ Drawn from our work in schools as part of the Worldwide Cultures of Thinking Project.
➤ Placed under the related principle to help you focus on the driving motivation behind each action though there is considerable overlap. For instance, building relationships also helps to foster belonging. Therefore, consider these top-level categories loosely.
➤ Modifiable to fit your local context.
➤ Connected to the most relevant cultural forces to which each specific action is associated. Both frameworks, the 8 cultural forces and the 10 mindsets, are synergistic and you can begin your journey either place.

Engaging in any of these actions will take time and a long-term investment on your part. These are not one-off actions. However, don't consider this time taken away from the teaching of content. Think about this time as an investment that will have payoffs through greater student engagement, cooperation, and less disruption.

Nurturing a Sense of Belonging. We want our students to feel that they belong at our school and in our classroom. This is particularly important for students from groups that might feel "belonging uncertainty" due to their ethnicity, socio-economic background, sexuality, or gender identity. Attending to the physical *environment* of the classroom can help this happen. For instance, we should ensure classroom displays have representations of *all* our students' various backgrounds, cultures, genders, neighborhoods, and sexualities in the visuals we put up. In addition, our choice of literature and examples should allow every student to "see themselves" represented. Consider too how the seating arrangement of your room might foster community and connection rather than individual silos. A classroom with ample flexible seating allows students to easily form groups, and move in and out of various social circles while also allowing space for quieter students to feel comfortable. New or transitioning students (going from elementary to middle school) are also likely to have "belonging uncertainty." Bringing these students into the school and classroom early and in small groups helps them to navigate and become familiar with the space so that they are not so overwhelmed on their first day.

Belonging is also about community building. We want students to get to know each other and interact in positive and supportive ways. However, we can't merely expect our students will know how to interact, collaborate, listen, or even talk to one another appropriately and effectively at the beginning of the year. Use *routines* and protocols that help students learn these behaviors. The Micro Lab protocol helps students learn to listen to one another and have conversations that build on the contributions of others (Ritchhart, Church, and Morrison 2011). You might want to identify criteria with your students that characterizes the qualities of a good conversation. For instance, listening to others, asking questions, making connections, building off what others say, making sure everyone participates, not dominating, and so on. You can find additional rubrics and self-assessment instruments by scanning the QR code for the website for the book *Morning Classroom Conversations: Build Your Students' Social-Emotional, Character, and Communication Skills Every Day* (2022).

Conversation rubrics and self-assessments QR code.

SCAN ME

Another example of a *routine* you might put in place to help students connect with each other and build community is "Daily Dedications." This simple classroom routine was developed by secondary history teacher Henry Seton and has become a ritual in his classroom that helps to build trust and focus the class. On a voluntary and rotating basis, students take 30–60 seconds at the beginning of the class to dedicate the day's learning to someone who inspires them to do their best in learning and life. This can be a real or fictional person, living or dead. Usually this is accompanied by a single photograph or image that is projected. Watch an example by scanning the QR code. As Seton explains, "These brief moments become the seeds for deeper relationship building, starting points for future conversations . . . it is culturally sustaining and student-centered in that students get to take the lead in honoring and celebrating their own diverse identities" (Seton 2021). Another take on this is one used by Kelly Gallagher in which he has students begin class by reading a one-minute poem or passage.

Daily Dedication video QR code.

SCAN ME

As mentioned earlier, one of the biggest threats to belonging is bullying. Nowadays, most schools have in place bullying prevention programs and/or wellness initiatives that can be useful in combating this very pervasive behavior. Such programs are important but not a panacea. Combating bullying requires vigilance and consistency on our part as teachers in all our *interactions* with students. In this regard, the words of Lieutenant General David Morrison in speaking to the public about incidents of sexism in the Australian Army are instructive (scan the QR code to watch). He emphasizes to all soldiers that "the standard you walk past is the standard you accept." When we hear a student say, "That's so gay" or make fun of someone's accent, we are condoning that behavior. Some call these "micro-aggressions" that set the stage for larger incidents of bullying. Victims take our silence as evidence that they aren't valued and don't really belong.

Lieutenant General David Morrison video QR code.

SCAN ME

Building Relationships. Relationships begin with creating *opportunities* for getting to know our students. There are many ways we might do this. At the start of the year, you might put together a short survey to find out about your students by asking them their past experiences in school, whom they admire, what their hopes and dreams are, what they like and dislike about school, and so on. Other teachers use letters, asking students to write to them about what they want their new teacher to know about them as individuals. Middle school teacher Erin Ott frames this differently, asking her students to create a "Take Care of Me" list in which they identify the specific things she might do to help support them as learners (Ott 2018). She also shares her own list of what things they can do to support her as a teacher. For instance, "contributing open and honestly from your own perspective and understanding." Mark Church asked the parents of his 5th graders to write a letter to him about their child to build a relationship with both the child and the family. Many said the assignment was both challenging and profound. Mathematics teacher Jeff Watson uses the "emotions chart" to provide quick check-ins. Others ask students to write down three words that describe themselves and then use this for a quick conference with the student. Repeating this process each term allows teachers and students to see changes.

Relationships are also built and sustained over time through our *interactions* with students. This means looking for various *opportunities* to connect with students, even briefly, one on one. One can start with greeting students at the door to the classroom each day by saying "Hello" and their name. It sounds like such a small thing, but research has shown that positive greetings at the classroom door increased students' academic engagement by 20% and decreased disruptive classroom behavior by 9%, potentially adding another hour onto the learning day (Cook et al. 2018).

Barry White Jr. of Charlotte, North Carolina, has taken greetings to a whole new level by inviting students to create and teach him their personalized handshake. Watch him demonstrate by scanning the QR code.

Barry White Jr. Handshakes video QR code.

SCAN ME

Of course, it is important to pronounce students' names correctly. Not doing so is a form of dismissal. It is a micro-aggression that communicates we don't care enough to get it right. If you are having trouble with this or have got it wrong in the past, ask the student for help by saying, "You know what? I think I've been messing up your name all year, and I'm sorry. I want to say it perfectly. Can you teach me?" If you struggle with this, as I do, video or audiotape the student pronouncing their name correctly so you can review it as needed. There are also pronunciation tools on the internet that can be useful.

Writing students individual notes periodically is another way to build connection. Middle school teacher John Tiersma sets himself the goal of writing and mailing at least one personalized note to each of his students each year. He breaks that down into smaller weekly goals. This allows him to focus on just a few students and really get curious about them. He finds he notices more as he looks for the positive in his students so that he can write things that are specific to the child, reveal a genuine appreciation, are honest, and perhaps even allude to future aspirations and goals, such as, "I can see you becoming a writer one day." John says, through the notes, "Students recognize that time was set aside for them, that they're worth being known. The handwritten card is something they can hold that shows that someone knows them and loves them" (Tiersma 2021). Other teachers have expanded this idea by involving students in writing notes of appreciation to each other on a regular basis.

At the school-wide level, it is important to look at how policies and practices might either encourage or inhibit relationship building. For instance, studies have shown a clear advantage of teachers looping with their students (teaching the same group for at least two years) versus platooning (specialist teachers for each subject) for elementary school students. Staying with the same teacher produces better academic success, fewer absences and suspensions, lower rates of retention, less disruptive behavior, and was of particular advantage to special needs students and non-white students (Fryer Jr. 2018; Hill and Jones 2018; Roberts 2001). Looping in the elementary grades is common in Germany, Italy, Israel, Sweden, and Japan as well as in Waldorf schools.

Cultivate a Climate of Fairness, Respect, and Value. Our *language* can be a major conveyor of respect and value. We need to be intentional about our words, body language, and tone so that all convey genuine interest, curiosity, and care. Sometimes this means making subtle shifts in what we say. For instance, while there is nothing wrong or harmful about phrases like "good girl/boy" or "I'm proud of you," they don't offer specifics, show genuine interest, encourage reflection, or promote dialog. They may inadvertently set up comparisons between students or put the focus on pleasing the teacher rather than students' personal growth. Instead, be specific about what was done well: "Great job of really puzzling that problem out" or "Thanks for cleaning up, I really appreciate that" instead of "good girl/boy." Rather than saying "I'm proud of you" or "well done," try to inquire more deeply by asking, "Tell me more about that," "What did you do that made that work?" or even "You must feel excited about that." All of these are more likely to spark conversation and provide students the opportunity to reflect and elaborate on their actions (Wilson 2021). In addition, phrases like "Thank you for your idea" or "I'm going to think about what you just said" can acknowledge contributions instead of "Great," "Good," or "Brilliant."

Language, tone, and presence are also key to what researcher Mary Rowe calls micro-affirmations. These "are tiny acts of opening doors to opportunity, gestures of inclusion and caring, and graceful acts of listening" (Rowe 2008). This could take the form of friendly gestures, smiling, or simple acknowledgments like: "Good to see you," "How are you today?" "We missed you yesterday," or "Glad you're here." These phrases acknowledge individuals and communicate that they are seen. Trying to use more micro-affirmations can also help inhibit micro-aggressions by providing new actions to replace old ones.

A simple *routine* to help students regularly show respect and value for each other is the 3 A's routine: Appreciation, Apologies, and Aha's! This routine need only take a couple of minutes at the end of a class. Invite students to share with the class any *appreciations* they have for anyone in the room (this could be someone who helped them or asked a great question that sparked conversation), offer an *apology* for their own behavior (this could be a recognition that they were distracting or unhelpful in a situation), or an *Aha* moment (this might be a new insight or learning they have). Not everyone will share, of course. You might only have a one or two students. However, by making this a routine you are providing space for students to show their respect and valuing of each other. Scan the QR code to watch a video of this routine.

3As Routine video QR code.

SCAN ME

We can demonstrate fairness in our dealings with students by being open and transparent about our decision-making process. This doesn't mean caving in or being lenient; it means sharing the information and constraints under which we are working and inviting students' input when appropriate. This could involve the scheduling of a test, policies around accepting late work, and so on. Perhaps no opportunity for fairness is bigger than when we are dealing with misbehavior. It is useful to approach transgressions with both empathy and curiosity, asking questions such as: What happened? What went through your mind at the time? How do you view the event now? Who was affected by your behavior? What do you need to do to repair the damage?

Students won't be able to restore a relationship if they don't understand how their behavior impacts others. Be wary of using words like *should* that carry judgment and avoid language that assigns blame. Don't say you're "shocked" or "appalled," for instance. Similarly, sarcasm, name-calling, and threats are unproductive and only serve to humiliate students. Watch your body language and tone to project both openness and caring. Using "restorative justice" practices help to maintain a sense of belonging and sends the message that students will not be excluded from the group just because they messed up (Anfara Jr., Evans, and Lester 2013; Fronius, Persson, Guckenburg, Hurley, and Petrosino 2016).

Fitting New Actions with Current Realities

Before you rush to implement the actions you are eager to try, step back and think about what you are currently doing at your school (see Figure 4.2):

➤ What actions, already in place, can be *amplified* and grown by applying some of the preceding identified principles?
➤ What practices need to be rethought or *modified* considering this mindset?
➤ What do you need to stop doing altogether and *remove* from our repertoire? Why? Does it run counter to this mindset? Is it ineffective? What "moveable barriers" are standing in the way of truly living this mindset?
➤ Finally, are there things that you need to *create*, totally new processes, structures, or actions to begin to put in place?

Figure 4.2 Amplify-Modify-Remove-Create.

Review of Current Practice: What do we need to...

AMPLIFY	MODIFY	REMOVE	CREATE

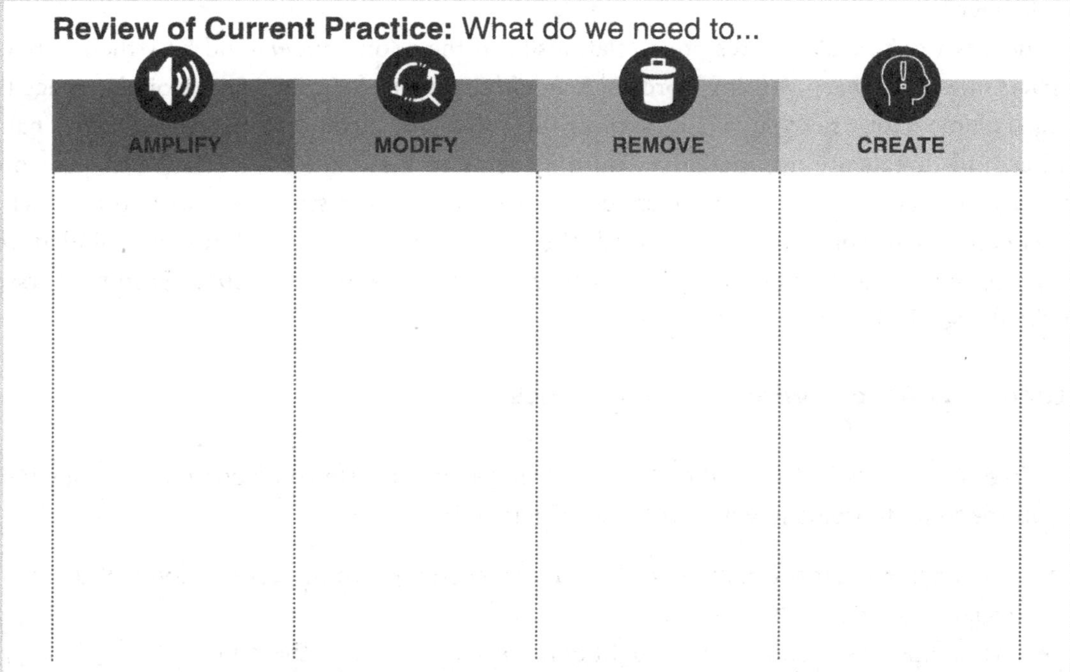

——— Conclusion: Our Theory of Action ———

We conclude our examination of this mindset "Students learn best when they feel known, valued, and respected by both the adults in the school and their peers" by formulating a "theory of action" in which we hypothesize the likely effects of our actions. What are we likely to see because of our acting on the principles we have laid out? A theory of action can be useful because it clarifies both what we are doing and why we are doing it. As such, it identifies particulars we might look for (street data) to know when and to what extent we have been successful. In this spirit of tying together our actions with anticipated outcomes, I offer the following theory of action for this mindset. Use it if it captures the actions you plan to take and the outcomes you expect. If it doesn't, feel free to craft your own theory of action that will better fit your context.

If **we focus on knowing our students, demonstrate that we value them as thinkers and learners, and develop positive relationships with them individually and collectively,** *then* **disruptive behavior will decrease, students will be more engaged, and they will feel more connected to the school community.**

Notes

Learning Is a Consequence of Thinking

"Learning is a consequence of thinking. Retention, understanding, and the active use of knowledge can be brought about only by learning experiences in which learners think about and think with what they are learning." This very succinct and straightforward statement by David Perkins in his book *Smart Schools* (1992, p. 8) perfectly sums up why we should care about thinking. While our curriculums may be full of knowledge to impart, we want students to remember that knowledge well past the test date and be able to effectively put it to use in the future. Thus, we want students to build robust understanding of the content. For this, we need thinking. Findings from cognitive science have shown that to build useable knowledge, we need to "play" with it, push it around, think through and with it, rather than merely memorize it. David Perkins drives home this point, "Thinking is what brings knowledge to life, what puts it to work, what tests it against the standard of evidence, what mobilizes it to make connection and predictions, what shapes it toward creative products and outcomes" (2010, p. x).

You might agree that the kind of *intentional* learning Perkins is talking about, the learning that we actively seek out and create for ourselves, the deeper learning rooted in meaning making and understanding does require thinking, and yet still be skeptical that all learning requires thinking. What about simple knowledge, occasional facts, and basic impressions? Surely, we can acquire this kind of knowledge without thought. We might refer to this as *incidental learning*, the learning that just seems to happen to us without much intentionality.

As a case of incidental learning, let's examine an excursion I used to lead my 3rd graders on—a hiking trip to the top of Twin Sisters Peak in Rocky Mountain National Park. I didn't give them worksheets or much instruction. We didn't stop along the way for mini-lectures or discussions. I wanted them to experience the setting, the hike, and feel a sense of accomplishment. My goal was to build community and set the stage for our year-long study of Colorado history. Therefore, their learning wasn't intentional in the same way other efforts to build thinking might be considered. Nonetheless, students were forming associations, detecting patterns, identifying causal relationships, and making observations and connections throughout our field trip. Later in the year, I would draw on this incidental learning to help expand students' understanding of the geography, geology, navigation, and exploration of Colorado through more explicit thinking. I could do this because they were, indeed, thinking during our hike.

What about training a skill? Isn't that just mindless repetition? In his book *Outliers*, Malcom Gladwell asserted that, on average, 10,000 hours of practice are needed to develop expertise in a field (Gladwell 2008). However, this isn't mindless training. It is thoughtful attention to areas that need improvement, breaking down one's actions, refined discernments of quality, analysis of problems, integrating feedback, and so on. In other words, *thoughtful* training.

Some might argue that the natural way in which we seem to learn language as an infant doesn't really require thinking. It seems so effortless. However, theorists and researchers have shown that even simple word learning is done through reasoning and association (Bloom 2001). Michael Luntley (2008) asserts, "The empirical evidence strongly supports the case for saying that some of the most basic learning that the human infant undertakes, the learning that first equips her with a stake in our shared culture, is learning by reasoning, not learning by training." What is more, Luntley emphasizes the importance of teachers acknowledging their students as active reasoners and sense-makers, for to do so is to empower and engage them as learners. Engaging students as thinkers, in the way Luntley calls us to do, allows students to be more sensitive to context and perspective, leading to more control and direction over their experiences.[1]

WHAT THE RESEARCH SAYS: *WHY* DOES IT MATTER?

The meta-analysis done by John Hattie reveals that teaching practices that engage students in thinking are associated with above-average effect sizes, and thus, more positive learning outcomes. An effect size of 0.5 can be thought of as equivalent to a one-grade-mark leap (from C to B), whereas an effect size of 1.0 is roughly equal to a two-grade-mark leap (from C to A) (Petty 2020). Producing at least a full grade increase is effective, and thus, effect sizes over 0.5 are considered high. The larger the effect size, the stronger the relationship between that teaching practice and student learning. Hattie identifies several thinking-based practices that have been shown to be highly effective, such as: cognitive task analysis in which teaching focuses on how to think about the content (effect size = 1.29), integration with prior knowledge (0.93), transfer strategies (0.86), classroom discussion (0.82), elaboration and organization (0.75), reciprocal teaching in which the thinking process is externalized through conversation (0.74), metacognitive strategies (0.69), self-verbalization and self-questioning (0.64), concept mapping (0.57), and comprehension strategies (0.77–0.58) (Hattie 2009; Waack 2014).[2] So even if one were only concerned with performance on exams, students do better when we focus on thinking.

Beware the Fluency Trap

One problem is that students themselves often don't believe this to be the case. They think they learn best when being lectured to, taking notes, and reviewing those notes. They have been enculturated that this is learning. In his book *How We Learn: The Surprising Truth about When, Where, and Why It Happens*, Benedict Carey calls this the *fluency trap*, "The belief that because facts or formulas or arguments are easy to remember *right now*, they'll remain that way tomorrow or the next day" (Carey 2015, p. 82). This is compounded by the fact that when learning requires a lot of thinking and deep processing, it can feel less certain, shakier, and more tentative. Physics professors at Harvard conducted a study in which they compared both students' perceptions of their learning and their actual learning. While students perceived that they learned more from the lecture, in actuality, they learned more when they were actively involved in thinking through discussion, prediction, experimentation, and problem solving (Deslauriers, McCarty, Miller, Callaghan, and Kestin 2019). Likewise, students often fall into the fluency trap when studying. They feel they know the material because they have gone over it, and it makes sense. Once again, research shows that studying for a test is most effectively done through thinking versus review, repetition, or memorization. Creating explanations, constructing new concept maps, and self-questioning have all been shown to be far superior to reviewing one's notes or engaging in last-minute cramming when it comes to knowledge retention, recall, and application (Carey 2015; Ebersbach, Feierabend, and Nazari 2020; Rendas, Fonseca, and Pinto 2006; Van Boxtel, van der Linden, Roelofs, and Erkens 2002).

Identifying Types of Thinking

Of course, merely helping students to do well on low-level exams is not the goal of this book. We strive to teach *beyond* the test. We recognize that most exams don't really get at students' understanding nor are they necessarily good measures of deeper learning (Yuan and Le 2012; Yuan and Le 2014). Furthermore, we realize that students don't only learn within the confines of schools or for the purposes of schooling. We hope our students will engage in learning and efforts to build understanding throughout their lives, and we want to prepare them for that. Therefore, it is important that we help students develop the tools for effective lifelong learning as well as an enjoyment of learning. To facilitate this, we must consider how understanding differs from knowledge and then turn our attention to identifying the types of thinking needed to build understanding.

Whereas we often talk about knowledge in a possessive sense—that is, something we have or can lay claim to—understanding is "a matter of being able to carry out a variety of performances concerning the topic" (Perkins 1993, p. 8). It requires us to go beyond the information given to produce something new (Bruner 1973). Rather than a reproductive, canonical response, one's understanding tends to lie in original, creative responses (Mehta and Fine 2019). Such responses require us to think with the information at hand as we construct new meaning. So, what kinds of thinking are most useful in promoting deeper learning and understanding? At Project Zero, we identified 8 thinking moves central to the enterprise of building understanding (Ritchhart et al. 2011):

- Observing closely and describing what is there.
- Building explanations and interpretations.
- Reasoning with evidence.
- Making connections.
- Considering different viewpoints and perspectives.
- Capturing the heart and forming conclusions.
- Wondering and asking questions
- Uncovering complexity and going below the surface of things.

Taken together, these 8 thinking moves form what we refer to as the *Understanding Map* (see Figure 5.1). We wouldn't necessarily engage in all of these in a single episode of learning, but over the course of a unit of study, it is certainly possible to make sure we provide students with opportunities to engage in all of them.

Figure 5.1 Understanding Map.

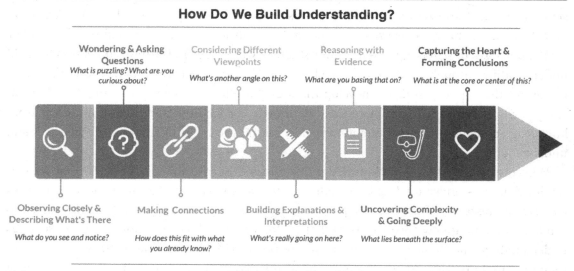

Although thinking is central to the enterprise of building understanding, we shouldn't draw too sharp a line between understanding and knowledge acquisition. Thinking yields benefits in knowledge acquisition as well (Coe, Rauch, Kime, and Singleton 2020). Information—what we have heard, read, or seen—that does not make sense to us is quickly forgotten. As Dewey said, "information is an undigested burden unless it is understood" (1933 p. 78). Furthermore, understanding benefits retention. When new knowledge is connected to prior knowledge, it is not only easier to recall but also easier to apply (Kuhn and Siegler 2006; Mayer 2003). The development of conceptual schema facilitates retrieval of information and the learning of new information (Wing, Burles, Ryan, and Gilboa 2022). Furthermore, the more connections we establish, the more powerful our learning becomes (Buschkuehl 2018). Engaging in self-questioning that takes one deeper into the content has been shown to be an effective study technique (Ebersbach et al. 2020). Trying to explain concepts to oneself or someone else, the central process in the Feynman Learning Technique, builds both understanding and knowledge (Parrish 2021). Thus, one can focus on imparting knowledge—in which understanding, long-term retention, and application are neglected—or one can focus on developing understanding that will also help to build knowledge. Why settle for one when you can have both?

VISIONS AND REFLECTIONS: *HOW* MIGHT IT LOOK?

As part of the "Teaching for Understanding" project conducted at Harvard Graduate School of Education from 1988–1995, we spent time engaging teachers in developing deeper appreciation for and insight into the topic of "understanding." We knew it wasn't enough to hand them new tools for teaching for understanding until they had a strong grasp of what understanding itself looks like, how it is created and nurtured, and how it might differ from knowledge. The following two visioning exercises come from this work. The first uses metaphors, which can be useful in helping us see things from new perspectives and identify key features. The second draws on one's own experience of developing understanding.

Constructing Our Vision

What does understanding look like? How does it feel? Open your smartphone and go to your "Photos." In the search feature (usually a looking glass icon at the bottom of the screen), enter a month and year chosen at random. I typed in "November 2018." A collection of pictures from that month will appear. You might have to choose "Select all." Scroll through the images and select one that, for you, captures "understanding." In essence, you are using this photo as a metaphor for what understanding means to you. I had some amazing choices: a Day of the Dead celebrant sitting alone on a bench with a ring of marigolds in her hair, a room full of

250 conference goers engaged in conversation, a white board full of writing, a car along a long dirt road stretching into the distance, a cabin covered in rusty tin, a hiking trail, hardy but delicate red flowers growing out of rocks on the trail, and many more. So many choices! I'm sure you will have as well. Once you have made your selection, explain to yourself why you selected that image as a good representation of what "understanding" is. For instance, I choose the image I took on my hike of the flowers growing from a rock. This makes me think that understanding often emerges from perseverance and when certain conditions are met, when the ecosystem is right. It's not always an easy process, however. The foothold of ideas is important. This gets me thinking about the importance of establishing roots for understanding. When understanding finally emerges, it is very apparent, it is almost like we can't help but see it. There is beauty in understanding. Make note of your selected image and why it is a good metaphor for understanding.

Now think of something you really understand well. Not perfectly, but well. Once you have identified a specific example, identify what you did to develop that understanding. How did you arrive at the understanding you now hold? Feel free to use the pages at the end of this chapter, the margins, a sheet of paper, or your electronic device to record your responses. Now, identify and record the type(s) of thinking you were doing for each of those activities. For example, you might have written that you watched videos of expert bakers to learn the process. Beside that activity, you could identify that you were observing closely and/or making connections, focused on process, and so on. Your thinking moves don't necessarily need to come from the Understanding Map, but if you are stuck that can be a useful tool.

Group Discussion

If you are reading this book with others, bring your lists, writings, and perhaps drawings to share and discuss.

➤ What do your collective reflections reveal about important features of understanding?
➤ What is revealed about the actions and thinking useful in developing understanding?
➤ What questions about understanding or thinking are emerging?

Contemplating Pictures of Practice

To extend your vision of the centrality of thinking to learning, we turn our attention to two case studies: one from a history lesson, the other from mathematics. As you read, keep your attention on how the teachers constantly engage their students in thinking and building understanding throughout the lesson. It might be easy to get caught up in the activity itself, but the power of these lessons depends upon keeping students thinking at every juncture.

Case One: From Facts to Understanding. Thalia Ormsby is about to introduce a new thinking routine to her 6th-grade class at Ashley Falls School in Del Mar, California. The +1 routine had just been chosen through a joint planning session with colleagues during a teacher "Learning Lab" conducted as part of the district's ongoing professional learning. Thalia had explained that her students had been learning about Emperor Qin Shi Huang through a lot of reading. Some of this reading had been done the previous day with a substitute teacher. Thalia knew the students seemed interested in what they were learning, but she was curious about how much they were retaining. More important than just recalling the facts, she wanted them to be able to use those facts to decide about Qin Shi Huang's effectiveness as an emperor. This was within the larger context of their study about "leadership." With these goals in mind, the +1 routine seemed like a good fit.

In presenting the routine, Thalia stands beside her self-created bulletin board of the Understanding Map. Beside each of the 8 thinking moves are note cards that identify the various thinking routines the class has used thus far that drew on that type of thinking. "You know whenever we do a new thinking routine, I like to introduce it by talking about the kind of thinking it helps us do so that we can understand why we are using them. Today, we are going to be doing the +1 routine to help us identify some of the facts and information we have been learning about Qin Shi Huang, and then we are going to use that information to help us think more about what kind of leader he was," Thalia explains. "The main types of thinking we will be doing are 'describing what's there' as we identify various things about Qin Shi Huang. Then we will be 'making some connections' and 'building explanations as well.'"

Next, Thalia clarifies the steps of the routine, explaining that students will first recall as much information as possible about Qin Shi Huang. She stresses that this is from memory and not by going back to notes or readings. "This is called retrieval practice, and it helps us build our memories," she explains. Retrieval practice is a well-researched learning technique for locking ideas into memory. When we retrieve a fact, we enhance our memory of that fact through more elaborate and deeper encoding. We form new connections to that fact, creating different paths for accessing that information (Bjork 1975; Roediger III and Karpicke 2006). As Benedict Carey eloquently states in his book *How We Learn*, "Using our memory changes our memory in ways we don't anticipate" (2015, p. 94).

Students busily begin writing down all that they can recall about Emperor Qin Shi Huang. Some students use dot points while others take a more narrative approach. After about five minutes, but before everyone is completely exhausted of ideas, Thalia stops the class, "Please pass your paper to the person sitting to your left. Clockwise. When you get your friend's paper, read over everything they have written, and your job is to add at least one new thing. That's the +1. You can add more if you have time. Your +1 might be an idea or fact that they don't have, or it could be adding an elaboration or detail onto something they already have." In this step, students enhance their peer's notes, but at the same time, they build their own memories. In trying to recall information, no doubt ideas were forgotten or were almost there but couldn't fully be recalled. By seeing these "near misses" at recall written on their friend's paper, the new information is ready to be encoded. The struggle to recall sets up the mind to encode that information more effectively once it is presented (Bjork and Bjork 2020).

The class is quiet as they read and then slowly the pencils come out and additions are made. After a few minutes, Thalia asks students to pass their papers once again and repeat the process. They pass twice more until everyone has their own paper back, at which point students are instructed to add anything else onto their page of notes that they might have read but isn't yet recorded. At this point, the thinking students are doing is all connected to building robust memory of the information. Now, Thalia transitions to getting students to use this information to help them build a better explanation of who Qin Shi Huang is as a leader: "Now, what I'd like you to do is some sorting of all this information from your table group. Look at all those facts and decide what each fact tells you about Qin Shi Huang as a leader. You can use this sheet of chart paper and create two columns. On one side, list the facts that you think support or provide evidence for him being a good leader, and on the other side, the cons or facts that might indicate he wasn't an effective leader."

The class erupts in activity. Students position themselves around their shared paper and begin to discuss their facts. "Well, he did start 'legalism' was one thing that I had down, but I don't know if that is good or not?" one student shares. The others jump in to offer opinions. "Well, it did create more order for people, so that's good." "Yeah, but if you followed Confucianism then it wouldn't be so good." A similar debate ensues at another table about the building of the Great Wall. Soon, students are engaged in thinking about perspectives: Good for whom? How does time change our perspective? As a result of these conversations, students begin to write qualifiers next to their facts, showing it can be both good and bad from a leadership perspective: "In the end, the Great Wall was good, but at the time, it cost so much money and people died." The conversations have quickly become complex. An exploration of which Thalia must cut off for now as the school day is about to end. "These conversations are so interesting, leading to lots of debate. We'll continue this tomorrow. I'm interested to hear more from groups about your decision-making process."

Case Two: Three-Act Math.[3] Mathematics educator Dan Meyer has popularized the idea of "Three-Act Math Tasks" that unfold much like a good story (Meyer 2011). Not only are stories evocative and create interest, but they also provide important hooks for our sustained attention and memory (Katz and Leirer 1980; Zak 2014). As social beings, we like stories, relationships, conflicts, and puzzles. In Act One, a central conflict is made visible and a problem uncovered, not by the teacher necessarily but often by the students. In Act Two, the students work to solve the problem, overcome obstacles, identify resources, and develop needed skills. Act Three is the resolution. The conflict/puzzle has been solved and discussed to arrive at closure and perhaps even point to a sequel.

When researchers Jal Mehta and Sarah Fine studied deeper learning in context, they visited lots of classrooms, one of which was a secondary math class in a high-poverty, urban school in the Northeast of the United States. Here, they stumbled into a "Three-Act Math" lesson unfolding in Nick Collins and Nathaniel Martin's algebra class. When they first walked into the classroom, they noticed a sign reading: "Math is an activity: questioning, noticing, calculating, exploring, organizing, persevering, making sense, understanding, applying connections." These verbs cued students into the thinking they would be doing in class each day and set them up for active learning.

The play begins. Projecting a package of balloons on the screen, student teacher Nathaniel Martin asks, "What do you notice? What do you wonder?" This is Act One, a perplexing problem found, in the seemingly ordinary, through careful observation and questioning. We sometimes neglect the importance of noticing, but it forms the basis for all analysis. The more we see, the more information we have with which to work. Questions, of course, are the catalyst for inquiry and one of the most powerful ways students become active autonomous learners (Aguiar, Mortimer, and Scott 2010). As students call out observations—"The balloon is red," "There are six"— Nathaniel is blowing up a balloon. One student jokes, "Don't pass out!" while another observes, "Hey, the picture of the balloon on the package is round but the one you are blowing up is not quite round."

"What other questions could you ask?" Nathaniel inquires. A student responds, "How can you measure a balloon?" From there, discussion ensues about diameter, circumference, and radius. Nathan asks them to define these terms and how they would use them to answer the question. His questions act not only to engage, but also as a quick assessment of students' skills and knowledge. He asks, "How many breaths will it take to fill this balloon? Is it fully inflated? How would you know?" These perplexing questions silence students as they think. Nathan then builds to the dramatic conflict that punctuates Act One: "How many breaths would it take to fill a much bigger balloon?" On cue, supervising teacher Nick Collins walks in with a huge purple balloon nearly as tall as he is. Problem set. Act One concludes. It takes all of five minutes.

The rest of the class is spent in Act Two. The students have a problem to solve by collecting data from an array of balloons, organizing it, looking at relationships, and plotting the data to derive a function that will resolve the puzzle of how many breaths to fill any balloon of a known dimension. This active learning combined with ambitious mathematical instruction has been shown to be key to supporting both engagement and academic performance (Blazar and

Pollard 2022). Act Three will have to wait till tomorrow. When asked about their math class compared to past mathematics courses they have taken, students tell researchers Mehta and Fine, that this class is "more fun" and "more thinking like a mathematician."

Reflecting on Current Practice

It is quite easy to give lip service to thinking. After all, who is going to say they don't value thinking? However, truly valuing thinking and seeing it as central to learning requires us to delve into our actual teaching on a deep level. The following questions are designed to help you interrogate your practice to uncover not only what thinking you value, but also how you actually show its value and make it central to students' learning.

Choosing Questions and Recording Responses

Different questions serve us at different times in our learning. Therefore, I suggest you read through the questions and identify:

➤ One or two that speak to you now. Questions that might challenge you or take your thinking in new directions.
➤ One or two you would most like to discuss with your colleagues.
➤ Circle and date the questions you select now so you can identify how your focus shifts with time and experience.
➤ Use the blank pages at the end of this chapter or your note-taking device to record your reflections.

- What kinds of thinking are essential within the discipline I teach? What role do these play in creating new knowledge and understanding in the field?
- What kinds of thinking am I trying (or do I want to try) to make so routine that students are automatically engaged in it?
- Could my students tell an outsider what kinds of thinking are important in our class?
- What are my "go to" routines and structures to support students' learning and thinking? Why these routines? What do I learn from them? What do my students learn? What makes them powerful for us as a class?
- Where, when, and how do I think aloud and make my own thinking visible?

- To what extent do my assessments require students to think? Which of my tasks, assignments, projects, and assessments can students complete without much thinking?

- How would my students answer the question: "Who have you become as a learner and thinker this year as a result of your time with me?"

- What tools, structures, and experiences have I given students to help them both develop and gain a sense of themselves as powerful and capable thinkers and learners?

- Do I always "lead with the thinking needed" when I explain assignments, tasks, and projects to students, or do I tend to explain all the "work" and mechanical components of the task? How can I shift?

- As a class, do we regularly reflect on our process as learners to adjust and fine tune our learning?

- How have I helped my students understand the importance of thinking in their studying and learning? How might I share some of the research on effective learning and studying?

- How have/might I create displays that highlight the kinds of thinking that are important?

- When, where, and how do I give students feedback on their thinking?

- When was the last time I noticed and named the thinking as it was happening?

DATA, PRINCIPLES, AND PRACTICES: *WHAT* ACTIONS CAN WE TAKE?

Having explored the connection between knowledge and understanding, and identified specific types of thinking that aid both, we have a better understanding of the centrality of thinking to learning. Thinking routines and the Understanding Map provide practical tools around which we can start to take action. To better situate these actions so that they will be successful, it is useful to understand the current role of thinking in our students' lives as learners. The following are three possible data collection techniques that can inform you about the role thinking is playing in your classroom and in students' perceptions.

Collecting Street Data

Street Data

➤ Helps us understand our own context as well as students' perspectives.
➤ Is relatively easy and quick to collect.
➤ Can be immediately analyzed and acted upon straightaway.

> ➤ Is meant to inform and suggest action.
> ➤ Is NOT an evaluation or measure of success but a snapshot of practice.
> ➤ Can take many forms: observations, interviews, surveys, exit tickets, recordings, and so on.

Street Data Action One: Reflections on Thinking. The following questions can be used either as exit tickets or a basis for a class discussion. You needn't use all these prompts. Likewise, you might want to modify or add new questions of your own to best engage your students.

- What kinds of thinking do you do the most of in school—not just this class but in all classes? Of these, which ones seem the most useful to you in your learning? *Note: As previously stated, students are not always good judges of what is most advantageous to their learning. Therefore, students' responses may be an opportunity to better explain how certain types of thinking help learning.*

- Who have you become as a learner and thinker this year as a result of your time with me? In what areas have you grown? What changes do you notice in yourself? What have you learned about yourself as a learner and thinker?

- What kinds of thinking do you think that I care about and value in this class? What kinds of thinking seem important in this subject area?

Street Data Action Two: In This Class. Use the In This Class survey to identify the kinds of thinking you are making a priority (and students are noticing) in a particular lesson (see Appendix E). At the end of a lesson have students complete the survey. This will take approximately five minutes, though it may take longer the first time. Complete the survey yourself *after* the class. If you have a colleague observing, have them complete the survey. Students might have a hard time identifying a type of thinking if it has not previously been discussed, explored, and examined so that they know what it looks like and feels like. If you get lots of questions about this, take that as useful information. Perhaps you will have more conversations about thinking later with your students. For now, just ask students to rely on their intuition.

In analyzing this data, don't worry about the rankings of 1, 2, and 3. Instead, just consider students' responses collectively as the top three kinds of thinking they noticed in class. In piloting this instrument, we found that ranking was easier for students than just identifying the three types of thinking they did the most. Students wanted to include them all. This may sound counterintuitive, but we found this easiest and quickest. You can download a spreadsheet in which to enter your data and generate a radar graph by scanning the QR code. You can also see examples of radar graphs generated from various classroom observations at the scanned weblink.

QR code for spreadsheets and radar graphs for in This Class data.

SCAN ME

Questions to Consider from the Quick Data:

- Do students' perceptions agree with your own? Why do you think this is the case?
- How much variation versus convergence is there?
- Are students able to identify specific and useful things they might do as learners (a sign of metacognition)? How might you help to support their ideas in the future?
- What useful advice have students given about things that they need as learners?
- Where, when, and how will you share your reactions and plans with students?
- How might you graphically display the results of this survey to better see patterns?

Keep in mind that results of this survey are only a snapshot of students', teacher's, and observers' perceptions of a single lesson. These results are useful for the questions they raise and the insights they suggest, not for making judgments or evaluations of the teaching. Over time, patterns might emerge within a class, department, or school that warrant additional investigation. For instance, there is nothing inherently problematic about a lesson focused on review and practice. However, if this is predominately the case, then it becomes an issue.

Street Data Action Three: Assessing Assessments. Review your assessments for the level of thinking you are asking of students. Gather a collection of tests, quizzes, and summative assessments for a unit or even a term. While this can be done with a single test, it is often more useful to consider your broader assessment repertoire. There is nothing wrong with asking knowledge-based questions per se on a single assessment. However, if these are dominant in the broader assessment repertoire it might be a concern. Use Norman Webb's "Depth of Knowledge" levels to rate how much thinking each question/task calls on students to do (Webb 2002). You are analyzing what it takes to be successful in terms of the task/question itself and not necessarily students' responses to it. Some students might respond to a more challenging task with a lower-level response. In other words, a student will receive top marks on a Level 3 task by giving a level 3 response, but they might give a level 2 response and receive a lower mark.

- Level 1: Recall of facts, definitions, terms, or information. Using basic skills, procedures, or abilities. Simply applying a known algorithm, formula, or approach. Keywords might include *name, identify, solve, complete, list, match, draw,* or *define.*

- Level 2: Requires some mental processing beyond recall. Students are asked to make decisions as to how to approach the question or problem. Keywords might include *classify, organize, estimate, make observations, collect and display data, summarize,* or *predict.*

- Level 3: Going beyond the text or what is given to explain, generalize, or connect ideas by using the evidence given. Reasoning and planning are required. There is complexity and abstraction. Keywords might include *synthesize, analyze, connect, generalize, provide evidence, support, formulate, hypothesize, explain,* or *reason.*

- Level 4: Tasks are very complex and often require an extended period to complete. They might also involve regular feedback to students over the course of the project. Students are often involved in designing, investigating, and creating something novel and unique that demonstrates their own voice. Analysis and considering of multiple variables and perspectives is often present as is a comprehensive critique of one's work. Keywords might include *design, critique, create, apply, identify alternatives, prove,* or *argue from multiple perspectives. Note: Even young children are capable of Level 4 work.*

Stating the Mindset as Principles for Action

What principles can help guide our efforts to breathe life into the mindset "Learning is a consequence of thinking"? As you will recall, principles do not provide specific actions, but guide our efforts in a broad sense. The following principles are major guideposts that can anchor your actions:

- Focus on understanding while making learning active.
- Make thinking explicit so that students are aware of it as a force in their learning.
- Scaffold, prompt, and push for thinking so that students feel both supported and challenged.

As you think about each of these principles, ask yourself: How does this apply to me? How might this look in my subject area, with my students, in my context? This will help you to derive actions that are personal and reflect the kind of guidance and direction that will best serve you and your students.

Possible Actions

It is important to keep in mind that all three of the preceding principles are synergistic and depend upon each other for maximum impact. Therefore, I suggest you identify actions from each of the three principles to enact at the *same* time rather than in sequential nature. This will help your efforts feel more cohesive to both you and your students. Feel free to bring in effective practices from other sources. The following actions described are:

➤ Drawn from our work in schools as part of the Worldwide Cultures of Thinking Project.
➤ Placed under the related principle to help you focus on the driving motivation behind each action.
➤ Modifiable to fit your local context.
➤ Connected to the most relevant cultural forces to which each specific action is associated. Both frameworks, the 8 cultural forces and the 10 mindsets, are synergistic and you can begin your journey either place.

Focus on Understanding while Making Learning Active. For students to engage in thinking, they need to encounter learning tasks that regularly go beyond the reproduction of knowledge. They need tasks that call for original thinking rather than the simple recall of facts. Therefore, a curriculum focused on big ideas, which builds students' conceptual understanding while promoting deeper learning, is more likely to be one in which thinking will play a central role. There are numerous guides available to support teachers in this work. See, for example: *The Teaching for Understanding Guide* (Blythe and Associates 1998), *Concept-Based Curriculum and Instruction for the Thinking Classroom* (Erickson 2006), and *Teaching for Deeper Learning: Tools to Engage Students in Meaning Making* (McTighe and Silver 2020). A key component of all these approaches is that teachers must craft and share clear understanding goals for each unit of instruction so that students are aware of what they are trying to understand. This provides direction for both students and teachers, allowing all to stay centered. In terms of specific practices, a focus on understanding will necessarily involve the activation of students' prior knowledge, ongoing elaboration of new learning, learning in authentic contexts, attention to transfer of learning to novel contexts, and organization of new knowledge in a way that stresses connections across ideas.

While research has shown the importance of ambitious instruction to build knowledge and understanding (and performance on tests), too often the challenge and intellectual effort involved are not always welcomed by students (Blazar and Pollard 2022). Therefore, it is important that learning be active, hands-on, and collaborative so that students are both engaged *and* building understanding. For example, in the preceding Case Two, math teachers Martin and Collins engaged their students in significant mathematics through active learning. Although your students might not be engaged in "Three-Act Math," make sure they are engaged actively in learning and not merely reading, watching, or listening for most of class time. Allow time for active processing of new information in the way Thalia Ormsby did in Case One. It is through active participation with others that students work with knowledge and information, adapting it for use and application. This process will build feelings of self-efficacy and independence. The challenge for teachers is to ensure that all students are engaged in the thinking and not just a few. This may mean rather than calling on just one student to answer a key question, you ask everyone to first write, then discuss their answers with a partner to reconcile and deepen their initial thoughts, and finally, randomly call on a pair to respond.

A key part of both building and assessing understanding is through application, creation, and performance. Make these the centerpiece of instruction. An understanding performance will both develop and demonstrate understanding (Wiske 1997). Look for ways for students to apply their burgeoning learning while also deepening it. This need not be a big project or summative assessment. Both the preceding Cases engaged students in understanding performances at the level of the lesson. When students are applying what they know in novel contexts, they are learning to transfer skills and knowledge and solve problems. Applications help to make the learning purposeful while leading to better retention. At the same time, these authentic opportunities will often provide the context in which new skills and knowledge might be introduced.

Make Thinking Explicit. The word *think* is one of the most frequently used words in the English language (Fry, Kress, and Fountoukidis 2000), and yet it is not always clear what we are talking about. Even if we are clear about what we mean, our students might not be. Therefore, it is important to develop a robust *language of learning and thinking* that enables us to talk about thinking explicitly with students. This might include displaying and using some version of the Understanding Map to identify key thinking moves as Thalia Ormsby did in Case One. Other graphical representations of the Understanding Map, including in different languages, can be accessed using the QR code. In addition, in most classrooms it will be important to unpack other learning words such as: *analyze, collaborate, persevering, making sense, going deeper, consolidate, discussion, assessment*, and so on. It is important that this be a co-construction done with students in an ongoing way and not just handing them a set of definitions. One way of building this language of learning is to notice and name when thinking is happening. A student makes a comment, a teacher might respond with, "That's a perspective we haven't yet considered" or "Thanks for synthesizing that idea for us."

QR code for alternative versions of understanding.

SCAN ME

When presenting a task, we need to make it a habit to lead with the thinking students will need to do and the purpose of that thinking. Teachers tend to explain an activity, task, or assignment in terms of the mechanical aspects or the steps of that task (Nuthall 2007). This might help students complete the task, but it won't activate their thinking and may leave the learning to chance. When introducing and explaining a task, it is useful to "locate the learning" in the task and name the thinking students will need to do as they carry it out. Using Kristen Kullberg's case from Mindset 4 as an example, a teacher might say, "Our goal over the next few lessons is to build our understanding of the concept of 'bravery.' We're going to be drawing on some of the ideas we already have about bravery, but a lot of learning *will be located in our discussion of the connections we can make between ideas and in our raising of questions about bravery.* Therefore, we are going to be spending a lot of time there. It's going to be important to go past your own ideas and consider the different perspectives offered by others to enrich your own understanding of the concept of bravery."

We can also make thinking explicit through Cognitive Task Analysis (CTA). John Hattie found this instructional strategy to be the most influential in supporting learning of all he studied, having a massive effect size of 1.29 (Visible-Learning 2019). While this may sound complex; it is just about making the thinking explicit by identifying the thinking needed to complete a task or assignment. This analysis should be done by us as teachers first, so that we know what thinking is involved in a task and can then scaffold and support it. At the same time, it is important to engage students in the process so that they can build their metacognitive and self-regulated learning skills. A teacher might ask, "What's the thinking we are going to need to do to solve this problem/ write this piece/accomplish this goal?" The aim is to ensure students are aware of the thinking skills they will need so that they can apply and monitor them as they solve problems, make decisions, or complete an assignment.

Ben Lawless from Aitken College in Melbourne, Australia, does this prior to writing an essay in history by asking his students: "What are the skills you use in writing a history essay?" Students identify writing, researching, using evidence, spelling, grammar, making a conclusion, looking at both sides, and using examples. He then zeros in on "researching" and asks the steps involved. Students' responses include asking questions, finding sources, taking notes, organizing notes, and rewriting notes. Finally, Ben has his students create a rubric that includes bad, middle level, and awesome examples of each of these practices (Barnett, Lawless, Kim, and Vista 2017).

Knowing the thinking one will need to do leads to better performance. CTA is a cognitive (as opposed to procedural) mapping of the task in which we identify the thinking to be done and the decision points that will arise. Teachers can also backwards map a task as a way of building this analytic skill. For instance, at the end of a class or project, ask students to identify the thinking that was done and how it contributed to our understanding and/or successful completion of the task.

Scaffold, Prompt, and Push for Thinking. Employ thinking routines regularly to help scaffold, structure, and support students' thinking. Studies have shown that the regular use of thinking routines to prompt, support, and scaffold student thinking produces better learning outcomes (Ritchhart and Church 2020; Sepulveda and Venegas-Muggli 2020). In introducing a routine, first lay out the goal of the activity and then introduce the thinking routine *as a tool for accomplishing that goal.* This helps to ensure that "doing a thinking routine" is not just an activity. It also supports students in learning when to use a thinking routine so that eventually they can use them independently across various contexts. Strategies and routines are most effective when students integrate and flexibly use thinking strategies across a wide variety of contexts that include challenging, engaging curriculum (Harvey and Goudvis 2013).

Press students for thinking so that they go beyond giving just information and answers. Use questions such as, "What makes you say that?" "What are you basing that idea on?" "Can you tell me more about that?" Teachers who regularly press for thinking set up the expectation that answers are not enough and that the thinking behind the answers, the reasoning, and the evidence one has marshalled are important. Years of interviews with at-risk students by Kathleen Cushman, indicate that students want their teachers to believe in them and that one way teachers signal this is by constantly pushing and pressing students to think (Cushman 2005; Cushman and Rogers 2009).

Prompting for thinking is not the same thing as prompting for answers: "You know, we talked about it yesterday. It begins with a 'B.'" When teachers focus on students getting the correct answer or completing the assignment correctly, there is a tendency to over-scaffold the task in such a way that it is stripped of learning. In contrast, when teachers pay attention to students' thinking, they are able to prompt the thinking students will need to be successful independently (Choppin 2011). For instance, a teacher might prompt a student having difficulty to "Try thinking about some of the connections between these two ideas." Similarly, teacher feedback should focus on giving feedback on students' thinking so that they are given information to help improve on their independent responses to problem solving and creative tasks.

Fitting New Actions with Current Realities

Before you rush to implement the actions you are eager to try, step back and think about what you are currently doing at your school (see Figure 5.2):

➤ What actions, already in place, can be *amplified* and grown by applying some of the previous principles identified?
➤ What practices need to be rethought or *modified* considering this mindset?
➤ What do you need to stop doing altogether and *remove* from our repertoire? Why? Does it run counter to this mindset? Is it ineffective? What "moveable barriers" are standing in the way of truly living this mindset?
➤ Finally, are there things that you need to *create*, totally new processes, structures, or actions to begin to put in place?

Figure 5.2 Amplify-Modify-Remove-Create.

Review of Current Practice: What do we need to...

AMPLIFY	MODIFY	REMOVE	CREATE

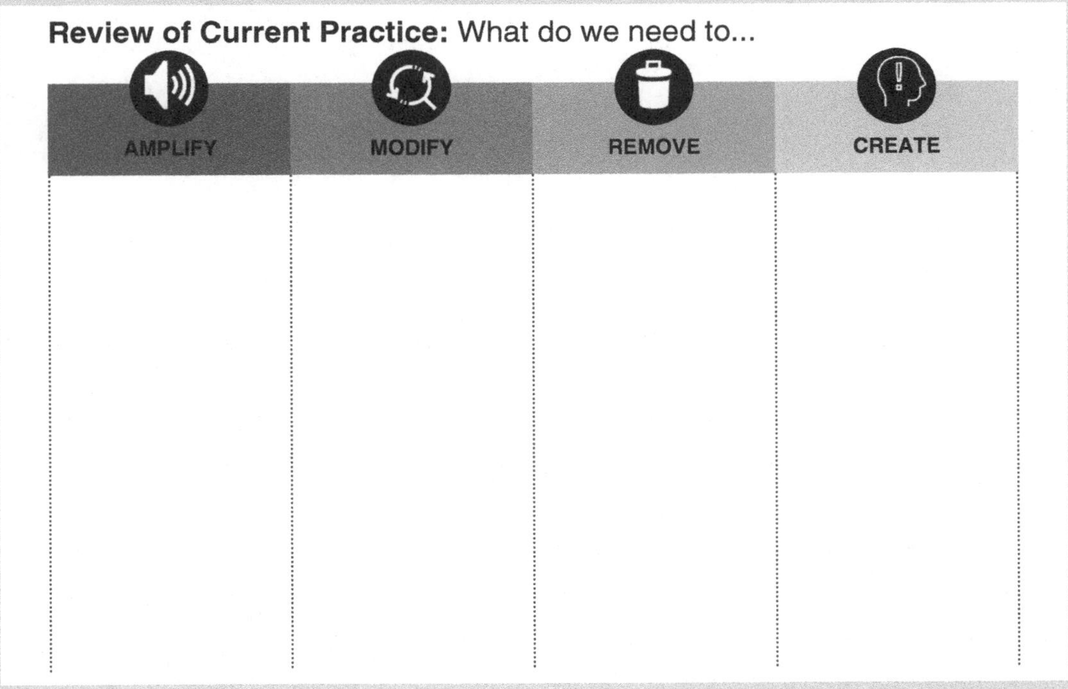

Conclusion: Our Theory of Action

We conclude our examination of this mindset "Learning is a consequence of thinking" by formulating a theory of action. What are we likely to see by fully embracing this mindset and act on the principles we have laid out? A theory of action clarifies both what we are doing and why we are doing it. As such, it identifies signposts we might look for to indicate when and to what extent we have been successful rather than merely what we have implemented. In this spirit of tying together our actions with anticipated outcomes, I offer the following theory of action for Mindset 5. Use it if it captures the actions you plan to take and the outcomes you expect. If it doesn't, feel free to craft your own theory of action that will better fit your context.

> *If* we identify, communicate, and scaffold the thinking needed in every lesson, assignment, and task to support students' development as effective thinkers, *then* student understanding will deepen, and students will focus primarily on the learning over the mere completion of work.

Notes

Learning and Thinking Are as Much a Collective Enterprise as They Are an Individual Endeavor

We are built to collaborate. Neuroscience has shown that it feels good (we release oxytocin) when we are connected and acting in alignment with others (Zak 2017). Furthermore, ideas get better when they are challenged, discussed, explored, and generally given a good workout. And yet schools tend to see learning as an individual endeavor built on compliance and competition and punctuated by awards, prizes, and levels of attainment (Elmore 2019). This is particularly prevalent in the United States, where the "prescription for success was and is a blend of pioneer spirit, self-assertion, individual ingenuity, and individual effort" (Webb and Palincsar 1996). Here, again, we see the grammar of schools reinforcing traditional roles for students and teachers.

Although this competitive and individualized view of learning has long been criticized by education reformers, scholars, philosophers, and theorists, some still voice concerns that too much attention on the group will lead to a loss of the individuality of each child (Krechevsky and Stork 2000). However, rather than seeing the individual and the group as opposing forces or contradictory approaches to teaching and learning, it is more useful to think of the symbiotic and dynamic relationship between the group and the individual. This recognizes that the individual grows in their relationship with the group without being subsumed by it. As Jerome Bruner powerfully states, "Mind is inside the head, but it is also with others" (Bruner 1996, p. 87).

It is useful here to distinguish between the common use of group work or team assignments in which students produce a project or complete a task as a team (often by merely dividing up the task) and the kind of true learning group, community of learners, or collective we are talking about here. Likewise, we are not talking about "cooperative learning" strategies with assigned roles done for a specific activity. Group work and cooperative learning are often one-off tasks or experiences whereas Mindset 6 focuses on developing an ongoing commitment to the way the class operates in order to foster and support each other as learners and thinkers. In other words, authentic collaboration. Group work maintains traditional teacher and student roles. Collaborative thinking requires rethinking those roles. Executive coach Yosh Beier defines *collaboration* as a committed, ongoing intention requiring consistent behaviors and attitudes (Beier 2019). This kind of learning in, from, and with groups is situated within Vygotsky's (Vygotsky 1978) sociocultural perspective, which theorizes that individuals gradually internalize new concepts, psychological tools, and skills that are first externalized in the social settings they experience (Shabani, Khatib, and Ebadi 2010). Thus, what happens in the group context affects the individual.

The concept of *collective* is useful in understanding the basis for this mindset. Douglas Thomas and John Seely Brown use the term *collective*, as opposed to *group* or *community*, to denote "a collection of people, skills, and talent that produces a result greater than the sum of its parts" (Thomas and Brown 2011, p. 52). They stress the active, goal-oriented, and participatory nature of the collective. The notion of *collective intelligence* has been around since Aristotle. Nowadays, it is being explored more formally in a wide variety of fields, including business, biology, computer science, democratic institutions, comedic improvisation, and design. This is not the same thing as groupthink, however. In fact, learning groups deliberately seek to combat both the notion of groupthink as well as individual cognitive bias to achieve a higher level of performance. Piere Lévy defines *collective intelligence* as "a form of universally distributed intelligence, constantly enhanced, coordinated in real time, and resulting in the effective mobilization of skills" with the goal of "mutual recognition and enrichment of individuals" as opposed to mindless, cult-like consensus (Murray 1999, p. 13). Thus, collective intelligence is emergent and synergistic as individuals share information and process ideas together, doing so with openness and an eye toward the common good.

WHAT THE RESEARCH SAYS: *WHY* DOES IT MATTER?

What makes an effective collaborative group? Of course, there is no single answer to this important question, but research points to several factors that we might consider and try to realize. Jerome Bruner (1996) identifies four factors at play in communities of learners: 1) *agency*, taking control of one's learning; 2) *reflection*, making the learning make sense; 3) *collaboration*, sharing the human resources of all those involved in the mix of teaching and learning; and 4) *culture*, the way of life and thought we construct, negotiate, and establish. In these factors, we see dynamic interplay between the group and the individual. Jo Boaler (2008) identifies three necessary components of effective learning groups that promote high levels of achievement for all individuals and promote "relational equity": 1) *respect* for other people's ideas, leading to positive intellectual relations; 2) *commitment* to the learning of others; and 3) learned methods of *communication* and support. Thomas and Brown (2011), in their exposition of naturally emergent collectives (blogs, study groups, informal networks), recognized several common factors were often present: shared purpose or interests, active engagement with the process of learning, distributed expertise, a flexible and fluid nature of the group, and playfulness and imagination.

What we see in all these factors is that learning (not work) must be central to the enterprise, good collaboration and communication skills are paramount, respect for and recognition of what others bring is foundational, and a sense of community must be built and maintained. When classrooms function as true learning groups, adults and children alike feel that they are part of something larger than themselves, which has meaning beyond the individual (Krechevsky and Stork 2000). Ample research has shown that within such learning communities, learners develop intellectually, socially, and academically.

Intellectual Development

Learning how to learn, growing intellectually, and learning to think are most effectively developed in a social context (Carr and Walton 2014; Ferlazzo 2019). Through the process of explaining, defending, and discussing with one another, children make use of their peers' ideas as "thinking devices," which enables them to reflect on and transform their own thinking (Webb and Palincsar 1996). When students learn alongside their more experienced peers, opportunities to "work together, brainstorm possibilities, pool knowledge and insights, conduct collective analyses, critique each other, and draw energy from a common goal" allow for deep learning to take place (Halpern, Heckman, and Larson 2013). Through talking to one another, students co-construct new knowledge. The "cognitive conflicts" that arise serve as the "power driving intellectual development" (Perret-Clermont 1980). Therefore, learning as a collective enterprise builds on or extends, rather than replaces, the work of individuals (Krechevsky and Stork 2000). Through working with others, students gain experiences that they would otherwise not have, including learning to "defend, negotiate and modify our ideas" (Krechevsky and Stork 2000).

Social Development

Under the right conditions, students are not only willing, but also capable of learning from one another. Furthermore, when learning is viewed as a collective endeavor and not an individual competition, students build their social and collaborative skills (Kilcher and Arends 2010). Interdependence is a key component of communities of learning. As students share ideas and resources, they assume joint responsibility for learning (Halpern et al. 2013). This creates a safe environment in which students view one another as "allies" rather than competitors, thereby increasing engagement (Boaler 2006) and academic achievement (Dana-Center 2020). In this context, students develop language and communication skills as well (Mercer 2003). Philosopher Michael Oakeshott describes conversation as an "unrehearsed intellectual adventure," which occurs when individuals respond, provoke, and play with ideas offered by others (Oakeshott 1959). This may take the form of "accountable talk," that helps students listen, respond to, and build off other's ideas in ways that build collective understanding (Resnick et al. 2018).

As students collaborate, they learn to "value the contribution of different methods, perspectives, and partially correct or even incorrect ideas" and develop open-mindedness (Boaler 2006). Thus, we cannot ignore developing the social skills needed for individuals to share, communicate, and explore ideas effectively with others. Learning to ask probing questions to elicit their peers' understanding of concepts as well as working with others across different ethnic and class backgrounds helps students develop important socio-emotional competencies (Boaler 2006). Students will only learn to communicate respectfully with others who have opinions different from theirs if they are given opportunities to interact with them (Schwartz 2018).

Academic Development

Employing peer instruction, Crouch and Mazur (2001) found university students more actively involved in their learning and more self-directed. They also attained higher levels of achievement and mastery when compared to traditional didactic instruction. Similar findings were reported by Richard Light in which university students who participated in study groups were dramatically more successful in their courses than those who did not. In Boaler's study of secondary mathematics classrooms, she found heterogeneously grouped students who regularly worked collaboratively to solve conceptual mathematics problems outperformed students in traditional, tracked math classes (Boaler 2008). The key to their learning was that every student felt commitment to the group's learning and those that struggled were not viewed as pulling the class down, but providing an opportunity to teach, explain, explore, and build understanding within the community. In a study of middle school students, collaborative learning led to improved problem-solving outcomes (Barron 2003). The collaborative nature of learning also allows students' thinking to be made visible as conversations often reveal more information than written work (Fiori, Boaler, Cleare, DiBrienza, and Sengupta 2004). This provides an opportunity for teachers to collect and analyze data about students' learning that are useful in informing their next steps in instruction (Fiori et al. 2004).

Professional Learning

To this point, we have focused on the benefits to students. Of course, teachers are learners as well. How does this mindset affect us as professionals learning together at a school? When teachers view teaching, and learning to teach, not just as an individual enterprise, but also as a collective endeavor, they are more likely to take risks, engage in innovative practices, develop a greater sense of efficacy, be more confident and empowered in their teaching, and increase their motivation (Fullan and Hargreaves 1996; Hattie 2009; Rosenholtz 1989; Webb and Ashton 1986). Not surprisingly, student outcomes also improve dramatically. Hattie identifies "collective teacher efficacy," that is, a shared belief in the group's ability to affect change together, as having an effect size of 1.57 (Eells 2011; Hattie 2015). This is the single highest effect size attained from his study of over 250 interventions and factors. In her seminal work defining collegial relationships among teachers, Judith Warren Little (1990) distinguishes between soft and strong forms of collegiality.

Soft forms are characterized by storytelling, sharing, and assistance. In contrast, strong collegiality has collaboration at its core. Little notes that such collaborations share the dynamic of the individual and the group learning in concert. These professional cultures of collaboration depend on and are characterized by the same qualities we seek to develop with students: helpfulness, support, trust, openness, and valuing of what people bring to the group (Nias, Southworth, and Yeomans 2002).

VISIONS AND REFLECTIONS: *HOW* MIGHT IT LOOK?

What does it truly mean to embrace thinking and learning as a collective endeavor? I expect almost everyone has the experience of doing group work or communal projects in schools. For many, this was a stressful rather than a pleasant or enriching experience. Perhaps someone didn't pull their weight, someone dominated, or the compromises required to complete the work left it disjointed. We certainly don't want to replicate that for our students. What we want is to engage students in joyful, purpose-driven work. To help us formulate such a vision, we first tap into our own experience to reflect on times when we were engaged in such a group.

Constructing Our Vision

In research into the neuroscience of trust, Paul Zak (2017) explains that when we connect with others, feel safe around them, and see them as partners looking out for our welfare, oxytocin is released. As a result, we feel good when we are connected to others, collaborating, and working toward common goals in which both the group and the individual benefit. Such environments build trust through the reinforcing feedback loop of extended oxytocin release. Zak sums up this effect by saying that joy "comes from doing purpose-driven work with a trusted team."

Recall a time in which you were engaged in joyful learning, that is, "doing purpose-driven work with a trusted team." With this specific example in mind, respond to the following prompts. Use the pages at the end of this chapter, the margins, a sheet of paper, or your electronic device to record your responses.

- What emotions were you feeling before, during, and after this process?
- How was trust built? How did you come to feel safe with these folks? What made this work feel purposeful? How was that purpose sustained and built? What role did you play in this process?
- What practices facilitated, not the work, but the collaboration? These might be facilitation moves by the leader, organization structures, norms, routines, or others. It might also be the language that was used.
- What kept this from turning into just another group project?

Contemplating Pictures of Practice

To further extend your vision of what true collaborative learning and thinking might look like, we now examine two case studies. The first comes from the Making Learning Visible project that was a collaboration between colleagues at Project Zero and the Reggio Emilia preschools in Italy. This case was crafted from the online account of "Documentation Examples" from the Making Learning Visible (Project_Zero 2006a) and its companion video (see QR code below). The quotes from the children are direct. The surrounding narrative and commentary are my own. The second example, from a grade 12 literature class, comes from our work in the Cultures of Thinking project centered at Bialik College in Melbourne, Australia.

Case One: The City of Reggio. A class in Reggio Emilia, Italy, has been exploring ideas around "cities" for months. Much discussion has ensued about the features and purpose of cities and how people interact within them. Many of these conversations have been documented through audio recordings. Today, a group of three five-year-old boys, Emiliano, Simone, and Giacomo gather to draw a city. They choose a large sheet of paper 60 square centimeters (roughly 2 square feet). Asked if they want to listen to their prior conversation, they decline. Still, having the documentation as part of the collective memory of the group allows them to build on their past efforts. It also stresses the continuity of the learning in which they are engaged.

Emiliano and Simone get right to work, shoulder to shoulder. Giacomo positions himself perpendicular to them and watches. At first there is not much conversation. Then comments are made about the importance of the town squares and streets to allow movement. Simone says, "The streets go to so many places, and there's one square after another in the city." Extending this line of thinking, Emiliano adds, "Yeah, otherwise you'd get lost."

Giacomo watches and listens intently, but does not participate. It's been nearly 20 minutes. At this point, Simone asks, "Why aren't you doing anything?" Giacomo fidgets slightly and then explains, "Cities have to work, and I have to see if it works." Emiliano takes this as an offer to explain more about the choices he and Simone have been making. "See, Giacomo, this is a different square," pointing to the new square he is working on. "It's the one with the field where the children play, and all the houses are different," he explains. He then makes a direct effort at inclusion, "Giacomo, can you draw the roofs of the houses? Come on, try!" Simone chimes in, "Will you help us then?" Finally, Giacomo perks up, "Okay!" he smiles. This effort to include all members, when they are ready, by drawing on their unique abilities, perspectives, and competencies is a hallmark of true learning groups.

Giacomo now begins to direct, "Let's make another square. I'm sure there are lots of squares in the city." The boys now work side by side, each contributing onto one another's drawings, perhaps by adding grass to a field, roofs to houses, or lines to roads. Again, there is no clear division of labor. There is a rationale behind their emerging city. Squares, each unique, are centers of activity and living, but they depend upon roads for movement in the city. Giacomo comments, "In the squares, there are people talking." Simone adds on, "There are pretty squares and ugly ones. There are also some squares for parked cars and for soccer players." Emiliano elaborates on the importance of squares, "I think cities that don't have squares are kind of strange." Giacomo extends this thought, "I think they don't work well because the people don't know where to be."

Work continues with additions of more streets and squares, a train station, and electrical poles. The central themes of connectivity, play, work, and movement emerge in their drawing and conversations with one another. The result is far greater than any individual could have produced. In sharing their map with their teacher, they discuss the aesthetics of their drawing, its quality, and its functionality. Giacomo comments, "We made a beautiful city even though it's a little bit messy." Emiliano highlights the functionality, "All the streets take you somewhere. It's a city where you can't get lost, where you're not afraid." Finally, Simone demonstrates that they have drawn upon their collective knowledge while also transcending it, "It's a city that could be Reggio Emilia because there's the Campo di Marte, but it isn't Reggio. Maybe it's called 'City of the World' because all the people in the world can live in this city." You can view a video of the boys' map developing by scanning the QR code.

QR code for The City of Reggio Video.

SCAN ME

Case Two: Collective Concept Maps. In preparing her students to write individual essays on Tim O'Brien's *In the Lake of the Woods*, Year 12 English teacher Ravi Grewal wanted to leverage the collective intelligence of the group and support students' deep dive into the book's protagonist John Wade. For this purpose, she chooses a thinking routine to enable collaboration and discussion. The routine Generate-Sort-Connect-Elaborate (GSCE) will help structure students' thoughts and analysis through collaborative discussion. Ravi explains her intention, "I want a structure that will give students the freedom to air different viewpoints, make connections, and arrive at conclusions without fear of being incorrect. I also want them to be the main participants in the discussion and not become a teacher directed one."

After explaining the purpose of today's lesson, Ravi guides students through the process of making an individual concept map using the steps of the routine. "Individually, I would like you to generate some ideas. Think of all the factors that impacted on John Wade as an individual and compile a list of those." Students take time to do this before Ravi gives the next instruction. "Now, place the ideas that you consider most important close to the center and those that are peripheral place further away from the center in descending order of importance." Ravi next directs students to draw connecting lines between factors that somehow complimented or influenced each other. Finally, she asks students to elaborate their ideas, adding details that would further their understanding.

Once students have completed individual concept maps, they are placed in heterogeneous groups of three to four and tasked with making a collective concept map following the same steps. By beginning with the individual, Ravi ensures that everyone will come to their group with ideas. No one can be a free rider. Using heterogeneous groups, students are exposed to different views, leading to richer learning (Okada and Simon 1997). She encourages students to share and discuss their ideas before arriving at "shared understandings." Ravi explains to students that much of their learning will come from their discussion, hearing other points of view, and justifying their choices rather than merely producing a final product. Producing the concept map, tangible as it is, is a means to an end and not the end itself.

Students drive the conversation in their groups as they clarify their understanding of the text and refine their thinking. This is an important part of a collaborative discussion (Barnett et al. 2017). Ravi notes, "They are having such passionate discussions. Each feels strongly that he or she has the most accurate 'spot.' That debate is exactly what I was looking for." One lively dispute occurs as a group of students discuss the question of whether it was Wade's experience in Vietnam that sent him over the brink or whether it was the result of his father's bullying during his childhood. The students discuss the possibility that if his father hadn't bullied him and taken away his self-esteem, then he might have grown up strong enough to withstand the trauma of the Vietnam war. There is great conflict over this idea with some students saying that no one could have experienced the trauma of My Lai and not been traumatized. In all groups, no one is willing merely to accept a classmate's placement of an idea unless they can justify and explain it.

As the class nears its end, groups present their maps to their peers. As they do, the class asks questions to understand their placements, choices, and connections rather than to agree or disagree with them. A lively discussion ensues about one group's choice of the word *murder* versus *killings*. Students question whether it is considered murder if it is done in war, or is an act of killing always murder? Sense-making and clarity comes through collective discussion. The class concludes with Ravi giving the homework assignment: "Write an essay discussing, 'Is John Wade a monster or is his only fault the fact that he is a man?'" Having discussed and explored the character of John Wade deeply and collaboratively, students are well prepared for this task. The assignment also provides individual accountability for learning while harnessing the power of collective thinking to build understanding. The homework assignment drives home that the goal of the lesson has been to "understand the character John Wade so that you will be able to write a thoughtful essay" and not, "create a group concept map we can hang on the wall." The individual learns in the context of the group. Scan the QR code to watch a video of this case.

QR code for GSCE video.

SCAN ME

Reflecting on Current Practice

Choosing Questions and Recording Responses

Different questions serve us at different times in our learning. Therefore, I suggest you read through the questions and identify:

➤ One or two that speak to you now. Questions that might challenge you or take your thinking in new directions.
➤ One or two you would most like to discuss with your colleagues.
➤ Circle and date the questions you select now so you can identify how your focus shifts with time and experience.
➤ Use the blank pages at the end of this chapter or your note-taking device to record your reflections.

• What would I expect to see and hear in a rich, fruitful, and respectful conversation in my class and subject area?

• How am I teaching and supporting students in having such rich, fruitful, and respectful conversations?

• Where, when, and how do I provide students feedback on their participation in classroom conversations? On their collaboration?

• How do I ensure all voices are heard in discussion and avoid gender, racial, perceived ability, or extrovert bias when I call on students?

- What opportunities do/might students have to exchange and share knowledge either formally or informally?

- In what ways am I modeling what it means to be a good listener, to treat others with respect and consideration, an effective collaborator?

- In group settings, what am I noticing with regards to students asking task-focused questions, providing justification for their statements, considering various options before coming to a decision, eliciting the opinion of everyone, and seeking agreement before acting? How can I teach, support, and reinforce these practices?

- How might I adapt an upcoming task so that it affords more than one starting point, requires more than one solution path, and makes thinking and learning visible?

- In thinking about an upcoming group task, does it require both positive interdependence and individual accountability?

- Where, when, and how am I providing thinking time before launching into group discussions? What am I noticing about the difference this makes with regards to who contributes and the quality of contributions?

- How am/might I use the space in the classroom to better facilitate student discussion and collaboration? Do students have the option to move somewhere other than their desks? Are flipcharts, poster boards, or whiteboards readily available to students?

- How do/might I provide students with feedback on their progress as a group?

- What routines and structures do I use to facilitate students' group discussion, problem solving, and learning? What makes these routines effective? Whom might they not be working for?

- How do/might I make use of documentation to capture group learning?

- How do I prepare students to work collaboratively with one another? What needs further reinforcement?

- Can my students describe what makes an effective learning group and group discussion?

- Where, when, and how do I ensure that students in my class work across different ability levels, ethnic groups, gender lines, and friendship groups?

- Where is the joy in my classroom?

- Where in my team, department, and school is there collaboration characterized by inquiry, reflection, examination of issues of teaching and learning?

DATA, PRINCIPLES, AND PRACTICES: *WHAT* ACTIONS CAN WE TAKE?

With a better understanding of how the group facilitates and deepens individual learning, making it richer and more meaningful, we are poised to act. But first, it is important to get some insights into where students are in terms of both their abilities and perceptions when it comes to participating actively and meaningfully in groups. The following two street data tools can be useful in this regard.

Collecting Street Data

Street Data

➤ Helps us understand our own context as well as students' perspectives.
➤ Is relatively easy and quick to collect.
➤ Can be immediately analyzed and acted upon straightaway.
➤ Is meant to inform and suggest action.
➤ Is NOT an evaluation or measure of success but a snapshot of practice.
➤ Can take many forms: observations, interviews, surveys, exit tickets, recordings, and so on.

Street Data Action One: Functioning in Groups. Use the "Functioning in Groups" observation checklist (see Appendix F) to identify the behaviors in which learning group members engage. The checklist could be used while students are working in small groups or during a whole-class discussion. Not all behaviors listed are likely to be observed in any single session. In addition, the more a group is led (for instance, by you in a whole-group discussion), the less likely some of the behaviors are to show up. Of course, this is data as well. As you look at the data, some questions to consider are:

- What actions were most/least prevalent? What might account for this?
- What questions or reflections does the data evoke?
- What possible factors contribute to the pattern of students' interaction?
- What skills/actions of group functioning need more attention, clarification, and practice? How might you do this?

- How might you share the data with the students?
- If used in a group discussion, how might you encourage some of the unseen behaviors to emerge?

Street Data Action Two: Collaborative Spirit. Conduct a quick survey of students' collaborative spirit and efficacy. The following two questions come from Peter Liljedahl's very practical research into *Building Thinking Classrooms in Mathematics* (Liljedahl 2020). Though the questions are targeted at mathematical problem solving, substitute the appropriate collaborative task so that the questions work for you. For example, creating a concept map, analyzing a primary source document, discussing a text, or conducting an experiment. These questions could be asked as an exit ticket or in an online poll.

1. If I told you that next class you are going to work in groups to solve a word problem, what is the likelihood that you would offer an idea?

   very likely   likely   highly unlikely   very unlikely

2. If you were to offer an idea, what is the likelihood that your idea would contribute to the solution of the problem?

   very likely   likely   highly unlikely   very unlikely

Students' responses to these two simple questions give you some baseline data of how they view themselves as group members in terms of active participation and confidence. Liljedahl (2020) found that 80% of the adolescent students in his sample rated themselves unlikely or very unlikely to contribute, and 90% said it was highly unlikely their ideas would contribute. Although discouraging results, Liljedahl observed dramatic improvement after just six weeks of students working in visibly random groupings for problem solving. This practice is elaborated in the "Possible Actions" section. At that time, all students reported they were either likely or very likely to offer an idea, and at least 50% felt it would contribute to the group's solution.

Stating the Mindset as Principles for Action

Advancing this mindset "Learning and thinking are as much a collective enterprise as they are an individual endeavor" calls us to first identify principles to guide and direct our efforts. Although there is no single way a collaborative thinking group must look and function, there is ample direction to be found in the research literature regarding useful guidelines and practices. Use these top-level principles in an overarching way to think about your current teaching and identify new practices to implement.

- Signal that collaboration is the expectation in your classroom.
- Teach communication skills that support students' effective listening and talking.
- Prepare students to be part of a team.
- Use structures and routines to support and practice collaborative thinking.

Possible Actions

While it is important to ensure actions are adapted and fitted to your context, be sure not to sell your students short as collaborative thinkers able to work effectively in groups when provided the right support and guidance. In the spirit of Peter Liljedahl, who developed a set of effective practices through testing, experimentation, and evaluation, try out an approach and see how it works. Adapt and iterate regularly based on the data you are getting about how things are working. Remember how we tend to be locked into the grammar of schools, and consequently, see the way things are currently as the way they are supposed to be. Don't be afraid to take risks. Give yourself and your students time to develop the tools and capacity for rich collaboration.

There are many strategies, tools, and resources for helping students to learn collaboratively. These will naturally take on an individual flavor since it is important that these efforts be authentic to who you are. The following actions can jump-start your thinking. These actions are:

➤ Drawn from our work in schools as part of the Worldwide Cultures of Thinking Project.
➤ Placed under the related principle to help you focus on the driving motivation behind each action though there is considerable overlap. For instance, building relationships helps to foster community. Therefore, consider these top-level categories loosely.
➤ Modifiable to fit your local context.
➤ Connected to the most relevant cultural forces to which each specific action is associated. Both frameworks, the 8 cultural forces and the 10 mindsets, are synergistic and you can begin your journey either place.

Signal Collaboration Is the Expectation. Setting expectations is not merely a matter of issuing a directive, "I expect you to collaborate." We must also construct a physical environment that makes collaboration easy, create regular opportunities for collaboration so it becomes the norm, and put students in charge of their learning. Each of these practices is examined in depth.

The *environment* is a powerful cultural force and sends messages about the kind of learning that will happen in a space. Make sure the physical setup of your classroom is designed and ready for cooperation and collaborative thinking, sending the message that this is how the class will operate. Be sure it sets the expectation that learning will happen through active discussion, the contribution of individual's ideas to the group, and that students are not solo agents but partners in a collective. Peter Liljedahl's research in collaborative, mathematical problem solving showed that students are very sensitive to environment and can predict both teaching and student behaviors based on the way a classroom is set up (Liljedahl 2020). Straight rows and highly organized space (even if beautiful) send the message of control and direction. Conversely, classrooms that are slightly less organized (though not chaotic or messy), that have furniture arranged in nonlinear and nonsymmetrical ways, and in which there is no clear "front of the room" are seen by students as more collaborative spaces. It's not hard to see why, when *all* students can see each other, discussion with others is easier. When the teacher is not the focus of attention, the learning group becomes the focus. Liljedahl calls this approach *defronting* the classroom. Some might ask, "But where will I teach?" You still have access to the white boards and projectors as needed, and of course, students can turn around their desks or move if necessary to view a presentation. Flexible seating arrangements make this easy. High school science teacher William Neuwirth in Santa Fe, New Mexico, found that when he defronted his classroom, most of his teaching happened from the center of the classroom, gathering students around in a circle and using the floor or a table to place objects for discussion.

One of the other environmental shifts arising from Liljedahl's research focuses on the best surface on which to write when working in groups. After much investigative research in classrooms, he concluded that work on vertical, nonpermanent surfaces (think a whiteboard) induced greater discussion, ease of getting started, participation, and time on task, among other things. When students are sitting and working at their desks, they may feel more anonymous, creating disengagement. Standing produces better blood flow to the brain, aiding concentration and alertness (Ouchi, Okada, Yoshikawa, Nobezawa, and Futatsubashi 1999). When standing, energy is enhanced, and students are better able to use their whole bodies in communicating. In addition, everyone can see the group's documentation more easily.

To make collaboration an ongoing, intentional practice, students must operate in learning groups often, not simply for one-off tasks. Create regular *opportunities* for collaboration. It is only then that students will begin to see the value in the collective thinking through of issues and problems. Thus, in building a culture of thinking, teachers need to regularly engage students in group analysis, problem solving, or experimentation. In these settings, the understandings constructed by the group through discussion and exploration support the learning of each individual who is then held accountable for their learning through individual assessments. We want students to see the group as a support for their learning, not a replacement of it. In creating such opportunities, design tasks that provide multiple entry points so all students can contribute. Group-worthy tasks focus on the co-construction of understanding and group interdependence. Such tasks generally address complex problems, issues, or projects and have several possible solution paths. They demand extensive interaction and discussion and cannot be completed through a divide-and-conquer strategy. If a task can be completed by dividing it into parts and assigning jobs to individuals, then it is unlikely to produce much learning. When you are observing students collaborate, be sure to name and notice when and how students learn from others, build on one another's ideas, or draw others into conversation. In debriefing these tasks, be sure to talk about the *group's* questions, insights, understandings rather than only that of individuals.

Whole-class discussions are also rich *opportunities* for collaboration. Stephen Brookfield describes class discussion as "the jewel crown of the engaged classroom" (Brookfield 2006, p. 115). In these discussions, we want students grappling with complexities, entertaining new perspectives, forming and expressing opinions, asking questions, making connections, building vocabulary, and developing understandings. However, to do so may require us to refrain from some common teaching practices, such as asking narrow questions or posing questions to which we already know the answer. It also means limiting our own talk so that students will have space to share their ideas. We want students talking to each other and not just to us or through us. In essence, we want whole-class discussions to mirror what we want to see in small groups. Dylan Wiliam (2009) calls this playing basketball, in which the ball is constantly passed, rather than ping-pong, in which the ball merely goes back and forth between two players. He uses the acronym PPPB for Pose, Pause, Pounce, and Bounce to denote the teaching moves in this kind of interaction. Whole-class discussion also gives us the opportunity to model what active listening looks like.

We all want students to be successful learners. However, we often undermine this when in our *interactions* with students we over-scaffold or over-simplify tasks to remove the very stretch that produces learning. This may make students more successful at completing a task, but less learning is happening. Another way in which we sometimes undermine our students' learning is by being *too* helpful. A student asks a question, and we immediately answer it out of habit. However, many times our answering the question will stop the student from thinking themselves or from going to their peers. What's the point in giving a collective thinking task if we answer all the questions related to how students might go about approaching that task? Sometimes we need to stop and ask ourselves: "Am I the only one who can answer this question?" "Will my answering promote more thinking on the part of the student or less?" The strategy, "Ask three before me," in which students are instructed to first approach three of their peers before asking the teacher a question encourages students to see their peers as resources for their learning, which is the heart of collaboration. This creates new patterns of *interaction* in the classroom

Teach Communication Skills. Teachers must invest time in building students' skills for productive interaction early in the year by explicitly teaching and debriefing group interactions and developing communication skills. Communication skills are consistently rated the most important and in-demand skills businesses seek in employees, so devoting time to developing them is a worthwhile endeavor (Berger 2016; GMAC Research Team 2020). Many conflicts and misunderstandings occur through misinterpretation of what others are trying to communicate. Learning the language of listening, accountable talk, how to identify discourse patterns, the language of feedback, and how to ask clarifying and probing questions are helpful tools to avoid such miscommunication. These approaches draw on the cultural forces of *language, modeling, time*, and *interactions*.

"Accountable Talk" is talk that holds the speaker accountable for providing reasons and evidence for their ideas and connecting it to the conversation (Resnick et al. 2018). This process helps students effectively engage in meaningful and respectful conversations mutually beneficial to both speaker and listener by teaching accountable talk. Scan the QR code to view a video of students using accountable talk. Accountable talk is developed through our *modeling*, providing sentence stems students can use, and reinforcing the importance of accountable talk through our feedback. Use *language* that is age-appropriate to create sentence stems based upon the following examples:

QR code for accountable talk video.

SCAN ME

- I want to add on to what ____ said.
- I have a connection to what ____ said.
- On page ____ it said ____.
- Could you clarify for me what you mean?
- I have another way of looking at this that is different from ____.
- Could you say more about that because I am having a hard time understanding ____.
- I agree/disagree with ____ because ____.

Many classroom conversations are of the popcorn variety in which individual contributions burst onto the scene. While there is a time and place for such conversations, such as the generation of ideas, these conversations often don't build, connect, or lead to better understanding of the topic. Instead, encourage conversations in which new ideas are carefully placed on top of and connect to the previous ideas, like a stacked ice cream cone. This visual metaphor can be useful for students of all ages and connects to the idea of accountable talk. Share, model, and promote "ice cream cone" more than "popcorn" conversations. Consider collecting data on classroom conversations by noting how many conversational additions were made to an idea or question before something new is introduced.

Using the Fishbowl technique allows us to *model* group *interactions* and make the implicit explicit. In a Fishbowl (sometimes called inner and outer circles), students stand in a circle around a small group that is engaging in the process to be learned, such as having an effective discussion. The group in the Fishbowl has generally been chosen strategically as a model. Teachers may be a part of this group. Those on the outside gather around in a circle (you should be able to see every student) and are given specific directions for observing. For example, they may be asked to pay attention to: Who talks and for how long? What questions sparked the most discussion? How do group members respond to each other? How are they using accountable talk? And so on. See an example of a 5th-grade teacher introducing the Ladder of Feedback routine using the Fishbowl technique by scanning the QR code.

QR code for Fishbowl Ladder of Feedback video.

SCAN ME

Many people simply are not good at talking "cold" as soon as a question is asked. A lot of us need *time* to process, organize, and rehearse. This might take the form of providing a few minutes to first jot notes individually and then having students talk to their neighbor or discuss in small groups before sharing in the whole-class setting. This allows time for both introverts and extroverts to develop their ideas. You might use the familiar Think-Pair-Share routine for this purpose or its partner, "1-2-4-All" in which individuals think or write alone (1), then discuss with a partner (2); next partner groups combine (4) and finally there is a whole-class discussion (All) (Casner-Lotto and Barrington 2006). Both formats allow students to develop their ideas and learn from others in a less public space, which may facilitate quieter students having more confidence to share. Remember, the first person to share in a group often sets the tone for what follows, so thinking and processing time can often assure a better start to a discussion. As useful as thinking time and rehearsal can be in discussion, sometimes thinking time is not needed if the focus is problem solving. Peter Liljedahl (2020) feels that if students think about a problem solution before getting in groups, they are more likely to hold on to their ideas than listen to others. In addition, more able students might already come to a solution before even entering the group, and less able students will just defer to them since they seem to know what they are doing. Liljedahl prefers to get students talking right away to ensure an equal footing.

Thus, experiment (and collect data on) the use of thinking time across various contexts to see what works for your students.

Teaching students about *clarifying* and *probing* questions and promoting their use can help students to build both their own and other's understanding. Clarifying questions are questions we ask *for ourselves* when something is not clear, or we are lacking background information. They don't do anything for the questionee, however. For example, if I were to ask you what grade level you teach, it would provide me useful information, but it doesn't personally help you. You already know the answer to that question. In fact, this is how we recognize that we have asked a clarifying question. The responder answers immediately in a few words because they have the answer. In contrast, a probing question is an *invitation to the questionee* to think more deeply. For instance, "What have you noticed as a result of defronting your classroom?" That question invites the responder's reflection.

Prepare Students to Be Part of a Team. To learn in, with, and through collaboration, we must teach our students positive ways of *interacting* in large and small group settings. We can't expect them to simply come prepared to productively engage with others. We must establish a culture of respect with attention to both community and agency, a culture in which everyone feels responsible for each other's learning. Students need to see one another as important resources in the classroom and actively seek help from others beyond the teacher. With this shared vision as our grounding, we can establish "ways of being" or group norms that support students' active and respectful participation. In setting norms, it is important to make sure students are clear about the goal of the group. If the goal is merely to get the work done, students are likely to suggest "Everyone has to do their part." In contrast, if the goal is collective thinking through problems and issues, a norm might be "Make sure you hear everyone's ideas." Identifying the goals of collaborative discussion allows students to anticipate the kind of contributions that are relevant and appropriate. Post these "Ways of Being" and have students revisit them regularly and revise if necessary. Posted norms help students monitor their behavior in a group and provide a common *language* for discussing group functioning.

In Preparing Students to Be Part of a Team, Focus on Actions over Roles. A hallmark of "cooperative learning" is the assignment of roles: facilitator, timekeeper, recorder, and so on. The idea is that roles clearly define actions for students and make accountability easier. However, assignment of such roles can be restrictive. Students focus only on their role and aren't really paying attention to the collective learning of the group. Thus, they don't really learn how to learn from, with, and in a group. What is more useful is identify the actions each group member needs to make to support the group's collective learning and thinking. For instance, posing questions of others, backing up ideas with evidence when you can, inviting others to share their perspective, listening to others, saying when you don't understand, and so on. Note that these actions necessarily cross over with "ways of being" and support positive *interactions*. This is why I like that term *ways of being* rather than *norms*. Norms often suggest rules.

The question of what size group and how to form groups is constantly on our minds as teachers. Advice on this topic is wide-ranging and contradictory. However, if we zero in on our goal, collaborative discussion, and collective thinking, the advice becomes clearer. Both Jo Boaler (2006) and Peter Liljedahl (2020) advocate for heterogeneous ability groups. They have found these groups work when the focus is on collective learning and a commitment to the learning of others is present. Liljedahl found that the formation of groups needs to be "visibly random." That means students can see there was no behind-the-scenes manipulation by the teacher. It was the luck of the draw, literally. In such situations, students worked with whom they were assigned that day and just got on with it. There was less moaning and groaning when groups were formed, and less off-task behavior than in self-selected groups. See the previous Street Data section for more of the results from such groups.

Use Structures and Routines for Collaborative Thinking. Support students in learning and thinking collaboratively through the use of *routines*, structures, and protocols that scaffold and consciously encourage the integration of ideas. In the book *The Power of Making Thinking Visible* (Ritchhart and Church 2020), there is a chapter on routines for engaging with others. Several of these have already been shared such as Making-Meaning (page 84), Generate-Sort-Connect-Elaborate (page 131), +1 (page 107). These all provide opportunities for students to learn from one another and to share their expertise. These routines also naturally document the group's learning, demonstrating how the group's understanding develops through the contributions of everyone.

The "Leaderless Discussion" routine creates an *opportunity* for students to own and drive the direction of a conversation. It gets more students involved in bringing their thinking to the group (Ritchhart and Church 2020). The Leaderless Discussion also provides teachers with opportunities to listen and observe, determining what ideas and concepts are coming to the surface for students in their efforts to develop understanding. Another central component of the routine is learning to ask good questions. Learning to frame questions that engage others in discussion is not easy. It takes time to develop.

Students seeing one another as resources for learning is one of the keys to developing a community of learners. Giving and receiving feedback is a way to both build and extend community cohesion. Feedback requires trust. Therefore, it is important to scaffold the feedback process so that it feels both substantive and safe. The Ladder of Feedback provides students with the

Figure 6.1 Ladder of Feedback.

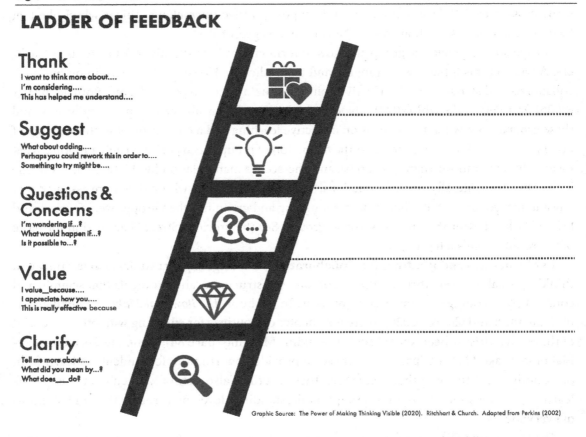

LADDER OF FEEDBACK

Thank
I want to think more about....
I'm considering....
This has helped me understand....

Suggest
What about adding....
Perhaps you could rework this in order to....
Something to try might be....

**Questions &
Concerns**
I'm wondering if...?
What would happen if...?
Is it possible to...?

Value
I value__because....
I appreciate how you....
This is really effective because

Clarify
Tell me more about....
What did you mean by...?
What does___do?

Graphic Source: The Power of Making Thinking Visible (2020). Ritchhart & Church. Adapted from Perkins (2002)

language and sentence stems to support positive and significant interactions (see Figure 6.1). The SAIL (Share-Ask-Ideas-Learned) routine is another routine for feedback. Here, the focus is on a presenter verbally *sharing* their plans, peers *asking* clarifying and probing questions while offering *ideas*, and the presenter sharing back to the group what they *learned* and will take away from the conversation (Ritchhart and Church 2020). Feedback can also be structured around the following simple prompts. After a student reads their work to a partner, the partner then responds by stating "What I heard is. . . ." and "What I wonder is. . . ."

Fitting New Actions with Current Realities

Before you rush to implement the actions you are eager to try, step back and think about what you are currently doing at your school (see Figure 6.2):

➤ What actions, already in place, can be *amplified* and grown by applying some of the principles identified above?
➤ What practices need to be rethought or *modified* considering this mindset?
➤ What do you need to stop doing altogether and *remove* from your repertoire? Why? Does it run counter to this mindset? Is it ineffective? What "moveable barriers" are standing in the way of truly living this mindset?
➤ Finally, are there things that you need to *create*, totally new processes, structures, or actions to begin to put in place?

Figure 6.2 Amplify-Modify-Remove-Create.

Review of Current Practice: What do we need to...

AMPLIFY	MODIFY	REMOVE	CREATE

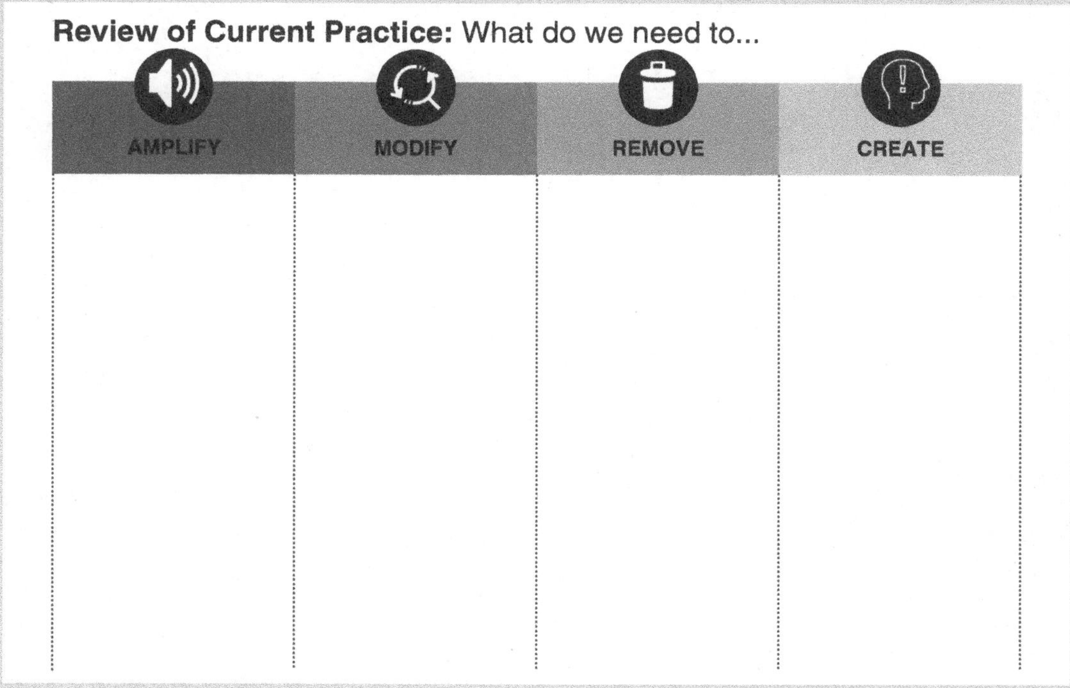

Conclusion: Our Theory of Action

We conclude our examination of this mindset by formulating a theory of action. What are we likely to see as a result of fully embracing the belief that "Learning and thinking are as much a collective enterprise as they are an individual endeavor"? If you act on the principles we have laid out, what is likely to occur in your classroom or across your school? This will constitute your theory of action. I offer the following theory of action for Mindset 6 that might be useful in shaping your own. Use it if it captures the actions you plan to take and the outcomes you expect.

If we engage students in learning from and with each other through active discussion and group exploration of content, then engagement will increase, students will become more self-directed learners, and a community of supportive learners able to engage in true collaboration will develop.

Notes

Learning Occurs at the Point of Challenge

The pressure for mastery of academic skills sometimes pushes teachers to focus on transferring information quickly rather than allowing students time to grapple with ideas, sort through ambiguities, and deal with complexities (Meyer 2010). Too often, teachers tend to reduce the challenge of tasks with the goal of making work more manageable for students (Cheeseman, Clarke, Roche, and Walker 2016b; Choppin 2011; Stein and Lane 1996). However, this simplification removes the very struggle that promotes students' learning and engagement (Meyer 2016). In fact, it is the struggle that fosters deep learning and understanding not the mere completion of the assignment (McGrath 2019; Terenzini 2020). The inclination to remove struggle, even to see it as bad, and to push students to demonstrate replication of skills quickly is rooted in our understanding of the purpose of schools, how learning happens, and what it means to have an education. In this book and across my decades of research and writing about developing cultures of thinking, I have advocated that the goal of a quality education is to develop students as powerful thinkers and learners who possess robust understanding ready to take their place in the world as active agents. Unfortunately, this is not yet a uniformly adopted view. Many teachers, students, parents, and policy makers see school as a competition to determine who can master a prescribed set of content as quickly as possible. Indeed, this view is part of the grammar of schools and is the basis for many of the practices we take for granted in our institutions. One of these practices is direct instruction.

In direct instruction, teachers set out clear intentions for a lesson, establish success criteria, model the skills, lead students through guided practice of the skill, and close the lesson with more independent practice (Hattie and Zierer 2017). Direct instruction, according to the National Institute for Direct Instruction (NIFDI.org 2012), is predicated on the idea that instruction *should* seek to eliminate misunderstanding, misconceptions, and misinterpretation to *accelerate* learning. Furthermore, it focuses on "small increments" and "prescribed tasks" given to students placed at their predetermined "skill level." Direct instruction is most effective when learners know very little about a domain and when instruction illuminates expert thinking (Keep 2021). Reviews of studies show it in the moderate range of effectiveness with an effect size of 0.59 (Hattie 2009).

However, direct instruction can *reduce* learning in several important ways. Rather than focusing on the big picture and complexity of ideas, content is narrowed to make it tame and easy to handle. Furthermore, this method of instruction is predicated on the belief that efficiency in acquiring a prescribed skill (assessed in the near term) is the goal of learning, rejecting the fact that teachers have a wide variety of goals beyond content transmission (Eppley, K. and C. Dudley-Marling 2019). In addition, there is often little attention given to long-term learning when teachers and students only focus on immediate success. Neuroscientist Robert Bjork makes an important distinction between learning, which is long lasting, and performance, which is the immediate, short-term functioning (Bjork 2015). Instruction that focuses on performance creates the illusion of learning, but the gains are soon lost.

The learning group, which is discussed in Mindset 6, is also reduced in this approach as students are taught in specific skill levels so the material will be easy to handle. Furthermore, the focus of direct instruction tends to be on the replication of other's ideas and skills. What gets lost is the opportunity for deeper learning and rich understanding of the material—the very things needed for long-term retention and robust transfer (Hattie and Zierer 2017; Mehta and Fine 2019). This focus on showing and telling also ignores the agency of learners and their ability to make sense of complexity. Sugata Mitra's famous "Hole-in-the-Wall" experiments in which he installed a computer kiosk in a Delhi slum, showed that, given opportunity, students could manage extreme complexity (Mitra 2003). Finally, reducing the challenge, struggle, and difficulty of learning neglects findings from neuroscience that show forcing our brains to work harder can result in better learning outcomes in terms of memory storage and memory retrieval (Bjork and Bjork 2020; Carey 2015).

The over-emphasis on direct instruction is not the only culprit, however. Another driver of both teachers' reduction of challenge and students' fear of challenge is that too many of us simply do not see the benefits of learning from our mistakes. We may have internalized society's message that mistakes are failures that reflect badly on us and should be avoided. Indeed, it seems like this view has become endemic in our modern society (Levine 2005; Lukianoff and Haidt 2019; Stixrud and Johnson 2019). However, research suggests that academic struggle is necessary for growth. Making mistakes, but more importantly *learning* from them, helps with brain growth and connectivity (Boaler 2019). Some of the highest-achieving people in the world are those who have struggled the most. Simply put: if we are not struggling, we are not learning.

WHAT THE RESEARCH SAYS: *WHY* DOES IT MATTER?

There is clear-cut evidence that producing results on tests is better achieved from challenge than simplification. In a study comparing American and Japanese teachers, researchers found that American teachers tended to demonstrate solutions to mathematical problems, whereas Japanese teachers permitted students to grapple with the problems and allowed time for solutions to be developed (Hiebert et al. 2005; Stigler and Perry 1988). Overall, students productively struggling and grappling with mathematics is less prevalent in U.S. classrooms than in other high-achieving countries (Banilower, Boyd, Pasley, and Weiss 2006). When teachers—whether in America or any other country—demonstrate solutions or "proceduralize" learning, they take away the challenge of problems, consequently converting problem-solving tasks into mere exercises in which students apply procedures/rules to a problem without the cognitive challenge that leads to deep learning (Cheeseman, Clarke, Roche, and Walker 2016; Cobb and Jackson 2011; Meyer 2010). The National Council of Mathematics has long advocated for more challenge in mathematics classrooms, though these ideas are still not widespread (Crosswhite, Dossey and Frye 1989). Efforts focusing on productive struggle through problem-based instruction conducted in Mississippi and Hawaii demonstrated that calculus students who experienced such instruction had higher levels of performance and demonstrated greater fluency, flexibility, and originality than their traditionally taught peers (Roble 2017).

Productive Struggle and Failure

A meta-analysis of 53 studies examining the effects of productive failure in which students received problem-solving tasks based on concepts students had *not yet studied* before instruction did better than the traditional direct instruction model of providing instruction followed by problem-solving applications (Sinha and Kapur 2021). This would be like Dan Meyer's "Three-Act Math" or the approach advocated by Peter Liljedahl, which are discussed in Mindsets 5 and 6, respectively. The key conditions were not just to produce failure, however. The problem-solving tasks were done collectively, allowing students to activate and differentiate prior knowledge. In addition, there was an emphasis on refining and critiquing both representations and solution paths, all occurring within the kind of collaborative learning as discussed in Mindset 6.

Unfortunately, this kind of challenging instruction is rare. John Hattie's research on teaching expertise showed that even experienced teachers focused on narrow surface-level goals centered on acquisition of knowledge over 70% of the time. In contrast, expert teachers, as defined by those having a National Board certification, focused more than 70% of their instruction on developing understanding in which knowledge was connected, extended, and abstracted (Hattie and Zierer 2017). Making sure students experience productive struggle is not simply mitigated by providing teachers with challenging tasks and goals focused on understanding, however. In studies of how teachers respond to students' struggles, teachers who evaluated students' responses as simply right or wrong tended to adapt tasks in ways that reduced the complexity of the tasks and simply made it possible for students to "get" right answers. In contrast, teachers who focused on understanding students' thinking were able to build on that thinking and make adaptations that enhanced both task complexity and students' opportunity to engage with the concepts (Choppin 2011). In studies of parents who regularly intervened to "help" children by taking over and completing the task for them, researchers found a negative effect on children's persistence and engagement with the tasks (Leonard, Martinez, Dashineau, Park, and Mackey 2019).

Desirable Difficulties

The fact is, a bit of difficulty and forcing the brain to work harder can lead to better memory and retention. Cognitive psychologist Robert Bjork coined the term *desirable difficulties* to describe those conditions that may be difficult and impeded performance in the short term, but led to better learning in the long run (Bjork and Bjork 2020). For example, research by Rohrer and Taylor compared a typical direct instruction technique in which a very narrow goal was taught and practiced, in this case, how to find the volume of only one figure, with a broader goal of teaching students to find volumes of several different types of figures. In the short run, the direct, narrow instruction group performed better. However, after a week the group with the "desirable difficulty" learning condition outperformed the direct instruction group by answering 63% of questions correctly to 20% for the direct instruction group (Rohrer and Taylor 2007). Similar studies and results have been produced comparing students taught algorithmically and those left to find their own creative solutions to problems (Wirebring et al. 2015). What is happening here is that the brain is not simply practicing a procedure and learning it by rote, but is actively exploring relationships, making connections, and processing information more deeply. This results in multiple pathways for retrieval and greater flexibility. fMRI scans have confirmed that students learning through struggle have more robust memories and easier recall. Another reason why this might be so is that students are more likely to stop their effort to learn when given narrow goals because it seems to them that they have mastered the material. However, this learning is weakly stored even though it can be adequately recalled in the short term.

Growth Mindset

In addition to being more engaging, developing thinking, and fostering understanding, regular encounters with challenge support student autonomy, creativity, and development of a growth mindset (Dweck 2006). As students learn to overcome challenges, they come to see struggle and setbacks as a natural step in learning (Dweck 2015). One study of students in Chile found that those with a growth mindset were three times more likely to score at the top 20% of the test, while students with a fixed mindset were four times more likely to score at the bottom 20%

(Romero 2015). Not only is a growth mindset associated with better performance and learning outcomes, but it also affects students' perceptions of schools. When students have a fixed mindset, schools are seen as threatening places where students must prove their intelligence. In contrast, when students have a growth mindset, schools are viewed as exciting places filled with challenge and growth (Romero 2015).

Desire for Challenge

Given many teachers' efforts to reduce complexity, it may come as a surprise to learn that students report that they actually like and value a degree of cognitive complexity as well as the feeling of being pushed and challenged—as long as it is accompanied with support (Cushman 2014; Hamari et al., 2016; Lamborn, Newmann, and Wehlage 1992; Meyer 2016). More demanding tasks encourage students to seek out connections in their learning, which keeps them more intrinsically interested, engaged, and motivated (Hamari et al. 2016). The flipside is that when students don't feel that they are being cognitively challenged, they are more likely to disengage. National studies confirm that lack of challenge is a major reason for disengagement in the classroom (Boaler 2019; Shernoff 2010; Shernoff 2013; Yazzie-Mintz 2007).

Perhaps this desire for more challenge shouldn't really surprise us based on what we intuitively know about engagement, fun, and "being in the zone." Mihaly Csikszentmihalyi's theory of "flow," the experience of being in the zone when performing an activity, has the idea of challenge at its core. If tasks are too easy, we disengage. If they are too hard, we get frustrated. Finding that point of challenge is key to creating a flow state in which we feel totally immersed, energized, and focused. Being in flow can have a powerful effect on learning. John Hattie states, "When a learner is deeply involved in the task, and in the zone, they can then experience the deepest and most lasting happiness. When in the zone, they have a sense of personal control over the activity, they seek and interpret immediate feedback, and they feel that they have the potential to achieve success" (Hattie and Zierer 2017). Flow is also a part of fun according to science journalist Catherine Price. She defines *fun* as "playful, connected, flow" (Price 2022). We enjoy being pushed and stretched by activities.

What constitutes a challenging task versus a task that is just hard? There are many ways in which tasks might be made both challenging and engaging. Dan Meyer argues that it is perplexity, not real-life application, that engages students in mathematics (Meyer 2016). Perplexity is something that piques interest, which makes us want to know more, that has a bit of both mystery and complexity. Creating cognitive conflict is another way to create the conditions in which students want to learn how to think (Nottingham 2017; Shernoff 2010). In science, challenging tasks require students to: 1) use knowledge to explain observable phenomenon; 2) reason with observations and data to construct or evaluate explanatory models or theory; and 3) use evidence to develop arguments (Kang 2017). Yet another way to challenge students is by placing them in the "zone of proximal development," the difference between what a learner can do without help and what they can achieve with guidance (McLeod 2012).

VISIONS AND REFLECTIONS: *HOW* MIGHT IT LOOK?

What constitutes productive struggle, challenge, or grappling with complexity? How can we understand these concepts and the conditions that give rise to them so that we can create them for our students? What do such tasks look like, and perhaps more importantly, what do they feel like to learners? If we are to help our students embrace challenge, then we must develop empathy for what they might be feeling as learners when they encounter and navigate their way through these experiences. To help us formulate such a vision, we tap into our own experience and then begin to define some terms.

Constructing Our Vision

When and where have you experienced moments where learning felt challenging? Perhaps you were forced to stretch yourself and engage in productive struggle. Take a moment and reflect on:

- What did it feel like at the time?
- How did it feel afterward?
- How did the struggle connect to your sense of accomplishment?

Use the pages at the end of this chapter, the margins, a sheet of paper, or your electronic device to record your reflections.

The words *challenge*, *struggle*, and *difficulty* are all familiar ones that we use frequently. Even with the addition of the modifiers *learning* challenge, *productive* struggle, and *desirable* difficulty the terms likely still resonate and feel familiar on some intuitive level. However, they are nuanced and complex in practice. Although our understanding of these terms will grow and evolve over time as we explore them and put them into practice, we want to define how we understand them now. Pick one of these terms. What would be your encapsulation of it right now if you had to explain it to someone else? If you'd rather not write, try to capture the heart and distill the essence of your chosen term by expressing it as a color, a symbol, and/or an image. Once again, record your responses in some way. As you work with these ideas, come back to what you recorded and see how you might modify it to better capture your new thinking.

Contemplating Pictures of Practice

Case One: Normalizing Struggle.[1] Fourth-grade teacher Kate Mills at the Knollwood School in Fair Haven, New Jersey, is very intentional in her efforts to normalize struggle and challenge in her classroom. "From the first day of school, I intentionally choose language and activities that help to create a classroom culture of problem solvers. I want to produce students who are able to think about achieving a particular goal and manage their mental processes," she explains. Consequently, she takes every opportunity to notice and name students' growth, struggle, problem-solving strategies, initiative, and cooperation. She also makes a point to step back and be sure she "highlights how the students—not the teacher—worked through those problems."

These strategies are vital to help students accept that struggle and failure are a normal part of learning and not something to avoid. At the same time, Kate recognizes the importance of stories and metaphors to ground concepts and provide a common reference. To this end, she shows students a two-minute video produced by a Canadian organization focused on heart health in which two people are riding up an escalator in an empty building (scan the QR code to view). The escalator suddenly stops. The people start calling for help, get out their mobile phones, and eventually sit down while waiting for help to arrive. Of course, as Kate's 4th graders quickly recognize, the couple could just walk the rest of the way. The absurdity of being "stuck" on an escalator is clearly apparent. Kate drives the metaphor home, "Many of us, probably all of us, are like the people in the video yelling for help when we get stuck. When we get stuck, we stop and

QR Code for Stuck on an Escalator video.

SCAN ME

immediately say 'Help!' instead of embracing the challenge and trying new ways to work through it." As the year progresses, the call to "just get off the escalator" becomes a familiar refrain in the classroom.

When Kate gives students a problem to solve, she does so with the admonition, "Your job is to get yourselves stuck—or to allow yourselves to get stuck on this problem—and then work through it, being mindful of how you're getting yourselves unstuck." As she checks in with students, she inquires: "How did you get yourself unstuck?" "What steps did you take?" "What didn't work?" "What did you learn from that?" These questions focus on process rather than product while helping students to be more metacognitive.

From these individual conversations and whole-class debriefings, Kate creates anchor charts with her students. One is labeled: "To get ourselves un-stuck we can try. . . ." This is followed by suggestions such as: reading the problem, restating what the problem is asking in your own words, highlighting important information, making a table, writing down important numbers, looking for patterns, drawing a picture, and so on. Another poster is titled: "We Can Get Ourselves Un-Stuck by Saying and Doing. . . ." What follows are useful sentence stems such as, "I think . . . ," "Maybe we could . . . ," "What about . . . ," "Let's try. . . ." In the "Doing" column are words like *revise, reread, ask questions, name the steps, explain*, and so on. Kate explains the usefulness of these charts, "The charts grow with us over time and are something that we refer to when students are stuck or struggling. They become a resource for students and a way for them to talk about their process when they are reflecting on and monitoring what did or did not work."

Case Two: A Formative Challenge.[2] Fractions, decimals, and percentages represent a big chunk of 6th-grade mathematics, but these topics aren't new to students. Students bring a lot with them in terms of procedures (for converting, ordering, and operating), contextual understandings, and even misconceptions. Mark Church, teaching at the International School of Amsterdam, sought to uncover this by dropping his students into a set of complex problems. He realized, "I need to see where students are both procedurally and conceptually. What representations are they using and how do they make sense of situations involving rational numbers? What kind of intuition and strategies do they bring into this space as problem solvers? Also, where are students' challenges? Where do they get hung up?"

Mark selected two problem scenarios from *Connected Mathematics* (Lappan, Fey, Fitzgerald, Friel, and Phillips 1997) to help him achieve this goal and provoke productive struggle:

- Samuel is getting a snack for himself and his little brother. There are two candy bars in the refrigerator. Samuel takes half of one candy bar for himself and half of the other candy bar for his little brother. His little brother complains that Samuel got more. Samuel says that he got half, and his brother got half. What might be the problem?

- Tisia made 19 out of 30 free throws in the warmup; Clarise made 8 out of 13; and Dorothea made 14 out of 21. Who would you say is the best free-throw shooter?

Mark didn't feel he needed to modify these problems to achieve his goals. He liked their complexity and accessibility, "I feel these problems have enough ambiguity to create some interesting thinking opportunities and perhaps some discussion. The candy bar problem taps into issues of 'fairness,' which early adolescent students are obsessed with, and the basketball problem has an element of figuring out 'Who's best?'" The problems also allowed students to get a sense of the stretch they were going to experience within this unit of study.

In anticipating how students might respond, Mark thought about the issue of part–whole relationships and the ambiguity of words like *half* and *out of*. He was curious to see if students would uncover the challenges. For instance, would students recognize that determining "best" is more complicated than just a simple average, that likelihood of performance as demonstrated over lots of occasions is also important?

Because Mark was using this as a formative assessment, he first had students complete the task individually in writing so he could spend time carefully assessing what each student was bringing to this topic in terms of procedures and reasoning. He then encouraged open-ended discussions to see how they would interact with and build on one another's ideas. Listening to these conversations, he felt that students were comfortable sharing their thinking, and lots of discussion and debate ensued. One student made the point of considering the whole by saying, "I'm not sure if a 'half' is always the same thing. If Oprah gave away half of her salary, it would be a lot more than if Mr. Church did." In another conversation, a student remarks, "But if you only shoot one free throw and make it, that's 100%, but that doesn't mean you are necessarily the best player."

As Mark reviews students' work later, he notes the reasoning, skills, and understandings they brought to the tasks:

- "If both of them get half, then Samuel's brother shouldn't be complaining." *Sticks with surface meaning of half.*
- "But Samuel might have just took a piece from a candy bar without making sure they were equal." *Issue of fractions as precise measures.*
- "Lots of children say, 'You've got the bigger half' but this isn't possible." *Preciseness but fails to see context of what is the whole.*
- "The two candy bars might be different sizes so you would get a different amount." *Considers the half in relation to the whole.*

- "I just reduced all the fractions to lowest terms; I didn't need to find a common denominator for this. Dorothea did the best." *Procedure skills and good perceptual understanding of relative magnitude of fractions.*
- "Clarise made 5 mistakes and the rest made 17 and 7, but I don't think that is right because they have different denominators." *Attempts straightforward comparisons but then recognizes the importance of common denominators though not sure how to deal with them procedurally.*

Reflecting on Current Practice

As we have examined, embracing challenge, complexity, and struggle run counter to our natural inclination both as teachers and as learners. In addition, the grammar of schools and the short-term emphasis on quick right answers biases us toward direct instruction. Consequently, embracing this mindset can feel a bit confronting. Current practices may not align or even be contradictory. Therefore, be easy on yourself in your examination. The point is to grow and develop over time. Use these questions to help you identify a good starting point for change.

Choosing Questions and Recording Responses

Different questions serve us at different times in our learning. Therefore, I suggest you read through the questions and identify:

➤ One or two that speak to you now. Questions that might challenge you or take your thinking in new directions.
➤ One or two you would most like to discuss with your colleagues.
➤ Circle and date the questions you select now so you can identify how your focus shifts with time and experience.
➤ Use the blank pages at the end of this chapter or your note-taking device to record your reflections.

- What beliefs about struggle, challenge, and failure are common in my school, community, and classroom?
- How do/might I normalize the idea of challenge, productive struggle, and learning from failure with my learners?
- How does my response to students' mistakes indicate that I see mistakes as a sign of failure or an opportunity for learning?

- When my students fail, do I seek to understand why, or do I simply assume it can always be attributed to either lack of effort or ability?

- Where was the challenge, the stretch, the press in my lesson today? Were all students challenged or just some?

- Am I comfortable giving students challenging tasks and problems that I have not yet "instructed" them on, or does it make me nervous to see them struggle when I could just show them? Where do these feelings come from?

- How am I finding the point of challenge for all my students?

- In what ways do I have a growth mindset, and where do I have a fixed mindset? *Note: Dweck (2015) has indicated we are all a mix of both mindsets, and no one is completely 100% one or the other.*

- Where and when do I give students time for structured, meaningful reflection on their learning? Do these reflections influence how students approach their learning in the next round? If so, how? If not, why not?

- How am I supporting my students to develop metacognitive skills for dealing with challenge and struggle?

- How do/might I document productive struggle in my classroom?

- What was the last big challenge I faced? How did I tackle it? When and how might I share this story with my students?

- Do I inadvertently put a ceiling or cap on tasks and assignments so that students stop working and learning once they have reached that ceiling? How might I raise or lift the ceiling so that all students can find their point of challenge?

- When students complete a task or assignment easily and quickly, do I simply give them something else to do or do I redesign the task so that it is appropriately challenging for them?

- Do I tend to rescue students when they struggle, or do I support their initiative by asking questions that will encourage them to do the thinking?

- How might I have conversations with students about how struggle and desirable difficulties affect the brain and influence learning?

DATA, PRINCIPLES, AND PRACTICES: *WHAT* ACTIONS CAN WE TAKE?

As you identify what you might do to move this mindset forward, it is useful to analyze the current state of things at your school and in your classrooms. With this mindset, students' perceptions can be a particularly useful area to examine. The first street data action focuses on having students identify moments of challenge. Their selections can tell you something about how they view challenges. The second action takes a whole-school approach to examine how messaging at a school might support or inhibit students' embrace of challenge.

Collecting Street Data

> ## Street Data
>
> ➤ Helps us understand our own context as well as students' perspectives.
> ➤ Is relatively easy and quick to collect.
> ➤ Can be immediately analyzed and acted upon straightaway.
> ➤ Is meant to inform and suggest action.
> ➤ Is NOT an evaluation or measure of success but a snapshot of practice.
> ➤ Can take many forms: observations, interviews, surveys, exit tickets, recordings, and so on.

Street Data Action One: Where's the Stretch? At the end of a week of instruction, ask students to complete an exit ticket or write a reflection on "Where's the Stretch?" Give students enough time to reflect on the entire week of learning, identify two events, and write a paragraph on each. If this is the first time using these prompts, you will need to talk about the idea of a *stretch* in one's learning: what it looks like, what it feels like, and why it is important to learning. This might include a discussion of why challenge matters and how it feeds learning. We use the word *stretch* to try and capture the sweet spot of learning, when things are not too easy, but also not so difficult that they become out of reach. Adapt the following prompts to fit your students and subject area:

- Where were you *stretched* this week in your learning by the lessons, activities, and learning that we/you did? Tell me about why you selected that moment/event.

- Where did you *stretch* or push yourself personally? Tell me about what you did, why, and how you felt about that.

If you are new to using Exit Tickets, a key part of their success is that teachers must show students that the time students spend on them matters—that we read them and use them in our planning as teachers. This means sharing our insights with students along with what we are planning to do with the information we gather. Some things to think about as you read through students' responses:

- What interesting or surprising details do you notice?

- Do students' responses reflect they understand the concept of a "stretch" versus something merely being difficult or hard? What lets you know that? If they don't, where, when, and how will you revisit that discussion?

- Do students' reactions to their stretches indicate that these moments produced joy, a sense of accomplishment, and a greater sense of self-efficacy as learners or were they experiencing frustration?

- What do you notice about the types of learning opportunities producing stretch? Are there some common factors or elements?

- Were you aware students were being stretched at the time? Had you planned on that to happen? Did you press into it? Were there ways you might have leveraged it even more?

- Are there students who cannot identify a stretch? Why do you think this is? How might you model, support, and help them to do so in the future?

- How will you share what you have learned with your students the next time you see them? How will you use this data in your planning?

Street Data Action Two: Walk-Throughs. Walk-throughs can be a useful data collection tool if they are used to better understand what is happening at a school and not as an evaluative measure. One valuable thing about walk-throughs is that they take a whole-school approach, focusing on collective rather than individual action. Walk-throughs can also be aspirational, helping us to develop a vision we can then work toward. This means abandoning the checklist of behaviors one expects to see if people are "implementing" things correctly, and instead focusing on developing a school-wide vision. To do this, begin by gathering a small group to do the walk-through. It could be as small as two people. Establish a vision by asking:

- In a school that believes learning occurs at the point of challenge, how would students get the message that people really do learn through struggle, difficulty, and challenge?

- What kinds of actions, language, environment, interactions, modeling, and opportunities would send this message? Be as specific and varied as possible. Record responses on a whiteboard or piece of chart paper.

- What are some counter-indicators to this mindset? What might we see and hear that would send students that opposite message? Again, record these responses.

With this vision in place, you are ready to do a walk-through. You have become more sensitive to messaging and counter messaging. Visit as many classrooms as you can in the time you allotted, knowing the goal is to pick up impressions and gather evidence that helps answer the question: "How would students here get the message that people really do learn through struggle, difficulty, and challenge?" Avoid taking notes when in a classroom because it can add a layer of unneeded tension for the observed teacher. Instead, record your reactions once back in the hallway. Gathered back in your meeting space, use the following prompts to help you discuss what you saw:

- What things did we see that send a message to students that we learn through challenge, struggle, and difficulty?
- What was it about these items that was important and powerful?
- How can we further enhance these elements?
- Where were there inklings of things that perhaps sent a positive message about challenge, but it was hard to tell?
- How might we tweak or bump up these practices so that they can be more powerful?
- What counter-indicators did we see that students might not be getting the message that learning occurs at the point of challenge? *Note: It's possible a teacher is doing everything right, but we still see in a student's behavior that a student doesn't embrace challenge.*
- Are there practices we need to review and examine because they are sending a counter message to what we want?

Stating the Mindset as Principles for Action

Turning the mindset "Learning occurs at the point of challenge" into principles for action is a way to guide and direct our efforts. These principles tell us what to do broadly in an overarching way. They are top-level guideposts that help orient us. Using these principles, we can then craft actions that fit our personal context. What is more, our principles provide touchstones by which to make sense of our current practices, looking at where and how we might bring them into alignment. Drawing on the research, I identify four principles:

- Define and explore productive struggle, challenge, productive failure, and desirable difficulties.
- Plan for struggle and challenge.
- Support the struggle in the moment
- Reflect on and celebrate struggles, challenges, and emerging learning.

Possible Actions

In this section, you will find a wealth of actions to help you move forward with Mindset 7. As useful as these have the potential to be, they are unlikely to be successful unless one truly believes that learning occurs at the point of challenge. If teachers don't hold this mindset, they may find themselves subtly subverting their own efforts. For instance, they may diminish task complexity because deep down they believe that students can't be expected to work on a problem they haven't been taught to solve. Teachers may over-scaffold and rescue students at the first hint of trouble because they fear the struggle is damaging to students' self-esteem, and they want them to be successful. Their language may focus on and praise products over process. They may default to direct instruction as soon as they feel a time crunch because it creates the illusion that they have taught, and students have learned. Therefore, make sure you understand the research behind this mindset and what it does to help students develop as powerful learners and thinkers before moving forward.

The shape, content, and form of challenge will naturally look quite different depending upon grade and subject area. In addition, individuals will differ in terms of what constitutes a challenge. The actions described in this section can jump-start your thinking. These actions are:

➤ Drawn from our work in schools as part of the Worldwide Cultures of Thinking Project.
➤ Placed under the related principle to help you focus on the driving motivation behind each action. "Note the sequential nature of these principles. Each helps to lay a foundation for what is to come next."
➤ Modifiable to fit your local context.
➤ Connected to the most relevant cultural forces to which each specific action is associated. Both frameworks, the 8 cultural forces and the 10 mindsets, are synergistic and you can begin your journey either place.

Define and Explore Productive Struggle, Challenge, Productive Failure, and Desirable Difficulties. Metaphors and analogies help us to understand and relate to new concepts. Therefore, introducing a guiding metaphor can be very useful to help students understand the meaning of these terms. In Kate Mills's class, the admonition to "get off the escalator" became a touchstone. Others have used James Nottingham's (Nottingham 2017) "Learning Pit" metaphor and visual for helping students understand that struggle, questions, and challenge should be an expected part of learning (scan the QR code to watch an explanation by James). In learning a

QR Code for Learning Pit video.

SCAN ME

sport or working out, students recognize that it is important to go beyond your current threshold regularly to make progress. All these metaphors help students visualize the learning process and understand why challenge is a necessary part of learning.

Building collective definitions can also help students to take ownership of a concept. You might want to discuss and define just one term you plan to use and reference often, such as *challenge, productive struggle, productive failure,* or *desirable difficulties.* The Making-Meaning thinking routine (p. 76 in *The Power of Making Thinking Visible*) can be useful for building both individual and collective definitions while exploring the complexities of a concept. In addition, it may be useful to identify examples and non-examples; for instance, looking at what makes a struggle productive versus destructive. Similarly, failure falls on a spectrum. Failure arising from defiance, inattention, or lack of effort is not to be encouraged. In contrast, failure related to exploration, prototyping, or processing complexities results in new learning and should be celebrated. Developing a *language* around these terms helps us to communicate about them.

You can further extend older students' understanding by exploring the science. A review of research studies has shown that when students are provided with *opportunities* to understand neuroplasticity and that the brain grows through challenging experience, they are more likely to embrace a growth mindset, accept challenge, and be more motivated (Sarrasin et al. 2018). There are lots of lesson plans online aimed at various grade levels that help students understand these concepts (scan the QR code to access). In addition, the idea of desirable difficulties is based upon the science of memory. Because desirable difficulty practices seem counterintuitive and students are likely to fall into the "fluency trap," it is important they be informed about the research and why these practices work. There are many excellent short videos online by Dr. Robert Bjork, director of the Bjork Learning and Forgetting Lab at UCLA (@gocognitive), the Lasting Learning Group (LastingLearning.com), and cognitive scientist and writer Dr. Benjamin Keep (@benjaminkeep). Dr. Keep produces teacher- and student-friendly videos on this concept.

QR Code for growth mindset lessons.

To sustain and extend these efforts, you may want to produce anchor charts that identify specific actions. Create evolving posters and anchor charts of what these concepts look and sound like as part of the physical *environment* of the classroom. Provide students with actions they can take when facing challenging situations. Generate *language* that learners can use as self-talk to indicate they have a growth mindset and accept challenge.

Plan for Struggle and Challenge. Challenge, productive struggle, and desirable difficulties do not just happen. They must be planned for and anticipated as part of the *opportunities* we create. To do this, we must avoid the tendency to over-scaffold and reduce challenge. We must learn to look at lessons as an episode of learning and not a final performance (Bjork 2013).

We must create, find, and modify tasks to make them appropriately challenging. How can we do this?

Look for tasks that provoke students to make sense, reason, connect ideas, establish their own ideas, struggle, and "get dirty" or "in the pit" with the concepts. Good tasks expose misconceptions or underdeveloped ideas and enable discussions that unpack and correct or enhance those ideas. Seek out tasks that create *opportunities* for different solutions or viewpoints and approaches. Good tasks provide students more opportunity to make conceptual connections and achieve deeper levels of understanding. One key feature of such tasks is that they require an original response, in methods if not solutions, rather than a reproductive response. Another quality is that the task offers an accessible entry point for all, but also a chance to stretch. These are often referred to as low-threshold, high-ceiling tasks, which allow students to naturally self-differentiate and find their own point of challenge.

You might modify a task by asking students to respond in more than one way, use different methods, or create different representations of their solution. In addition, asking students to analyze for efficiency, generalizability, effectiveness, or other criteria can make a task more challenging. Sometimes simply asking: "What *might* be a solution?" rather than: "What *is* the answer?" can open up a task. Using *conditional language*, such as *might,* signals that you aren't interested in a single solution. The Claim-Support-Question routine in *Making Thinking Visible* (Ritchhart, Church, and Morrison 2011) is a good way of opening up a task to explore complexity and underlying concepts. For instance, Caitlin Faiman asked her Year 6 students: "The sum of two fractions is 11 2/3. What *might* the fractions be?" After five minutes of grappling with all the possible solutions to this problem, the students make "claims" (generalizable features) around what must be true in all the possible solutions. For instance, "At least one of the numbers will have to be a fraction or mixed number." They then collectively look for supports and questions to further refine their claims.

Support the Struggle and Encourage Challenge. To adequately support students, we need to *anticipate student responses*. Do the task yourself and try approaching it from different perspectives. This will help you to learn your way around the task, clarify the question or problem, and unearth less obvious challenges. It will also allow you to identify what you want to ask students to provide that will make their decisions and reasoning visible to you. Having done the task, you can anticipate how students might represent the problem, what language they might use or struggle with, and what misconceptions might surface. This will help you to plan your responses. Too often, teachers want to immediately correct any misconceptions, errors, or misapplied strategies. This comes from a place of: "If I don't tell them, how will they know?" Another approach is to raise these as a tension, dispute, perspective, or challenge with the class for discussion. For instance, "I notice some people saying that 'a half is always a half,' but others are saying 'the size of a half can differ.' What do you think?" Most of the time, students will work through the misunderstandings collectively themselves with only minor guidance through questioning on our part.

In our *interactions* with students as they work, we can offer invitations to think and explain through open-ended prompts such as:

- "Talk to me about what you're doing."
- "I'm interested in your thinking on this one, can you explain it to me?"
- "Where's the challenge in this for you?"
- "Is there another way you might approach this?"
- "What does this remind you of?"
- "What is something you know about this problem/issue?"
- "What's a solution that you know would be wrong?"

These metacognitive prompts might not seem like we are offering much, but many times when students verbalize their thinking and speak about their actions, they clarify for themselves what they are doing and get themselves unstuck. Of course, we can ask probing questions to push further: "Why might that be useful?" "What would be the logic in that approach?" "What would that yield?"

In the same way that you can use the class to help confront misconceptions; other students are a huge help in tackling challenges. Working in groups allows for much of the thinking to be externalized through discussion. It can then be debated, analyzed, parsed, and refined. When students are working in groups, encourage them to check in with other groups to learn from them. This is facilitated if students are working on vertical surfaces around the room. Make help-seeking the norm so that learning is not viewed as a competitive contest (Webb 2013).

Finally, offer scaffolding only as needed. We might think of scaffolding not as structuring a task to ensure it will be completed successfully, but as navigating the terrain between frustration (the challenge is too much) and boredom (the challenge is too little). This means being ready with prompts, hints, or modifications that preserve the learning but make the task more accessible for some and more challenging for others. Researchers identify two different types of hints: ones that decrease the challenge and ones that increase students' ability (Liljedahl 2020; Choppin 2011; Kang 2017). The first type is often our default as a teacher. It focuses on getting the work done by giving partial answers or simplifying the task. The second type, though more time-consuming, provides for more learning. These might take the form of reminding students of a strategy, identifying the type of thinking that might be useful, or providing a tool that helps them to visualize the problem in a new way.

Reflect and Celebrate. We need to regularly celebrate mistakes, difficulties, and failures so that students come to see these as learning *opportunities*. Teachers need to regularly name and notice productive struggle and learning from mistakes. This key *language* move draws attention to behaviors we wish to reinforce (Johnston 2004). As more experienced learners, we can *model* how we deal with mistakes, frustrations, and failures when we encounter them ourselves. We can talk about our own embrace of challenge, showing our students how we are stretching ourselves, trying new things, growing, and learning. The organization Fail Fest (www.failfest.us) provides resources and sponsors events for celebrating failure. The *routine* My Favorite No (scan the QR code to view) sends the message that learning is always a process, and we can show understanding even though we are not 100% accurate. Likewise, the "I used to think. . . . Now I think" routine communicates that our learning, our thinking, our understanding is always changing, growing, and developing (see *Making Thinking Visible*). The ESP+I routine (Experience Struggles-Puzzles-Insights) identifies struggles as a key component in our reflection as learners (see *The Power of Making Thinking Visible)*. In addition, we want to provide feedback that acknowledges effort and actions more than ability. For instance, you might begin a feedback session by saying: *"Let's talk about what you tried, and what you can try next."* This helps students understand that making mistakes is okay and that they can overcome them.

QR Code for My Favorite No video.

SCAN ME

Fitting New Actions with Current Realities

Before you rush to implement actions you are eager to try, step back and think about what you are currently doing at your school (see Figure 7.1):

➤ What actions, already in place, can be *amplified* and grown by applying some of the identified principles?

➤ What practices need to be rethought or *modified* considering this mindset?

➤ What do you need to stop doing altogether and *remove* from your repertoire? Why? Does it run counter to this mindset? Is it ineffective? What "moveable barriers" are standing in the way of truly living this mindset?

➤ Finally, are there things that you need to *create*, totally new processes, structures, or actions to begin to put in place?

Figure 7.1 Amplify-Modify-Remove-Create.

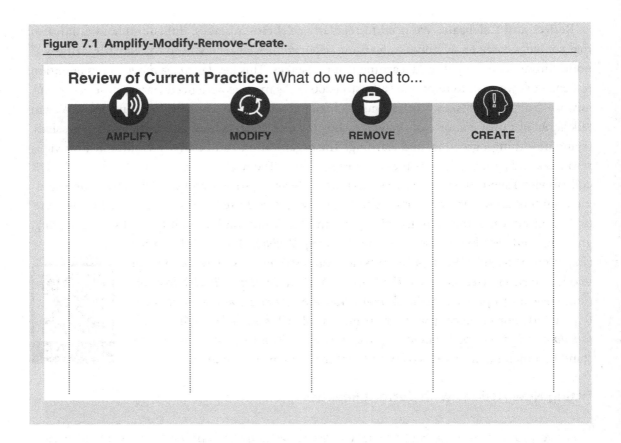

Review of Current Practice: What do we need to...

AMPLIFY	MODIFY	REMOVE	CREATE

────── Conclusion: Our Theory of Action ──────

What are we likely to see as a result of acting from the mindset "Learning occurs at the point of challenge"? How do we tie together the natural actions this mindset gives rise to and the outcomes we would expect for students? The research on challenge suggests that it must be normalized as part of students' regular experience, so they develop confidence in themselves as learners. This means the regular use of challenging tasks and teaching interactions that will support learners' agency. The research and neuroscience suggest that more robust learning outcomes ensue from these actions as well as a greater sense of efficacy, direction, engagement, and control. Tying together our actions with anticipated outcomes, I offer the following theory of action for Mindset 7.

Use it if it captures the actions you plan to take and the outcomes you expect to see from your learners. If it doesn't, feel free to craft your own theory of action that will better fit your context.

If we normalize learning from mistakes and make struggle and failure a regular part of learning by creating tasks that are purposeful, engaging, challenging, and self-differentiating, *then* all students will experience deeper, more long-lasting, and robust learning outcomes while developing as self-directed learners with a growth mindset.

Notes

Questions Drive Thinking and Learning

In an Australian primary school, 5th graders gather in a literature circle. The teacher begins by asking a wonderfully open-ended question, "What is the cost of war?" What an expansive question with so much nuance. As the students offer rich and varied responses, the teacher merely takes each reply in turn until they get to the last student. "Childhood?" a girl responds with a hint of uncertainty in her voice. "Yes," the teacher responds, "That's the one I like." And with that, "discussion" ends. Across the hall, another teacher stops her group's reading after a passage in which one character is compared to a vulture. "What is a vulture?" she asks, merely trying to clarify the analogy. A simple, knowledge-based question. What ensues is a rich discussion of the traits of vultures and how the character has some of these traits. Afterward, the group generates alternative metaphors and has a rich discussion of which best fit for the character.

These two vignettes from my colleague Sally Godinho at the University of Melbourne in Australia come from her research on learning through dialogue (Godinho and Wilson 2006). They demonstrate the complex nature of questions as vehicles to promote thinking and learning, emphasizing the point made by J.T. Dillon, "It makes no difference whether the question is higher or lower cognitive, whether it is simple or complex, whether it is fact or interpretation. What makes the difference is whether the answer to the question is predetermined to be right, whether it is to be recited or discussed" (Dillon 1994, p. 22). Martin Nystrand refers to these as *authentic questions*, that is, they authentically "invite students to contribute something new to the discussion that can change or modify it in some way" (Nystrand, Gamoran, Kachur, and Prendergast 1997).

As Sally's examples illustrate, the kind of questions that drive learning don't necessarily come from some prescribed list in the teacher's manual or a simplistic set of guidelines: "Use Bloom's taxonomy to create your questions" or "Ask more open-ended questions." They arise from our *motives* as teachers and *exist as part of a dialogue* we initiate with students. Chad Littlefield and Will Wise, co-authors of *Ask Powerful Questions: Create Conversations That Matter* (2017), explain that our *intentions* are the basis for our questions, and we will not really generate connected conversations if our intentions are not right. Furthermore, by sharing our intentions openly and honestly with others, we build trust and develop the rapport needed for dialogue. Will explains, "As a teacher, as soon as I walk into a room, my intent has a direct impact on what happens. When my intent is to share knowledge, I become the expert, and everyone else becomes objects or faces with numbers associated with them. When I walk in with the intent to create an experience in which people realize what is possible for themselves, then magic happens" (Wise 2017, p. 6). When the intent is wrong—narrow, manipulative, superficial, or hidden—it is much harder ground on which to grow good questions that spark conversation. Teachers knowing the purpose behind their questions and sharing it is a crucial factor in improving their questioning practice (Renton 2020).

Consider a scenario in which a teacher asks a challenging question. For instance, "Was Truman correct in dropping the atomic bomb?" and is greeted with silence. Some students might view the question as a trick, thinking the teacher is trying to expose their ignorance. They don't know the intent of the question. However, if the question is framed with intent: "I'm really interested in your perspective on this issue before we jump into what historians think: Was Truman correct in dropping the atomic bomb?" Here students know they are not being tricked. They know the intent and know the teacher is genuinely interested in their responses. The more our students know us and the more they feel known (Mindset 4), the more rapport we will have built. Although we may not always need to explicitly share our intention, our intention is the driving force behind our questions, nonetheless.

In our research on teacher questioning as part of the Worldwide Cultures of Thinking project, we identified five types of questions teachers ask related to their motives, intent, and goals. These are to review content (review), manage the class (procedural), build understanding (constructive), spark exploration and inquiry (generative), and make thinking visible (facilitative) (see Figure 8.1). All these goals are reasonable instructionally at different times. Thus, we shouldn't consider one type of question good and one bad; rather, it is the balance of question types that matters. In our studies, we saw the balance of question types shift as classrooms became cultures of thinking. Over time, we noticed teachers asked fewer review and procedural questions and more facilitative questions (Ritchhart 2015). Constructive questions remained about the same. This shift makes sense. When your intent becomes to make students' thinking visible, when you are genuinely curious about students' thinking, then you become less interested in merely testing students' knowledge (review), and you naturally begin to ask more facilitative questions.

WHAT THE RESEARCH SAYS: *WHY* DOES IT MATTER?

Questions are drivers of inquiry, catalysts for changing perceptions, vehicles for developing understanding, promoters of action, and opportunities to clarify our thinking (Berger 2014; Murdoch 2022). Questions allow us to express our curiosity and recognize curiosity in others. What is more, questions are often the spark for discussions and tools for connecting with others

Figure 8.1 Typology of questions.

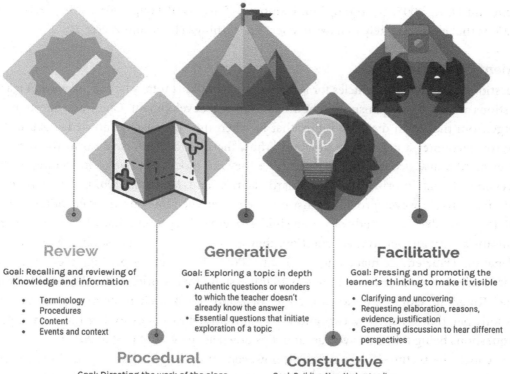

A Typology of Question Types

Review

Goal: Recalling and reviewing of Knowledge and information

- Terminology
- Procedures
- Content
- Events and context

Procedural

Goal: Directing the work of the class

- Clarifying
- Going over directions and assignments
- Organizational and management related
- Checking for attention, agreement.
- Task completion

Generative

Goal: Exploring a topic in depth

- Authentic questions or wonders to which the teacher doesn't already know the answer
- Essential questions that initiate exploration of a topic

Constructive

Goal: Building New Understanding

- Connecting and linking
- Orienting and focusing on big ideas, central concepts, or purpose
- Evaluating
- Extending, interpreting, explaining
- Considering perspectives

Facilitative

Goal: Pressing and promoting the learner's thinking to make it visible

- Clarifying and uncovering
- Requesting elaboration, reasons, evidence, justification
- Generating discussion to hear different perspectives

(Aguiar et al. 2010). It is not surprising, then, that questions are a major way that teachers interact with their students. It's been estimated that teacher questions consume between 10%–20% of the time students spend in classrooms (Carlsen 1991) and that teachers ask up to 120 questions per hour (Vogler 2008). However, assessments of teachers' questions indicate that between 80%–90% of teacher questions only require students to recall facts (Christoph and Nystrand 2001;

Hattie and Zierer 2017). Such questions may help students to test memory and review content, but they do little to deepen understanding or engagement. In contrast, generative, authentic questions—those questions to which teachers do not already know the answer—have historically been the least-asked type of question despite evidence that they are positively associated with student engagement, critical thinking, and academic achievement (Busching and Slesinger 1995; Caram and Davis 2005; Nystrand, Wu, Gamoran, Zeiser, and Long 2003). It is precisely these questions that are most likely to have an effect on learning (Hattie and Zierer 2017).

Student Questions

If questions are important vehicles for learning, they shouldn't totally be the purview of teachers. Questions are a key mechanism for children's cognitive development. Children's questions often emerge from their own disequilibrium; that is, when they perceive a knowledge gap in themselves or encounter a perplexing situation. Thus, the provided information in the form of an answer or response occurs exactly at the time they are most receptive to it, leading to deeper processing of that information (Chouinard, Harris, and Maratsos 2007). Far from making children passive, however, providing answers to children's genuine questions encourages them to think for themselves. In a study of young children, researchers found that when children receive an unsatisfactory answer to their question, they either reframe the question or pose their own explanation (Frazier, Gelman, and Wellman 2009). It is not surprising, then, that young children ask a lot of questions as they seek to understand their world. According to a study in the United Kingdom, children between the ages of 2 and 10 ask their mothers approximately 300 questions per day. One every two and a half minutes! Peak questioning hits at age 4, with 390 questions being asked on average, and dips down at age 9 to 144 (Staff 2013).

In school, the picture is very different, however. Susan Engel, studying curiosity in schools over a three-month period, found on average only two to five curiosity episodes in kindergarten classrooms within a two-hour period (Engel 2011). In 5th grade, the picture was even more bleak, with zero to two episodes. It's not that students aren't asking questions; it is that their questions are focused on getting work done (Carlsen 1991): "What do I write here?" "Is this correct?" "Can you help me?" "What are we supposed to do next?" Peter Liljedahl's research found that students ask, and teachers answer, up to 400 questions a day (Liljedahl 2020). However, over 90% of these fell in the category of either "proximity questions" or "stop thinking questions." Proximity questions are asked simply because the teacher is close by. However, students rarely make use of the information they receive. Such questions are more about conforming to the role of student. "Studenting" is what Liljedahl calls this. "Stop thinking questions" aim to minimize the work or effort, such as, "Is this going to be on the test?" "Do we have to explain our thinking?" The solution to this problem of poor questioning is two-fold: 1) stop answering the proximity and stop-thinking questions, and 2) make more room for students to ask authentic questions that can move their learning and thinking forward.

There is ample research to suggest it is beneficial to make room for students' genuine questions. Questions are one of the most powerful ways students express their thinking, enhance problem solving, monitor understanding, and improve as active and autonomous learners (Aguiar et al. 2010). Questions are also a major way in which we express and recognize curiosity. Fostering students' disposition toward curiosity (see Mindset 2) involves creating opportunities for authentic problem solving, robust inquiry, and rich discussion within a classroom culture where questioning is valued (Thomas and Brown 2011; Toyani 2015). To accomplish this, we need to provide more room for student questions. As one of my mentors, Dennie Palmer Wolf, so eloquently stated, "Question finding is the ability to go to a poem, a painting, a piece of music or a document, a mathematical description, a science experiment and locate a novel direction for investigation. The ability is difficult to teach directly, yet it may be one of the most important by-products of learning in an educational climate in which questions are varied, worth pursuit, authentic and humanely posed" (Wolf 1987).

Across most disciplines, providing structures and opportunities for students' questions is cited as essential for comprehension, self-assessment of content and intellectual engagement (Engel 2016). In addition, student self-generated questions related to study material is more beneficial to recall than restudying of the material (Ebersbach et al. 2020). It is not enough to merely encourage students to ask questions more frequently, however. Research shows that the *quality* of questions is crucial (Aguiar et al. 2010). Therefore, it is important that teachers model critical thinking and curiosity in their questions, specifically employing deep-level, constructive questions (Murdoch 2015). Such questions ask students to explain and predict, apply learning across contexts, evaluate information, and wonder about the world around them. Many teachers use the "Question Formulation Technique" (QFT), developed by the Right Question Institute (Rothstein and Santana 2011), or the "Question Sorts" routines (Ritchhart and Church 2020) as vehicles for helping students ask good questions. Once adequate conditions are established, students' questions tend to improve both in frequency and in quality (Aguiar et al. 2010).

Listening

Returning to the issue of motives, intentions, and goals; we situate rich, authentic questions within a larger classroom culture that privileges the exploration of ideas. Of course, asking good questions is only a start when it comes to promoting thinking; one must also listen to students' answers and continually prod, probe, and press students' thinking (Ritchhart and Church 2020). Teachers who press students to think are seen as more caring, likeable, and interested (Cornelius-White 2007; O'Hara and Sternberg 2001). However, if we don't listen to students' thoughts, then it will be hard to pose questions that push them. A good question can lead students down a certain path, but teachers must be ready to follow. But, this doesn't mean we grab hold of the student's question and use it as an opportunity for exposition. Rather it is using their question to open doors for their exploration. Once again, we see the power of our intentions. If we are simply listening for answers or for correctness, or opportunities for us to talk, that is what we will respond to. But if we are listening for thinking, burgeoning understanding, curiosity, new perspectives, and engagement, then we will pick up on those things. Will Wise captures the idea of intentional listening beautifully, "When this type of listening occurs, there is also a shift in the world of the speaker. When we listen as if someone's life depends on it, something radical can happen. We can listen them *into being*. We listen them into a new space—a space where they can recreate themselves in the current moment" (Wise 2017, p. 135).

VISIONS AND REFLECTIONS: *HOW* MIGHT IT LOOK?

We all know what questions sound like. We hear them every day from our students and ask a lot of them ourselves. But what does it mean for questions to act as drivers of thinking and learning? In constructing a vision of the power of questions, we need to explore this terrain. This allows us to think about how intention shapes our questions and how our own curiosity is a source of questioning.

Constructing Our Vision

The Latin root for the word *intention* is *intendere*, which means to direct one's attention, to stretch out, or extend. We can think of our intentions as allowing us to stretch toward our students, to lean forward with our goals, and to pursue a purpose beyond ourselves as we seek to connect with our students. However, too often, the intention behind our question is hidden from students. What if we made a habit of leading with intention and purpose?

1. Think of a few questions (aim for three or four) you recall asking from a recent lesson. They could have been asked to a whole class, a small group, or an individual. Make note of these.

2. Now think about your intention behind asking each question. Note: We ask so many questions reflexively that sometimes it may take some effort to uncover our intention. Why was it that I asked that? What was I hoping to accomplish?

3. Once you have uncovered your intention, rewrite your questions in a way that clearly states the intention first. For instance, "To help me better understand, I'd like to know. . . ." Or "I'm really interested in what might be tricky about this problem, can you explain . . . ?" Lead with intention.

4. Looking at your newly formed questions, consider: How might students' responses have been different if I had used this framing? How might it have helped build trust and engagement? Are my intentions aimed at understanding where students are as learners?

The ubiquity of answers at our fingertips has contributed to a curiosity deficit both in ourselves and our students. When was the last time you were in a group and someone asked a question, but instead of the group exploring it, someone just googled the answer? What happened to that conversation thread? Likely it didn't go much further. Answers can sometimes (though not always) kill questions and the opportunity to explore. Yes, it may be nice to know who recorded that song you are listening to, but hearing people share their connections and associations to that song and how it connected to their lives is much more interesting. As adults we are so used to speaking in declarative statements, that we ask fewer and fewer questions. Some estimate adults only ask 6–20 questions in a day (Cox 2020; Wise 2017) compared with the 390 of 4-year-olds! And yet, we know the power of curiosity to make us happier, more productive, and more successful (Gino 2018; Hsee, Ruan, and Y Lu 2015). Furthermore, if we want our students to be curious, we need to lead with curiosity and be models they can emulate. So where was your curiosity today?

1. What questions did you ask today, not of your students but of others in your life?
2. Which would you say reflected genuine curiosity? What makes you say that? What do you notice about these types of questions?
3. If you have a scarcity of curiosity questions in your life, what are some questions you might ask around anything you have seen or been engaged with today?

Group Discussion

If you are reading this book with others, bring your questions (original and rewritten) to share and discuss.

➤ What is your reaction to your colleagues' rewritten questions? What do you notice about them? Do they invite a different response from the original?
➤ Was it difficult to uncover the intention behind your questions?
➤ What kinds of things were you and your colleagues curious about? What do you notice about these questions? How do they resemble or differ from questions occurring in the classroom?

Contemplating Pictures of Practice

To expand our vision of the role questions might play in the classroom as drivers of learning and thinking, we examine two case studies. The first is from a middle school humanities class in which the teacher invites her students to ask and investigate big questions. The second is from a secondary math teacher who makes use of the Question Formulation Technique (QFT) as a formative tool to give her insights into her students' understanding.

Case One: Unanswerable Questions.[1] How did the world begin? Is there a God? Why do hate and evil exist? Why do we smile when we are happy? Are there parallel universes? These questions are the kinds of universal, philosophical quandaries humankind has always pursued—not exactly the typical fare for a middle school humanities class. Yet, there they were, written on cardstock sentence strips and hanging on the wall of Heather Woodcock's 7th-grade classroom in Cambridge, Massachusetts. Heather explained their origin, "I was doing some writing in my journal, and I started asking myself some of these [kinds of] questions and was intrigued by them. I thought, well, why can't 7th graders do this? I was trying to get them to really focus on something that they were curious about and then bring that into school a little bit and make it more formal. Make them [the students] more aware of the bigger questions. Because there are so many answers to things we do in school."

Heather designed the assignment with the intent to foster engagement, personalization, and connection. As homework, students generated three or four big questions that didn't have obvious answers. Then, the class shared and discussed their questions, exploring: "What makes a question unanswerable? Are they important questions if you can't find the answers? Are these kinds of questions the most important questions to be asking? Are they important at all? Why?" Students then formulated a question that really intrigued them and wrote about why they were drawn to that question along with their initial thoughts. This personalization ensured a high degree of ownership.

Next, students shared their preliminary writings in small groups and received comments and suggestions on how to improve their response papers in their second draft. The final step of the project was for each student to use his or her response paper as the basis for a performance piece, perhaps a poem, a dramatic reading, or a visual piece of art. As with the beginning of the assignment, this final performance offered a lot of choice and opportunity for personalization. Reflecting on the assignment, Heather felt the spark of curiosity and deep thinking had been ignited. "The kids were intrigued. They enjoyed it. They thought it was a little bit strange to be doing in school, but they really liked hearing each other's questions and their responses to the questions. And it's been great to have the questions up in the classroom because so many people come in and say, 'What's up with those questions? That's so interesting.'"

Case Two: The Question Formulation Technique.[2] We often think of questions as guiding inquiry and exploration; however, research has shown that generating questions is a very effective study technique (Ebersbach et al. 2020). In addition, questions reveal quite a lot about someone's level of understanding. The 17th-century French writer Voltaire famously said that one should judge a man by his questions rather than his answers. Questions reveal the edge of our understanding and where we are headed as learners. Therefore, asking students to generate questions at the end of a unit can be both a useful formative assessment as well as an effective study technique. High school math teacher Megan Gretzinger from Appleton City, Missouri, uses students' questions in just this way.

Employing the Question Formulation Technique (QFT), Megan begins the process by designating a question focus. In this case, "Volume," the topic of the current lesson. She then asks students, working in groups of four or five, to generate as many questions as they can without stopping to discuss, judge, or answer them. Every question is written down exactly as stated. If statements appear, these are rewritten as questions. Megan notices many of students' initial questions are a bit generic and attach to real-word relevance: "Why is volume important?" "When will we use it in our lives?" After these initial questions warm students up, deeper curiosity begins to emerge. Questions begin to focus on the concept itself, its origins, and the steps needed to take understanding it further: "How is volume related to math?" "Who came up with all the different formulas?" "Is there more than one way to find volume?" "Who invented volume?" Some groups identify practical questions related to the calculation of volume in different instances.

After students generate their questions, Megan brings the class together and has each group share their most important question. This leads to a flurry of quick discussion in the groups as students weigh the various merits of each question to determine which question seems to really dig deep and take them somewhere as learners. Of course, each group wants to be able to share a provocative, probing question that will get their classmates to think. As students share, Megan can see that some student's questions have gone well beyond what the class has studied on the topic and are more abstract: "What if the base is a cross-section?" She makes note of this so that she can follow up with challenging volume problems for these students. In the next round, students share their second most important question. This process continues until all the questions are shared. Once all questions have been shared aloud, Megan collects each group's documented lists to help her set topics for the class to review the next day.

Reflecting on Current Practice

The intent of the following questions is to push your thinking. They might even make you a bit uncomfortable. Living with and going deeply into questions and puzzles of teaching allows us to enter into a space of inquiry into our own practice. Questioning our questioning! Pick a few questions that will help you better understand the effects of your actions, critically reflect on those actions, provoke additional questions, and/or help you think about future actions and possibilities. If you find yourself merely explaining what you currently are doing, chances are you might be *reporting* more than *reflecting*. Consider selecting another prompt that might take you deeper into examining your practice.

Choosing Questions and Recording Responses

Different questions serve us at different times in our learning. Therefore, I suggest you read through the questions and identify:

➤ One or two that speak to you now. Questions that might challenge you or take your thinking in new directions.
➤ One or two you would most like to discuss with your colleagues.
➤ Circle and date the questions you select now so you can identify how your focus shifts with time and experience.
➤ Use the blank pages at the end of this chapter or your note-taking device to record your reflections.

- Where am I making use of generative/essential questions to guide my instruction? How do I keep these questions alive throughout our unit as beacons or guides for our learning versus just hooks to get us started?
- What are examples of my most effective essential questions over the years? What do I notice about what makes a good guiding, essential question in my subject area for my students?
- How do/might I use student questions in my teaching? How might I take this to the next level?
- Where and how am I modeling my own curiosity? Do I regularly ask authentic questions that reveal that I am curious?
- Where do students' questions live in my classroom? If someone walked into my classroom, how would they be able to tell from the displays and documentation that I care about curiosity, inquiry, and questioning?

- What is my pattern of questioning? Is it ping-pong style with me hitting every question back to the student or are we playing basketball with lots of people involved? Where and how can I further encourage students to respond to each other? Where and how might I do more to promote students asking questions to one another?

- Do I give sufficient thinking time when I ask constructive questions so that students have a chance to develop their thinking? Do all students have an opportunity to share their response in some way?

- Am I answering student questions that don't need answering (proximity and non-thinking questions)? How might I respond differently?

- Reflecting on a particular lesson you have just taught or after an observation of a colleague's classroom:
  - What questions did I/they ask that I thought were particularly provocative or useful?
  - What questions did I/they ask that sparked discussion and engagement?
  - What student questions about the content emerged in this lesson? Where did opportunities exist for student questions to emerge? Where and how might I/they have made more room for students' questions?
  - Where and when did I/they ask follow-up facilitative questions? Is there a particular facilitative question that seemed to be effective?
  - Did I/they ask any authentic questions (ones to which I/they didn't already know the answer)? Where might I/they have done so?

DATA, PRINCIPLES, AND PRACTICES: *WHAT* ACTIONS CAN WE TAKE?

This mindset might be one in which we have blind spots, precisely because we are so used to asking questions. We may naturally assume that we are asking good and effective questions. However, how can we truly know this? What is the current state of questioning in your classroom and at your school? What kinds of questions are students asking? What data would be useful to inform your future work? Although typically street data can take many forms, you will find that observations or audio recordings are particularly useful as so many questions get asked so quickly. Since changing our questioning or discourse patterns takes time, it is important to constantly take stock of where you are both individually and as a school in promoting this mindset.

Collecting Street Data

> ## Street Data
>
> ➤ Helps us understand our own context as well as students' perspectives.
> ➤ Is relatively easy and quick to collect.
> ➤ Can be immediately analyzed and acted upon straightaway.
> ➤ Is meant to inform and suggest action.
> ➤ Is NOT an evaluation or measure of success but a snapshot of practice.
> ➤ Can take many forms: observations, interviews, surveys, exit tickets, recordings, and so on.

Street Data Action One: The First 10 Questions. It is often difficult to assess our questioning real time when we are in the midst of teaching. One reason for this is that teachers simply ask a lot of questions. Our research and that of others found teachers typically ask between 50–100 questions in a class period. Therefore, it just isn't possible to remember all of them. What we do tend to remember are those powerful or effective questions because they resonate and register more. Consequently, we overestimate the overall quality of our questioning. "The First 10 Questions" is a process for collecting street data on a school's collective "question asking" to identify the kinds of questions our students are generally experiencing across the school.

The protocol for collecting "The First 10 Questions" is simple. A documenter, who could be a school leader, coach, teacher, or some combination thereof, goes into a classroom and simply records the first 10 questions they hear (by teacher or students). They leave the room and go to the next classroom, recording the first 10 questions heard. This process continues for the rest of the class period. It is generally possible to visit 8 to 12 classrooms in a single class period. Note: This process could be carried out to collect questions across the school, within a particular department, or at a single grade level. Questions are then compiled and copied to be shared. Often, questions are mixed up so that individual classrooms are not readily identifiable. The point is not to assess teachers but to get a sense of the school community's collective questioning. The questions are then shared with teachers as a snapshot of questioning to determine what can be gleaned about the kinds of questions students are encountering. Some questions to consider from the data are:

- What types of questions (see Figure 8.1) are we asking our students?
- Which questions from this data snapshot push and press students to think? What makes you say that?

- Is there another way to frame a particular question to engage students more deeply?

- What is the minimum required of a student in answering a particular question?

- How many student questions were there, and how might they be categorized?

- If you were a student encountering these questions, what would you feel your teachers cared about? What would you think they are listening for?

- How many questions begin with what or how? These tend to provoke more elaborate responses (Wise, 2017). Which questions might be productively reworded to begin with what or how?

Street Data Action Two: Student Questions. There are, of course, many ways to parse questions in a classroom. Thinking about students' questions, Peter Liljedahl's framework (keep-thinking questions, stop-thinking questions, and proximity question) can be useful as it helps us sort out the questions we want to encourage and those we perhaps needn't respond to. The most powerful questions students ask are the "keep-thinking" questions. These may be new lines of inquiry that have sparked their imagination, quandaries emerging for the current topic, proposals for next steps, or so on. What they aren't are questions of clarification about the work or questions that try to negotiate the work and get out of the thinking (stop-thinking questions). Nor are they the "Studenting" questions that serve no real purpose other than to signal one is a conscientious student (proximity questions). Proximity questions can be a bit hard to spot at first as the student is trying to signal conscientiousness. Thus, we are pleased when we hear them. However, ask yourself: Was this question only asked because I was close by? Do students need the information they are asking for? For instance, when a student asks, "Is this question asking us to come up with an alternative method?" This is most likely a proximity question. They have already identified what the question is asking and are asking you to confirm it only because you happened to walk by their desk.

Pick one of these three types of questions on which to focus on an upcoming lesson. Having only one type on which to concentrate will make it easier to identify and track them. Your mind will be primed to hear them. Throughout the lesson, notice when these questions come up and how you respond. For instance, Liljedahl suggests not answering proximity or stop-thinking questions, but perhaps just smiling or turning it back to the student: "I think you can answer that for yourself." You might want to try your hand at counting the number of questions of your selected type that come up in a lesson. One way to do this is to just count the first five in your head as they occur. Make a tally mark somewhere to indicate five questions of that type have been asked and continue counting the next five in your head. Don't worry if you can't keep an accurate count; the point is to raise your general awareness of what is happening regarding the targeted type of question in your classroom. As you are aware of these questions and the way you typically respond, you can better understand the role these questions are playing in your classroom. If you have a trusted colleague who can observe you, it will be possible to get a more accurate count. While you will benefit from the data, your colleague will benefit from becoming more aware of students' questions.

Stating the Mindset as Principles for Action

The mindset "Questions drive thinking and learning" clearly grounds questioning as a key practice. However, there are a few guiding principles that will be useful in making your questioning more effective. These principles provide top-level guidance that will need to be fleshed out through specific actions. Such actions should be personal and reflect what will be useful in your context and help you personally move forward. The following guiding principles emerge from the research:

- Use questions to both launch and propel the learning.
- Deepen and extend discourse through questions, time, and listening.
- Celebrate and support students' questioning.

Possible Actions

Because our own questioning and discourse can be difficult to notice in the moment, it is often helpful to reflect immediately after you have tried something to create greater awareness. Collecting some street data can also be useful. Consider pairing up with a colleague who can support you, going into each other's classrooms to help act as data collectors.

Our questioning and that of students will reflect our subject area and grade. In addition, what counts as a review question in one classroom may be considered constructive in another depending on the teacher's intent. Use the described actions to jump-start your thinking. These actions are:

- ➤ Drawn from our work in schools as part of the Worldwide Cultures of Thinking Project.
- ➤ Placed under the related principle to help you focus on the driving motivation behind each action. *In selecting actions, you may choose to zero in on just one principle. For instance, supporting and celebrating students' questioning. Of course, it is also fine to take a more varied approach, trying actions related to each principle.*
- ➤ Modifiable to fit your local context.
- ➤ Connected primarily to the cultural forces of *language, interactions, modeling,* and *time.*

Use Questions to Both Launch and Propel Learning. Plan units around generative questions, which act as the "legs" that propel learning. These could be essential questions, questions of inquiry, or debatable questions. These will be questions that are:

- Open-ended (recall openness comes from our intent).
- Thought-provoking (you can't just look up an answer).
- Forcing student to go well beyond knowledge (e.g., analysis, prediction, inference).
- Likely to spark imagination and discussion.
- Require support and evidence.
- Invite an original response.
- Centered on big ideas in the discipline and the world that are worth understanding.

Essential and generative questions are also big frames for learning at the unit level. Some textbooks now include an essential question for each lesson, which is a misuse of the term since these questions get asked and answered in a single lesson with very little student direction. Keep in mind that learning to form generative or essential questions is a skill that develops. Don't get hung up on crafting the perfect question. Likewise, don't feel like you must stick with a question that isn't working. Allow yourself to reframe a question in the middle of unit if needed. Just be sure to share the intent of your reframing with your students. For more resources on generative and essential questions, see Wiggins 2005, Blythe and Associates 1998, and McTighe 2013. To hear essential questions from High Tech High teachers, scan the QR code.

QR Code for Essential Questions video.

SCAN ME

Review Figure 8.1 to get more familiar with the range of questions teachers ask. If you find yourself asking a preponderance of review or procedural questions, you may need to tilt the balance of your questions. It is important to use constructive questions to support students in building understanding. You can recognize constructive questions because they engage students with the content in novel ways and require thinking. On the other hand, try to limit review questions. While these questions have a place in classrooms and can be useful in consolidating knowledge and information, they should not dominate. Likewise, limit procedural questions (questions that have to do with the running of the class) by using simple directives. Instead of asking, "Does everyone have their pencil?" Direct: "Everyone, please get out your pencils." Finally, facilitative questions that help to make students' thinking visible should be one of your most common question types. Asking a follow-up question such as "What makes you say that?" can encourage students to explain their thinking. Facilitative questions show that you are interested in students' thinking more than just correct answers.

To make curiosity and questioning the norm, we must be *models* of curiosity for our students. Our ability to ask questions about content that takes us deeper and sparks interest serves as a model of what intellectual questioning sounds like. Look for *opportunities* to ask authentic questions as you teach, that is, questions to which you don't already know the answer. Such questions model your own engagement with the content and send a signal that you are a learner too. When a teacher is curious and interested, it often prompts deeper engagement by students (Christoph and Nystrand 2001; Engel 2011). We want to demonstrate curiosity in our students' learning as well. We want to be students of our students. This kind of curiosity drives good listening and sends the message that it is the thinking that matters more than the answers.

Deepen and Extend Conversation through Questions, Time, and Listening. Practice sharing your intentions when you ask questions. Knowing why we are asking a question, what we hope to gain from doing so, how it will move us forward, or what useful information will emerge, helps us to ask better questions. Sharing the intention/motive behind our question will help to build trust and spark dialogue as well. Students are so used to viewing teacher questions as a test of their knowledge that they will, by default, assume that is your intent. That assumption may cause them to freeze up if they don't know the answer. Sharing our intent first—"I want to gather lots of possibilities," "I'm interested in your perspectives," "I'm curious about what is immediately coming to mind for you"—helps students know how to respond and how their responses will be used. Using conditional language, "What might a solution to this be?" rather than absolute language, "What is the answer?" is another way of communicating intention. The conditional "might" conveys that we are looking for possibilities, not answers. Absolute language, on the other hand, communicates that there is a specific answer we are after, and the game being played is "guess what's in the teacher's head."

The "reflective toss" is an effective strategy to change our *interactions* with students and place them in the role, not of answer giver, but of elaborator, evidence provider, and explanation giver. The reflective toss is a pattern of questioning identified by teacher researcher Jim Minstrell (Van Zee and Minstrell 1997). He said that a teacher's first move in creating discourse should be to try and "catch" student's meaning. What are they saying? Do I understand what they have said? The teacher then "tosses" or throws responsivity for thinking back to the student by asking them to elaborate, explain, or justify their response. The simple question, "What makes you say that?" is a great example of a simple but powerful "toss." The toss question is always going to be a facilitative question as its aim is to facilitate making the student's thinking visible. The ball is now back in the student's court, and they elaborate, justify, explain, provide evidence, or support their initial answer. In doing so, they make their thinking more visible to the teacher, the class, and themselves.

If we want students to think, we need to give them *time* to do so. The traditional research on wait time came from an era when almost all teacher questions were review, knowledge-based questions. That research focused on fractions of a second. As our teaching focuses more on understanding and getting students to think, we need to provide students with more time to do so, particularly after asking constructive questions. Consider the question and how much thinking it needs. Do students need time to write? Allocate time accordingly and be clear about how much time you are giving. This sends a signal that one is not expected to know the answer but to engage with the question.

It is easy for a few voices to dominate in a classroom. Some students process quickly or like to process out loud and so are ready to talk at a moment's notice. However, we want to make sure all students are engaged with the questions we ask. Use strategies like think-pair-share or its extension 1-2-4-All in which individuals think or write alone (1), then discusses with a partner (2), then partner groups combine (4), and finally a whole class discussion ensues (All) to allow everyone to share the progress of their thinking. Informal sharing as "table talks" can work as well. To make these informal sharings more effective, you might announce the following: "If you are a person that tends to find yourself talking first in a group, I want to invite you to be a listener first before sharing. Likewise, if you are a person that tends to be a listener, I want to invite you to be the first to share at your table." Note, this is an invitation that not everyone will take up, but it signals that we all have different patterns in group conversations, and it is useful to sometimes switch those up.

Are you playing basketball or ping-pong in your classroom? Ping-pong conversations just go back and forth between you and a single student. We need to start passing the ball and playing basketball! This means bringing other students into the conversation with invitations such as:

- Who would like to respond to what ___ just said?
- What are other people's thoughts?
- Can someone build on ___'s idea?
- Who has a different take on this?
- Who can offer another perspective?
- Who sees a connection between what ___ just said and what ___ said?

Although these direct invitations can be helpful, they aren't always necessary. If we avoid the tendency to jump in and comment as soon as a student has given a response, but instead let some silence into that space, then often another student will automatically jump in. Our fear of silence and need to fill the air with teacher talk often robs students of the *opportunity* to converse directly with their classmates in a whole class conversation. This fear, and our desire to complete the planned lesson, sometimes causes us to answer our own questions. If you get no response from a deep, important, constructive question you have just asked, consider responding: "I'm going to let that question hang in the air for now, and perhaps we will return to it later in the lesson."

In every conversation, we are listening for something: correctness, misconceptions, misunderstandings, new perspectives, thinking, reasoning, alternative ideas, conformity, approval, agreement, next steps, problems to be fixed, what we can add, and so on. Many times, we are seeking to validate ourselves. Listening for what we want to hear. Sometimes teachers have a hard time hearing students' thinking because all they hear is correctness or incorrectness. We can change that. We can begin to listen for things that validate the responder, that give them reason and endorsement, that make them feel heard. We can listen our students "into being" powerful thinkers and learners. When we expand our listening in this way and are in touch with what we are listening for, we begin to hear more. We are primed to notice it more. As Henry David Thoreau said, "We cannot see anything until we are possessed with the idea of it, take it into our heads—and then we can hardly see anything else" (Thoreau 1862).

To facilitate more student questioning, it can be useful to employ question-based structures and routines. Structures like the Socratic Seminar, Harkness Method, Leaderless Discussion (see Mindset 6), Reciprocal Teaching (see Mindset 5), and World Café are all structures that foreground student questioning as the basis for discussion. You can find more resources on each of these through an internet search. In addition, several thinking routines (see *Making Thinking Visible* and *The Power of Making Thinking Visible*) put questioning at the center of the experience, for instance, the 3 Y's, Question Sorts, SAIL, Think-Puzzle-Explore, See-Think-Wonder, and Take Note.

Celebrate and Support Students' Questioning. It is often useful to teach students about different types of questions so that we can solicit them, and students will be comfortable offering them. For instance, the difference between clarifying and probing questions. Clarifying questions are questions we ask for our own benefit. Something is not clear or there is missing information we need, and we ask for it. Stopping after directions and asking, "What clarification questions are there?" gives students the opportunity to seek information. Likewise, when a student has spoken in class and what they have said is not clear to us or to another student, we might open the conversation by stating, "I have a clarifying question." The idea here is that we need to seek first to understand others (Covey 1989). Probing questions, on the other hand, seek to get the speaker or presenter to think more deeply about things. The speaker doesn't already know the answer but must stop and think. We recognize we are being helpful to the speaker by asking these types of questions. Many protocols (Descriptive Consultancy, SAIL) that aim to help others sort through problems, difficulties, or design challenges make use of these two types of questions.

Questions of inquiry are another type of question to teach students. Inquiry questions help set a direction for either individual or class exploration. Inquiry questions have the same characteristics as generative and essential questions previously mentioned. However, since one of the reasons behind inquiry as a method is to help students to *become inquirers*, we want students involved in the process of crafting the questions of inquiry that will guide them rather than to do it for them. Of course, there can be teacher-led inquiries, but they are often a stepping stone to teach students the process so that they can assume more independence over time (MacKenzie and Bathurst-Hunt 2019; Murdoch 2022). The Question Sorts routine, which asks students to sort questions based on how much new learning a question is likely to produce (generativeness) and how interested students are in them (genuineness) can be a useful technique for identifying good questions for inquiry.

We must work to create a culture of questioning. Warren Berger, author of *A More Beautiful Question*, says that, as teachers, we need to recognize that asking questions can be scary for some students (Berger 2014). Therefore, we need to normalize and support that process of asking those "keep-thinking questions." We need to give students a chance to exercise their questioning muscles. The Question Formulation Technique (QFT) previously discussed in Case Two is one way to do this. Questions also need to be valued for students to see their worth. Honor students' questions by incorporating them into the learning as much as possible and giving them an *opportunity* to pursue them. Have a place in the physical *environment* where such questions reside so they linger in our collective consciousness: a wonder wall, an inquiry notebook, or an online document. Being playful with questioning and allowing questions to push us and take us deeper also shows student the value of questioning. Design thinking, used to better understand users and redefine problem spaces, requires us to generate questions that can take us beyond our assumptions. Looking at something familiar as being new can help us playfully generate questions about it. The world's greatest inventors were often working from a question. Wild questions sometimes result in great breakthroughs. Eliot Eisner famously said, "The most significant intellectual achievement is not so much in problem solving, but in question posing" (Eisner 2001). Questioning techniques like the "5 Why's" in which every answer is met with, "And why is that important?" or "Why did that happen?" keep pushing for a deeper level of understanding.

To help students become better questioners, we must provide students with feedback on their questions or have them provide feedback to one another. Critical feedback can help students refine their questions and get better at asking higher-level questions. Feedback for improvement doesn't need to be critical or feel harsh. Often rewriting questions, framing them in a new way, or suggesting alternative words can be useful. These are parts of the QFT process. A gallery walk focused on "Asking Questions about Questions" can create new ideas. The Question Sorts routine provides built-in criteria (genuine and generative) to help create better questions. Asking students, "What was a favorite question you heard someone ask today? And why?" can spark discussion about what makes a good question. In "The Descriptive Consultancy," the person sharing the problem is often asked to identify the questions that were most helpful in moving them forward.

Model self-questioning as a metacognitive technique for advancing one's own learning such as, "The first thing I ask myself when confronted with a problem like this is. . . ." It can be useful to build a question bank of such questions. The Understanding Map, which is discussed in Mindset 5, has a question with each type of thinking. These are just starter questions. A class could generate a whole host of questions to ask around each type of thinking. Anchor charts, like those created by Kate Mills in Mindset 7, can be created around issues like problem solving, analysis, story revision, and/or the phases of inquiry. These should be questions learners can ask themselves during each phase of a project or cycle to help them evaluate, reflect on, and direct their learning.

Fitting New Actions with Current Realities

Before you rush to implement the actions you are eager to try, step back and think about what you are currently doing at your school (see Figure 8.2):

➤ What actions, already in place, can be *amplified* and grown by applying some of the identified principles?

➤ What practices need to be rethought or *modified* considering this mindset?

➤ What do you need to stop doing altogether and *remove* from our repertoire? Why? Does it run counter to this mindset? Is it ineffective? What "moveable barriers" are standing in the way of truly living this mindset?

➤ Finally, are there things that you need to *create*, totally new processes, structures, or actions to begin to put in place?

Figure 8.2 Amplify-Modify-Remove-Create.

Review of Current Practice: What do we need to...

AMPLIFY	MODIFY	REMOVE	CREATE

———— Conclusion: Our Theory of Action ————

Contemplating a theory of action for this mindset, "Questions drive thinking and learning," brings us back to the importance of intention, motives, and goals. Just as the intention behind our question will either cause them to land with a thud or soar into rich conversation, our intention behind this mindset will determine how far it can go. What is it that we are trying to accomplish from our questioning? What do we hope to see because of our actions? In this spirit of being transparent about intention, I offer the following theory of action for Mindset 8. Use it if it captures the actions you plan to take and the outcomes you expect. If it doesn't, feel free to craft your own theory of action that will better fit your context.

> *If* we make effective questioning a hallmark of our instruction and encourage student questioning around ideas, *then* we will deepen student understanding and promote their curiosity, engagement, and self-direction.

Notes

The Opportunities We Create for Our Students Matter to Their Engagement, Empowerment, and Learning

Over 40 years ago, Walter Doyle remarked on the connection between students' learning and the opportunities in which they are engaged. "Students will learn what a task leads them to do, that is, they will acquire information and operations that are necessary to accomplish the tasks they encounter" (Doyle 1983, p. 8). Two decades later, educational visionary Elliot Eisner wrote, "The activities in which youngsters participate in classes are the means through which their thinking is promoted" (Eisner 2001, p. 301). He elaborates that students in a quality school should regularly experience opportunities to formulate their own purpose, to work collaboratively on problems that concern them, to serve the community, to work in depth, and to apply their learning in new contexts. In their work on "Instructional Rounds," Richard Elmore and Elizabeth City distilled these sentiments further into one of their core tenets: "The task predicts performance" (City et al. 2009, p. 30). Clearly, opportunities—that is to say, the tasks, activities, lessons, assignments, work, and projects we design and to which we invite our students to engage—matter.

It shouldn't come as a surprise that students themselves recognize the significance of opportunities to their learning and that they equate a teacher's provision of such opportunities as a key attribute of good teaching. In a study of how student evaluations correlate with teacher effectiveness, Stephen Irving found that students were able to accurately distinguish expert teachers (those Nationally Board-Certified) from those that were not based on the *opportunities* teachers created for cognitive engagement and the development of thinking (Irving 2004). Irving found that it was *what teachers got their students to do* in class rather than what the teacher did instructionally that emerged as the key factor in students distinguishing expertise. If educators want students to be able to analyze, interpret, create, solve problems, think critically, apply knowledge, detect patterns, and make sense of new information, then we must engage them in "a constant flux of doing" these very things (Sfard 1998, p. 6). Echoing the importance of thinking to understanding, Fred Newmann, founder of the Authentic Intellectual Work Institute, emphasizes that we need to focus on the actual intellectual demands placed on students in the opportunities we create (Newmann, Bryk, and Nagaoka 2001). Furthermore, we must make sure students' work is authentic to the disciplines and of use in the broader world—rather than merely contrived, superficial schoolwork. Producing powerful learning, then, "requires not just a mind at work but a mind working on meaningful tasks" (Lampert 2015, p. 2).

Similarly, if we want students to develop understanding, then they must regularly be involved in "performances of understanding," that is, to actively participate in the process of building and demonstrating understanding (Blythe and Associates 1998). Understanding is not some hoped-for outcome at the end of instruction but an ongoing process of participation in the act of building understanding. Developing understanding is both the goal and the means of reaching the goal. Are we creating such opportunities in our classrooms?

Since the opportunities we create clearly matter to students' learning, what kinds of opportunities do students typically experience in schools? Decades of research yield a very clear and consistent picture. It isn't pretty. It remains the norm in most classes to learn passively, engage in low-level tasks requiring little thinking, and focus on short-term surface learning for tests (Doyle 1983; Graff 2008; Eisner 2001; Hazra 2022; Lampert 2015; Santelises and Dabrowski 2015). Estimates from a diverse range of researchers over time have judged that roughly 80% of students' time at school is spent in this way (Hattie 2009; Doyle 1983; Kane and Staiger 2012), meaning a student might only experience deeper, engaged learning in one out of five classes . . . if they are lucky. This is true even at schools striving to teach for deeper learning, high academic standards, and understanding (Mehta and Fine 2019). The situation is even more dire in less affluent, more at-risk, and historically low-performing schools (Newmann et al. 2001; Santelises and Dabrowski 2015).

Magdalene Lampert sketches an all-too-familiar picture of what learning in such settings looks like drawn from a secondary mathematics class:

Students need to demonstrate knowledge of the system the teacher presents. They are learning that "doing mathematics" means following the rules laid down by the teacher, and "knowing mathematics"—and being successful in this subject—means remembering and applying the correct terms and the correct rule when doing an assignment. They are also learning that mathematical truth is determined when their answers are ratified as correct by the teacher or the textbook. The ratio of right answers to wrong ones on their graded papers will signal whether or not they belong among those who are "good at math." (Lampert 2015, p. 7)

In this context, we don't see powerful learning happening as much as we see students "doing school" (Pope 2008) or "studenting" (Liljedahl 2020). Students simply learn to play the game of school, which is generally understood to be a quest for top marks and high achievement, or they exit the game. Consequently, meaningful learning, engagement, curiosity, and even personal integrity (cheating is often high in such contexts) are seen as distractions in the quest for grades.

Elliot Eisner sums up the problem of focusing on test scores as a measure of learning: "If what students are learning is simply used as a means to increase their scores on the next test, we may win the battle and lose the war. . . . We need to determine whether students can use what they have learned" (Eisner 2001, p. 302). In creating a culture of thinking, we strive to change the game, to write a new story of learning, disrupt the status quo, and break the entrenched grammar of schools. Taking seriously the outside influence of the opportunities we create for our students is fundamental to this process.

WHAT THE RESEARCH SAYS: *WHY* DOES IT MATTER?

As teachers, we all want to create powerful learning for our students. Even so, most of us accept tests as part of our reality. The good news is that there need be no trade-off between providing students with rich, powerful learning and making sure students are prepared for tests. In a large-scale study conducted in Chicago Public Schools at grades 3, 6, and 8, Fred Newmann and his associates found that the best preparation for tests, even tests of knowledge and basic skills, is the regular engagement in learning opportunities that focuses on developing understanding, is connected to students' lives, has meaning for students, stresses application, and involves communication of one's thinking and expression of one's ideas in the language of the disciplines (Newmann et al. 2001).

Of course, if we are after understanding and deeper learning, engaging students in powerful opportunities becomes even more important. In a comparison of National Board-Certified teachers with their noncertified peers (those who applied but didn't receive certification), researchers found that Board-Certified teachers were much more likely to engage their students in challenge, deep understanding, ownership, application, and problem solving (effect sizes ranged between 0.80 and 1.38) (Smith, Baker, Hattie, and Bond 2008). As a consequence, student work from the Board-Certified teachers' classrooms was two and half times more likely to reflect deeper understanding as measured using Biggs' SOLO (Structure of the Observed Learning Outcome) taxonomy (Hattie 2009).

In the Deeper Learning Network of schools, teachers seek to create opportunities that will empower learners, contextualize knowledge, connect learning to the real world, extend learning beyond school, and personalize learning (Martínez, McGrath, and Foster 2016). In an evaluation of Network schools compared to matched schools (similar student population located in the same area), researchers found students attending a network school performed about a full grade level ahead in reading and science (one year's additional growth), and about two-thirds of a grade level ahead (six months additional growth) in mathematics when compared to matched sample of students in regular public schools (Zeiser, Taylor, Rickles, Garet, and Segeritz 2014).

Qualities of Powerful Learning Opportunities

So, what constitutes a Powerful Learning Opportunity? There are many qualities and ingredients one might consider. At the most foundational level, all researchers and theorists tend to look for the thinking involved and the degree to which the task focuses on developing understanding as opposed to knowledge acquisition. This is not to say that knowledge is neglected, but the focus is on integrating, connecting, applying, and extending knowledge (UQx 2017). Often, the components of complexity and challenge (see Mindset 7) and questioning (see Mindset 8) are also mentioned (Hofstadter 1963). Sometimes the degree of student ownership, connection to the real world, communication, and production of quality products are identified as well (Berger, Gardner, Meier, Sizer, and Lieberman 2003; Patton 2012).

Thus, there are certainly a lot of potential ingredients to consider in the design of Powerful Learning Opportunities. However, a laundry list of ingredients is not practically useful. In the Worldwide Cultures of Thinking Project (Ritchhart 2015), we draw on the work of Fred Newmann, both his research on authentic intellectual work and his evaluation of opportunities in Chicago Public Schools mentioned earlier (Newmann 1996; Newmann et al. 2001), as well as the groundbreaking research of the Teaching for Understanding Project (Wiske 1997) to identify four key components of Powerful Learning Opportunities: novel application, meaningful inquiry, effective communication, and perceived worth (see Figure 9.1).

Looking at the verbs associated with each of these components (see Figure 9.1), thinking is embedded throughout but in different ways. "Novel application" focuses on the central issue of transfer, a major aim of education. Knowledge and skills are important, but the bigger question is *whether students can apply their learning to new situations*. The element of "meaningful inquiry" suggests that tasks should allow students to extend their understanding, not just practice what they can already do. "Effective communication" pushes students to express their learning successfully to others. This requires them to develop their own voice. While there is originality and uniqueness here, there is also the expectation that such communication shows a grasp of the language, symbols, and forms of the discipline in which students are immersed. Finally, "perceived worth," connects to the idea that learning must be seen as valuable and worthwhile to the learner. It's not enough for teachers to feel it is valuable. Here, elements of quality, excellence, audience, and connection to the world outside of school come into play. Jal Mehta sums up the importance of worthwhile tasks, "Most people do not persevere at things because they are good at persevering; they persevere because they find things that are worth investing in. The implication for schools is that they should spend less time trying to boost students' grit, and more time trying to think about how their offerings could help students develop purpose and passion" (Mehta 2015).

Figure 9.1 Elements of Powerful Learning Opportunities.

DESIGN for POWERFUL LEARNING

Novel
Application

Applying, organizing, interpreting, evaluating, or synthesizing prior knowledge to solve novel problems or form new judgments.

Meaningful
Inquiry

Develop new understandings and insights that go beyond the obvious and extend one's current understanding.

Effective
Communication

Expressing, representing, justifying, supporting, and communicating one's ideas, understandings, methods, and processes effectively using disciplinary tools, symbols & language.

Perceived
Worth

Producing discourse, products, or performances that have some sense of personal meaning and value beyond merely "doing work for the teacher." The activity is imbued with purpose. At the highest level, such efforts may even have utilitarian, aesthetic, or social value that transcends the classroom and connects students' learning to the larger world.

Engagement

When teachers create learning opportunities that have these four components, we find that they both *engage* and *empower* students as well as produce deeper learning (Ritchhart and Church 2020). Thus, engagement and empowerment are emergent characteristics of Powerful Learning Opportunities rather than as separate design features. However, this is not to say we can merely take their appearance for granted. They must be cultivated. Therefore, it is worth understanding exactly how these two attributes serve deeper learning and how they can be nurtured in the "flux of doing," as Sfard (1998, p. 6) says.

We all want our students to be engaged. Engaged students are more fun to teach, and they actually learn more (Goss, Sonnemann, and Griffiths 2017). This occurs not simply because they are having "fun," but is due to the fact that "engaged students make a psychological investment in learning" (Newmann 1992, p. 2). Furthermore, a longitudinal study of elementary mathematics students in 53 schools found that students who had engaging teachers who helped them to enjoy and love doing mathematics performed better in high school than their peers who experienced less engaging opportunities (Blazar and Pollard 2022). This, despite students not always realizing high levels of achievement as elementary math students. This may seem a contradictory finding. Isn't the goal of teaching to get students to their highest level of achievement? Isn't this what is needed for success? Perhaps not if we are concerned with the long term. If performance comes at the cost of engagement, it may turn students off to future learning. We win the battle but lose the war as Eisner (2001) said. Of course, we should strive for both outcomes: high performance and high engagement. Not surprisingly, the students in the study who had teachers who both fostered deep, challenging learning and engaged students did the best in both the near and long term. This group was small, however, comprising only 6 of 53 teachers in the study.

Just as engagement promotes learning, disengagement diminishes it, and student disengagement is a problem. In a longitudinal study of 1,300 Australian students in grades 2 through 11, teachers reported 40% of students displayed unproductive behaviors regularly (Angus et al. 2009). A Gallop study found U.S. students' self-reported overall engagement with school diminished over time. While 75% of 5th graders report being engaged by school, this drops to 42% by grade 9 and 32% by grade 11 (Brenneman 2016). It may be tempting to blame students for their lack of engagement. After all, it is their behavior (or lack thereof) that we are noticing. However, research by David Shernoff found that 75% of the variation in student engagement was attributable to differences in the classroom context while only 25% could be explained by students' own background characteristics (Shernoff 2010).

Interestingly, Shernoff and colleagues found that involving high school students in *thinking* led to greater levels of student-reported engagement. These findings mirror those of researchers assessing urban middle school students' perceptions of their teachers. When teachers engaged students in independent thinking, students recognized this as useful to their development of understanding and their empowerment as learners (Shernoff 2013). The importance of deep engagement and thinking opportunities emerged as a commonality among teachers Mehta and Fine studied in their search for deeper learning as well (Mehta and Fine 2019). They found that teachers who promoted deeper learning viewed thinking and engagement as a necessary part of learning and as something of which *all* students were capable. This contrasted with teachers who failed to engage students in deep learning consistently. Those teachers were more likely to view understanding and thinking as being beyond the reach of some of their students.

When it comes to the opportunities we create, it is useful to consider three specific types of engagement: 1) engagement with others, 2) engagement with ideas, and 3) engagement in action (Ritchhart and Church 2020). In engaging with others, we recognize that learning unfolds in the company of others and is a social endeavor. We learn in, from, and with groups (see Mindset 6). The group supports our learning as well as challenges it, allowing us to reach higher levels of performance. At the same time, learning demands a personal engagement with ideas. Whereas we might be able to receive new information passively, building understanding is an active process that involves digging in and making "a psychological investment in learning" (Newmann 1992, p. 2). We bring ourselves to the learning moment. Sometimes this is identified as cognitive engagement, to distinguish it from mere engagement in activity (Fredricks, Blumenfeld, and Paris 2004). It is cognitive engagement with ideas that leads to learning. Finally, exploring meaningful issues and ideas connected to the world often means students want to act on their learning. Providing opportunities and structures for them to do so encourages students' agency and power while enhancing relevance.

Empowerment

Empowering students is not necessarily about handing over control, it is about supporting students in finding their place in the world. As with engagement, many factors go into creating conditions for empowerment, such as creating original work of high quality about which one is proud, having a sense of purpose, connecting one's learning to the world, developing a sense of identity as a learner, and feeling a sense of ownership and control over one's learning. Early empowerment theorists Thomas and Velthouse identified four components to empowerment: *meaningfulness* of the task, *competence*, *impact*, and *choice/ownership* (Thomas and Velthouse 1990). While a sense of one's competence is a trait that learners develop through time and experience, the other qualities relate to attributes of the learning task itself and connect to previously mentioned elements: perceived worth, engaging in action, and ownership.

Nurturing ownership is not merely giving students superficial choices and options; it is an ongoing process of relinquishing control so that students can step forward. In their book, *A Passion for Excellence*, Thomas Peters and Nancy Austin quip that "nobody washes a rental car" (Peters and Austin 1985). Why, then, would we expect students to care about, take pride in, and strive for excellence in activities they do not feel they own? It's hard to feel empowered when you're just learning for a test, when all you are asked to do is reproduce answers or procedures that you have been shown. Moving beyond merely reproductive tasks to those that require an *original* response allows students to find their voice, share their insights, and show their new understanding (Doyle 1983; Lukehart 2019).

Empowering students requires us to move beyond merely teaching *about* a subject. We need to engage students *authentically* in the disciplines, focusing on the processes, the ways of thinking, and the ways of creating new knowledge and understanding in the various fields of study (Gardner and Boix-Mansilla 1994; Newmann, Marks, and Gamoran 1996). When we do so, we encourage the development of *identity* (Lukehart 2019; Mehta and Fine 2019). Students come to see themselves as mathematicians, scientist, historians, artist, and writers. In short, they learn to view themselves as powerful thinkers and learners able to create new knowledge and build new understanding in the varied endeavors in which they engage. Finally, when the opportunities we create connect to who students are as individuals, connect them to their community, and allow students to stretch into the world beyond, then the learning no longer sits outside themselves but resides within (Jones, Valdez, Nowakowski, and Rasmussen 1994).

VISIONS AND REFLECTIONS: *HOW* MIGHT IT LOOK?

We have all experienced Powerful Learning Opportunities as learners. What is more, we have all had occasions of creating, participating in, or helping to realize Powerful Learning Opportunities. It is useful to tap into those occasions to help us develop our vision of key components, features, and teaching practices connected with such opportunities.

Constructing Our Vision

Use the "Success Analysis Protocol: Powerful Learning Opportunities" (see Appendix G) to guide your reflections and analysis of a Powerful Learning Opportunity you played an active role in helping to realize. This protocol is adapted from a collection of protocols by the School Reform Initiative (www.schoolreforminitiative.org). If you are reading alone, you might just do Steps 1 and 2 of the protocol. If you are reading this book with colleagues, consider doing the first two steps on your own and then use Steps 3 through 7 to share, discuss, and develop a deeper understanding of what constitutes a Powerful Learning Opportunity and the importance of the tasks we create.

Contemplating Pictures of Practice

Case One: Children Are Citizens.[1] In 2014, the Children Are Citizens (CAC) project was launched with the goal of building informed, meaningful, and reciprocal relationships between children and the city of Washington, D.C. Seventeen classrooms from PreK3 through 1st grade at five different schools throughout the city spent a semester discovering and researching places in D.C. that interested them and that they felt made the city unique and useful to people. Teachers further focused students' attention by asking them, "What would you want to share about the city with other children who might be visiting for the first time?" However, CAC students were not simply learning "about" the city. The core of this project aimed to explore the idea of young children as citizens in the here and now with the capacity to contribute to their community in powerful ways—not future, would-be citizens with possible contributions later in life, but active, engaged citizens right now.

In Anna Ramirez's early PreK3 class (three-year-olds), the children decided it was the Metro that made Washington, D.C., special. To engage students in thinking more deeply about the Metro, Anna showed them interesting and unusual images of the Metro, using the See-Think-Wonder routine as a structure for discussion. Their interest was piqued. They had lots of questions. The children suggested the class ride the Metro to explore further and see if they could find the answer to some of their questions. Of course, as researchers, students would need to document and record their findings. Clipboards and iPads for taking pictures were secured. When the station manager inquired what this group of 13 three-year-olds were up to, students had a ready reply: "Investigating the Metro."

Debriefing with the children afterward, Anna noted they were impressed by the speed of the train, by the Metro traveling above as well as below ground, and by the number of train lines meeting at the Metro Center stop. In addition, they were engaged by the color-coded maps showing where trains traveled. Looking at the collected documentation, Anna chose a collection of iPad images taken by students and printed them for the class to review. Based on these photos, children drew pictures that allowed them to elaborate details and express their emotions. Several students began to create their own, color-coded Metro maps. Anna listened intently to students' conversations while they drew, noting emerging ideas and theories. For instance, students questioned where trains "slept" after working so hard all day and proposed a theory that it must be "in the tunnels where it was dark."

Through the monthly Children Are Citizens seminars, Anna learned that Rebecca Courouble's PreK4 (four-year olds) class from Washington International School was also studying the Metro. Anna shared her students' early drafts of the Metro map with Rebecca. Anna requested photographs of Rebecca's students looking at the maps because she wanted her students "to be able to see and feel what it's like to have someone you don't know, look [at] something you created." The feedback from Rebecca's class was specific and direct. Their comments helped Anna's children create better maps and realize they could change their ideas if other suggestions appealed to them.

This early round of sharing with an audience and receiving feedback added meaning. Knowing that others are interested in their learning helped students focus on the quality of their drawings and their aesthetic decisions. Having collectively learned so much about the Metro, students were eager to personalize their learning and share it more widely by writing a story about a special Metro train named Rayo. Students chose this name because *Rayo* means "lightning" in Spanish "and because he is so fast!" Their story was combined with other classes participating in the CAC project in a book, *Washington, D.C., Belongs to Everyone!* You can read an e-version of the full book by scanning the QR code. (The metro investigation can be found on pages 61–77.) At the celebratory book launch at the National Gallery of Art, every child received a copy of the group book and an author's sticker. The joy, wonder, and excitement of both adults and children at the event were palpable.

QR Code for *Washington, D.C., Belongs to Everyone!* book.

Case Two: Learning through Material Culture: "The Industrial Revolution fundamentally changed American society and culture throughout the nineteenth and twentieth centuries." Sounds like a typical introduction one might find in a secondary history textbook. How, then, to make this topic more generative, engaging, and worthwhile to students? Adam Hellebuyck and Mike Medvinksy at the University Liggett School outside of Detroit, Michigan, thought this could be accomplished by grounding the larger issues emerging during the Industrial Revolution in the particulars of one specific object. They chose one of the most iconic symbols of that era, which also connected well to their locale: the Ford Model T. As Mike reflects, "When thinking about our locality and what physical object best represents our history, the Ford Model T rose to the top. From understanding the internal combustion engine to the $5 a day labor law, we both felt that the Model T was the object that could anchor students' research, interactions, and grow their ideas." Through the examination of the role this bit of "material culture" from the period played in the economics, daily life, and rituals of the time, they felt there would be many opportunities for student-led inquiry. They were right.

As a new elective course at a school committed to inquiry, Mike and Adam had ideas but didn't want a scripted course. They wanted to co-construct the course with students. "Our commitment was to have as many hands-on experiences with the Model T as possible," Mike explains. "When designing learning experiences, we would ask ourselves, 'How can learners use the physical vehicle to learn this?'" Mike and Adam knew that just being around the actual vehicle would spark curiosity and so they wrote a grant to procure an actual Model T. They wanted students to sit inside and think about how people would have interacted with the Model T. Their hope was that this would help students to transcend time and the remoteness of history and consequently begin to think differently.

Adam and Mike began the first day with an immersive, hands-on experience, inviting students to create a model of the combustion engine using various found materials the teachers had gathered. This hands-on project gave learners the opportunity to represent combustion in many ways, while also encouraging close looking, originality, and attention to design. These constructions, and the curiosity they provoked, laid the groundwork for the class's first home reading assignment about different engine types designed and built in the early 1900s.

The next day, Adam and Mike set in place a routine they would use throughout the course: Insights and Questions (IQ). Using two mobile whiteboards, they invited students to write on one whiteboard the new insights they had from the reading and on the other the questions that were emerging. While this routine allowed for active but low-stake processing of the new content, Mike and Adam also wanted to use the questions that emerged as springboards for inquiry. The first time with the routine, only a few learners contributed, but there were enough to build on. One student wrote, "What would our world be like if we stuck with electric motors?" This prompted a rich discussion about business, environmental choices, and cause and effect. Mike commented, "Our class would not have been focused on this if this student question was not posed. That caused learners to realize that their inquiry mattered and that the class would be guided by their contributions." As the semester progressed, the Insights and Questions boards became more robust, and by the final weeks of class, everyone was contributing.

It didn't take students long to realize that one of the most iconic parts of an automobile is its hood ornament. With that insight there were questions: "Were these devices merely ornamentation?" "Were they functional?" "Who designed them?" These questions led to a new line of inquiry. As small groups researched the function and purpose of hood ornaments, students discovered that hood ornaments were both decorative as well as utilitarian, and that they represented either a metaphor for the car or mission of the company.

Keeping the learning hands-on and thinking-rich, Adam and Mike invited students to design and create a working prototype of an original hood ornament for the class's Ford Model T that would showcase their group's aspirations and goals for the course. Once designs were finished on paper, students next used 3D modeling software to create a working hood ornament. However, when students printed their designs and fitted them on the car, they discovered they needed to have threads to screw into place. Mike and Adam didn't know how to help students with that bit of engineering, so they partnered with an advanced math class that met during the same time block and paired up one student-mathematician with one student-designer. This partnership led to new learning and members of both classes were quite proud when they screwed their hood ornament into the 1922 Ford Model T and it fit!

Learning history through the material culture of the time opens up one's imagination. As one student, Caden, reflected "You just gotta immerse yourself with the history of the car. In the other history classes that I've had it's hard to imagine yourself there, but in this class when you're hands-on and you're doing the stuff and you can imagine like what it was like to build that car or to really drive that car."

Reflecting on Current Practice

Choosing Questions and Recording Responses

Not every question will fit your context or spark deep reflection. Seek out those questions likely to push your thinking and propel you forward as you consider the importance of the opportunities you create for students. I suggest you read through the questions and identify:

➤ One or two that speak to you now. Questions that might challenge you or take your thinking in new directions.
➤ One or two you would most like to discuss with your colleagues.
➤ Circle and date the questions you select now so you can identify how your focus shifts with time and experience.
➤ Use the blank pages at the end of this chapter or your note-taking device to record your reflections.

- How might I help students better engage productively with others? What skills or structures might I need to help them do this more effectively?

- Looking ahead through curricular topics, where might there be opportunities for my students to engage in action? What might these look like?

- What are the big ideas I want students to engage in this year? Why are these important? How will I help my students to find them meaningful?

- Where, when, and how might I allow for students' voices in shaping their learning? Will my students view these as significant opportunities to direct their learning? How might these opportunities be further enhanced?

- How can I tell if my students are developing the identity of a mathematician, scientist, artist, critic, writer (or whatever applicable identity) in my classroom? Where am I noticing it? What might I look for? What might I do to enhance this?

- What is a past assignment or lesson I taught in which students' responses were simple replications of what I had taught? How might I bump that up so to encourage, allow, and support more original responses?

- How might I make an upcoming lesson/unit more connected to students' lives and community?

- Where and how might I take my students' learning beyond the classroom?

- How am I engaging my students in the authentic process of people in my discipline? What are these processes? Do my students see these processes as a key part of their learning?

- How am I supporting and giving time to students' production of quality work through ongoing revision and feedback?

- Where, when, and how do I give my students opportunities to become experts and share their expertise?

- Do I consider my first responsibility as a teacher to empower my students as learners?

- How do I make sure my students are not just learning "about" my subject area?

DATA, PRINCIPLES, AND PRACTICES: *WHAT* ACTIONS CAN WE TAKE?

Having enhanced our understanding of the central role learning opportunities play in students' development of understanding as well as their engagement and empowerment, we are ready to move forward. The elements uncovered from the Success Analysis Protocol can inform this action as well as the four design elements of Powerful Learning Opportunities (see Figure 9.1).

There is one last piece of information we need: a better understanding of the opportunities our students are encountering now. As with the topic of questioning, teachers might overestimate the richness of the opportunities they are creating. There is a natural tendency to remember only the rich opportunities because they are so evocative and salient. Often, this is not a true representation of students' experience. Therefore, it can be instructive to collect some street data before jumping into action.

Collecting Street Data

Street Data

➤ Helps us understand our own context as well as students' perspectives.
➤ Is relatively easy and quick to collect.
➤ Can be immediately analyzed and acted upon straightaway.
➤ Is meant to inform and suggest action.
➤ Is NOT an evaluation or measure of success but a snapshot of practice.
➤ Can take many forms: observations, interviews, surveys, exit tickets, recordings, and so on.

There are many types of opportunities on which you might want to collect data. For instance, what kinds of opportunities do students have to collaborate, to revise, to produce quality work, to connect to the world, to study topics in depth, to give feedback, and so on. All are worthy of understanding better through the design and collection of street data. Whatever your focus, there are three main areas that might provide useful data: examining the tasks (both learning and assessment), analyzing the tasks as realized by students, and uncovering students' perceptions of the opportunities afforded. The following three street data actions described address these areas, but, having grown comfortable with collecting street data yourself, you may well have useful ideas of your own

Street Data Action One: The Slice. A Slice Protocol looks at a targeted selection or "slice" of student work, assignments, tasks, or assessments. The purpose is to look at student work across time and/or across classrooms, to gain new insights and perspectives on the kinds of opportunities teachers are creating for students across a grade, department, or school. There are many variations of Slice Protocols: Vertical, Day in the Life, Minnesota, and Longfellow, among them (Protocols n.d.;

Cushman 1997). Appendix H provides a general format that can be scaled up or down for your purposes. Keep in mind that the wider the slice—a whole-school look at homework, for instance—the longer it will take to analyze, perhaps even a full day. An outline of the basic steps follows:

1. **Determine the Slice focus.** You might choose to look at homework, assessments, or tasks from period 3. The larger the sample, the longer the time needed for analysis.
2. **Identify an analytical frame.** You may want to use the four design elements from Figure 9.1, consider originality versus reproduction, or look at issues of engagement and empowerment. Additional foci are provided in Appendix H.
3. **Analyze the work.** This is typically done first individually but could also happen in pairs. Analysis is based on the purpose of the slice and uses the appropriate analytical frame.
4. **Share noticings, questions, and insights.** Individuals or pairs share their analysis with the larger group to answer the guiding question: What can we say about the opportunities our students are experiencing?

Street Data Action Two: Analyze a Task or Project from the Perspective of the Students' "Doing." Select one assignment/activity/project/assessment. Read through the task and make a list of the verbs that best describe what students are required to do in completing the task. Then, rank those verbs according to the amount of time students are likely to spend doing each. Next, review a collection of student work from the completed task. For each work sample, identify the verbs that best describe what students actually did in completing the assignment. Again, rank these verbs according to the amount of time you estimate students spent on each.

- What does the list of verbs describing what students will do reveal about the task/project in terms of learning potential?
- How will these actions, identified through the verbs, help students develop understanding?
- Does the balance of actions as defined by your ranking suggest that students will be learning versus merely completing work?
- How does your identification of verbs and ratings correspond to the way students spent their time? Why do you think this is? What might help students better focus their energies on what is important if they haven't done so?

With older students, you may consider having them come up with their own verbs to capture what they did, and then rank them in terms of how they spent their time. How were students' verbs and ranking different from your own? Having students identify the verbs corresponding to their action is similar to the cognitive task analysis discussed in Mindset 5.

Street Data Action Three: Survey of Opportunities. There is often a discrepancy between what teachers think they are doing and what students think they are doing (Brown 2002). Therefore, it can be useful to survey students about their perceptions. Pick and choose items from the following list that match your interests. Have students respond to these by indicating the number of classes in which they engage in activities relevant to that opportunity: 0 = none of my classes; 1 = one of my classes; 2 = two of my classes; 3 = three or more of my classes. For elementary students, it could be 1 time a day, 2 times a day, and so on.

Opportunities for Learning Survey Prompts[2]

1. Opportunities for complex problem solving. This might include analyzing ideas, evaluating the reliability of sources, constructing new ideas, or applying knowledge/skills to solve new problems.

2. Opportunities for creative thinking. This might include creating an original response or solution to a problem, approaching things in new ways, creating new ideas, and using your imagination.

3. Opportunities to communicate. This might include expressing your thoughts and learning in your own voice through writing, speaking, drawing graphs, or pictures.

4. Opportunities to collaborate. This might include collaborating on assignments with others, getting and giving feedback, learning from classmates in discussion.

5. Opportunities to receive feedback, engage in revision, and produce quality work. This might include receiving feedback you can use to improve your work from teachers, peers, or experts, as well as time to revise your work to produce something you are proud of.

6. Opportunities for real-world connections: This might include learning that emphasizes real-world connections, takes place outside school, or involves taking action as a result of your learning.

7. Opportunities for ownership. This might include projects and work that is self-directed, open-ended, personally meaningful, and sustained over time.

Stating the Mindset as Principles for Action

Based on our examination of what constitutes a Powerful Learning Opportunity, I identified four key components that can serve as principles to help guide our teaching and instructional planning:

1. Novel Application: Attending to the transfer of skills and knowledge.
2. Meaningful Inquiry: Focusing on continually deepening students' understanding.
3. Effective Communication: Producing quality work through revision and feedback, which employs the language of the discipline.
4. Perceived Worth: Ensuring the learning is authentic, purposeful, has an audience, and/or is connected to the world so students develop ownership.

Drawing on the research it is certainly possible to identify other principles. For example, reviews of teachers focused on deeper learning found they "see their first responsibility as empowering students as learners" (Martínez et al. 2016). Thus, one might identify "empowerment" as a guiding principle. Similarly, engagement surfaced as an important construct, and this too might be flagged. However, I feel these constructs already sit within the four components of Powerful Learning Opportunities. Of course, you may choose to use a different approach in your formulation.

Possible Actions

The actions that follow are loosely grouped to correspond to the four key components of Powerful Learning Opportunities identified as our guiding principles. However, as with most of our actions as teachers, many of these will cross over into other realms and do double duty so consider this categorization as only a loose framing. These actions are:

➤ Drawn from our work in schools as part of the Worldwide Cultures of Thinking Project.
➤ Placed under the related principle to help you focus on the driving motivation behind each action though there is considerable overlap. For instance, having an audience for one's work both forces effective communication and makes it feel more worthwhile.
➤ Modifiable to fit your local context.
➤ This particular mindset is centered on the cultural force of *opportunities*, though you will find that *time* and *expectations* also play a role.

Novel Application. We must attend to the issue of transfer directly rather than assuming it will just occur. "Hugging" and "Bridging" are two transfer strategies identified by David Perkins and Gavriel Salomon (Perkins and Salomon 1988). "Hugging" is keeping the learning one seeks close to the context. This facilitates "near transfer" as learners have seen the skill in context and are accustomed to its application. It is almost reflexive. "Bridging," on the other hand, focuses on "far transfer," to new or original situations. Here, we make mindful abstractions, actively seek out connections, generalize learning, and analyze situations for common features. Interdisciplinary work and design thinking often target this kind of transfer by applying what one knows to a new situation.

Problem-based learning provides an authentic, meaningful context for students' learning and development of skills and is an example of "hugging." Consequently, the learned skills are easier to retain and apply (Dochy, Segers, Van den Bossche, and Gijbels 2003). Knowledge developed is often more elaborated, and thus, easier to recall, though research suggests directly teaching knowledge as part of problem-based learning may be even more effective (Hattie 2009). Dan Meyer's Three-Act Math (see Mindset 5, Case Two) and Peter Liljedahl's approach (see Mindset 6) are good examples of problem-based learning. Another example of hugging is case-based learning. Case Two on the Model T Ford is an example of a case. Cases provide a meaningful context for learning, with a memorable anchoring experience on which to situate further learning. In analyzing a case, one learns to pose or articulate a problem, engage in problem solving, and persuade one's peers of the suitability of one's approach. These approaches tend to involve students working as teams.

Project-based learning tends to be longer term, to integrate more subject areas, and involve a larger project that might be shared with an audience. These factors allow students to exert more control and ownership. Depending on the project and when and where it is situated in students' learning, it can be a case of either hugging or bridging. The preceding two cases presented, Children Are Citizens and the hood ornament design, make use of project-based learning. Project-based learning has an effect size of 0.71 based on recent meta-analyses (Chen and Yang 2019). In comparison to problem-based learning, it is more effective at developing knowledge and concepts, perhaps because projects are longer term and more integrated. In addition, project-based learning has positive effects on students' attitudes, efficacy, and motivation (Shin 2018). The Buck Institute for Education (www.pblworks.org) provides excellent resources for getting started and deepening project-based learning.

Meaningful Inquiry. Ensure students are engaged in the kinds of thinking, problem solving, decision making, and knowledge creation that people in the discipline authentically engage in as opposed to merely learning *about* the subject as an outsider. It might be useful to make a list of both the kinds of activities in which professionals in your subject area engage, the kinds of products they produce, and the thinking that they are required to do as part of these endeavors. Look for ways to engage students in all these actions. Choose topics of study that are central to the discipline or domain under study, are relatable and interesting to students, pique interest and curiosity, and are richly connected to other ideas in and outside the discipline.

Meaningful inquiry often involves students learning from experts and becoming experts themselves. Fourth-grade teachers Zach Rondot and Grayson McKinney (2021) have developed a simple three-part system to connect students with the outside world. Part one is leveraging outside experts to provide information and knowledge about which students are curious. Part two focuses students on becoming experts on a topic through project-based learning and inquiry. Part three is students teaching others as the experts they have become. You can see this process playing out in Jenna Gampel's 2nd-grade classroom at the Conservatory Lab Charter School in Boston, Massachusetts, by scanning the QR code.

QR Code for The Truth about Snakes video.

As is discussed in Mindset 7, it is important to allow students to grapple as they are building understanding. Thus, we need to avoid over-scaffolding. Over-scaffolding is a severe impediment to students' development as learners and thinkers. In a desire to help students "complete the work," teachers too often reduce or eliminate the opportunity for students to grapple with complexity, make decisions, learn from mistakes, and engage meaningfully, productively, and independently. Over-scaffolding is essentially micro-managing. Over-scaffolding occurs in two ways: 1) we may narrow tasks in terms of both depth and time to explore, giving students small steps they complete one by one. This can make it hard to see the big picture or work toward a goal. Instead, we need to create a sense of ongoing, fluid work that has purpose and in which there will be lots of opportunities for feedback and revision; 2) we reduce complexity (of texts, problems, projects) and do most of the thinking for students on the front-end rather than supporting students in an as-needed basis.

Effective Communication. Identify an audience for students' learning beyond just you. Having an audience makes effective communication of one's ideas, learning, and thinking necessary. An audience can sometimes be found in less experienced learners by having your students teach, explain, model, show, or demonstrate their learning. Having an audience also builds a sense of purpose. It isn't just work for the teacher. How might your students' learning find an audience within the classroom, beyond the classroom, and beyond the school?

Communicating effectively to others demands that we revise our work. Too often, students turn in first drafts or marginal work, whether this be paintings by young children or essays by seniors. Not surprisingly, this work seldom represents their best effort or constitutes work of which they are proud. Consequently, it is quickly discarded after it has been graded and returned.

However, when the quality of one's work matters, one almost always submits multiple drafts. Of course, producing quality work requires one be given the *time* to do so and perhaps a target audience for whom one is producing. Lenz identifies "revision toward mastery" as a key component of deeper teaching and learning (Lenz, Wells, and Kingston 2015). Revision doesn't happen in isolation, however. One needs feedback on one's efforts, trial runs, and prototypes that provide additional input and information on how the work can be improved.

A long line of research has identified feedback as an important factor in fostering learning (Hattie and Timperley 2007; Wiliam 2014). For feedback to be useful, it needs to be specific, honest, and action oriented. In addition, feedback is only useful when there are opportunities to revise one's work. You can see the power of feedback, revision, and a focus on quality work in Ron Berger's video, Austin's Butterfly, by scanning the QR code. There are lots of tools that can be useful in providing feedback. Project Zero's Ladder of Feedback (see Ritchhart and Church 2020) can be used effectively at all grade levels. Others use the TAG structure: **T**ell something you liked, **A**sk a question, **G**ive a suggestion. Ron Berger lays down some useful ground rules for any feedback/critique session: Be kind. Be specific. Be helpful.

QR Code for Austin's Butterfly video.

SCAN ME

Perceived worth. Involve students in the co-construction of the curriculum. This might mean bringing in students' voices, interests, and questions to help shape a unit built more on inquiry than delivery of information. It might also take the form of attending to the clues found in students' conversations and actions with regards to their interests and potential questions as was done in the previous two cases. Look for opportunities and occasions for students to determine their own directions and learning path to investigate something they want to understand and explore. Engage students in setting and evaluating their own learning goals. To help students own their learning, give them freedom in how to respond to a task and what they will produce. Students can also be involved in setting criteria for what a quality outcome should entail.

Situating learning in the world can make it more meaningful. When learning is connected to issues and events in students' homes, their immediate community, or in the larger world, it will take on more significance. In addition, if we can bring in outside voices (videoconference or guest speakers) or take students out of the school (field trips and excursions), we break the walls of the classroom and help students develop relationships in the community. Of course, such work is best when it is meaningful and sustained over time. Students often view one-off field trips as a chance to take a break from learning, whereas sustained engagement with a place or organization builds depth of understanding and engagement. When learning seeks to address issues, it is natural to think about taking action. Engage students in action by finding opportunities to take learning beyond the classroom to make a difference in the world as advocates and/or change agents. Where might this learning go? Who might we be able to help? How can we share what we have learned?

In his book, *The Path to Purpose*, William Damon (2008) reports that purpose gives us energy, satisfaction, persistence, joy, hope, direction, and meaning. He defines *purpose* as "engagement in the world beyond the self," which has two components: 1) meaning to oneself, and 2) intention to accomplish something of consequence beyond oneself (Damon and Malin 2020). Clearly, purpose is much more than stating a learning intention or rattling off the objective for the lesson. Furthermore, it is not about, "Next year you will need to know this." Or "This is important for your exams." Purpose is the bigger picture. What will this learning allow us to do? How will it shape us? How will it allow us to accomplish something worthwhile? How will it help us find our place in the world? How will it allow us to make a meaningful contribution to the world? Keeping our eyes on the big picture, communicating where our learning is headed, and how even this small lesson connects to that bigger picture is all part of an ongoing commitment to lead with purpose.

Fitting New Actions with Current Realities

Before you rush to implement the new actions that you are eager to try, step back and think about what you are currently doing at your school (see Figure 9.2):

➤ What actions, already in place, can be *amplified* and grown by applying some of the principles identified above?

➤ What practices need to be rethought or *modified* considering this mindset?

➤ What do you need to stop doing altogether and *remove* from our repertoire? Why? Does it run counter to this mindset? Is it ineffective? What "moveable barriers" are standing in the way of truly living this mindset?

➤ Finally, are there things that you need to *create,* totally new processes, structures, or actions to begin to put in place?

Figure 9.2 Amplify-Modify-Remove-Create.

Review of Current Practice: What do we need to...

AMPLIFY	MODIFY	REMOVE	CREATE

Conclusion: Our Theory of Action

Once we take on the mindset that the opportunities we create for our students matter to their engagement, empowerment, and learning, then we begin to look not only at our curriculum, lessons, and plans differently, but also at the whole of our teaching. Since an individual lesson can encapsulate lots of opportunities, we need to be strategic in embedding the kinds of opportunities that will lead to the outcomes we truly desire. Too often, this has meant schools providing opportunities to acquire and practice knowledge and skills so that students can do well on tests. This needn't be the case. The following theory of action suggests that if we provide different kinds of opportunities, we can achieve much more:

> *If* we consistently engage students with big ideas connected to their lives and provide opportunities for them to set goals, display agency, make choices, pursue passions, create, and innovate in their production of quality work, *then* our students will build understanding and become engaged, empowered, self-directed learners able to find purpose in their lives.

Notes

We Make Thinking and Learning Visible to Demystify, Inform, and Illuminate These Processes

Thinking and learning can seem mysterious, opaque, and veiled processes locked in a learner's head and difficult to access. As a result, we often focus on the tests and the work students produce as evidence of learning and thinking. This feels easier and certainly familiar to our own experience of schooling. However, in doing so we deprive students of opportunities to grow fully both as thinkers and as a learning community. In addition, we rob ourselves as teachers of the very information needed to enrich and guide students' learning. We need that window into the messiness and budding formation of students' thoughts so that we can appropriately nudge them forward.

Furthermore, relying only on tests to tell the story of learning in our schools and classrooms presents a wildly distorted and inaccurate picture. As Daniel Koretz points out in *The Testing Charade*, when test scores improve, we don't know if students really are learning more or if these gains come at the expense of them no longer learning in arts classes because they have been cut back, or the gains could be the result of extensive test prep, which doesn't produce more learning just better test takers (Koretz 2017). Thus, tests not only distort, but also limit students' learning. Moreover, tests blind stakeholders to all the other things that are important in schools: the level of student engagement, the community being built, the growing independence of learners, and the development of passion. When test scores become *the single story*, it is reductive. As author Chimamanda Adichie says, "The single story creates stereotypes, and the problem with stereotypes is not that they are untrue, but that they are incomplete. They make one story become the only story" (Adichie 2009). We have a responsibility to ourselves, to our students, to parents, and to the community to make more of the story of learning visible.

If we don't choose to let tests be the whole story of learning and thinking, how do we shed light on the real learning?[1] How do we look beyond products, tests, and scores? What will our evidence be? As Vea Vecchi from Reggio Schools emphatically states, "We feel it is necessary, once again, to deny the assertion that learning, and how we learn, is a process that cannot be seen, that cannot be activated and observed, leaving the school with the sole task of eliciting learning and then verifying it after the fact. What we are interested in is precisely an attempt to see this process and to understand how the construction of doing, thinking, and knowing takes place, as well as what sort of influences or modifications can occur in these processes" (Project Zero 2006b). Note the shift Vea Vecchi is making away from dependence on products and toward a greater understanding and appreciation of the process. Of course, process is dynamic, ongoing, and even fast-moving whereas generating products (tests) allows us to halt the messiness of learning and force an outcome. The mechanisms for making learning and thinking visible don't occur post hoc but are an integral component that cannot be separated from our teaching. On one hand, this embedding adds a new layer of complexity to teaching. On the other, it is an interesting, informative, and enhancing layer that elevates both our teaching and students' learning. Accordingly, we take the idea of making learning and thinking visible as a central goal of teaching and a mindset worth cultivating.

What exactly are the mechanisms for making learning and thinking visible? Four useful practices are: thinking routines, documentation, listening, and questioning (Ritchhart and Church 2020). While each can be engaged in as a discrete practice, they are better thought of as a synergistic, dynamic, and supportive constellation. Figure 10.1 shows how these practices might be conceptualized as a cohesive, overlapping, interconnected whole.

WHAT THE RESEARCH SAYS: *WHY* DOES IT MATTER?

As Vea Vechhi argues, informing instruction and understanding learning better are two very important goals of making learning and thinking visible. When thinking and learning are more visible, we can provide better feedback. In addition, the process of formative assessment directly depends upon understanding the learning that is happening. This is not done by merely looking at the correctness of responses on a paper (i.e., just feedback on performance), but through the careful examination of students' learning and thinking. At the same time, research has shown additional benefits. Visibility helps to develop effective learners, enhance expertise and deep learning, as well as promote academic achievement.

Developing Effective Learners

We know that how students think about the enterprise of learning and the process of thinking affects the way they approach new learning tasks (Dart et al. 2000; Schoenfeld 1983; Van Rossum and Schenk 1984; Vermunt and Verloop 1999). When students view learning as chiefly about memorization, they apply memory strategies to the task even if understanding is required. This mismatch between the task and the application of appropriate thinking is a major obstacle to learning (Carey 2015). Thus, it is important for teachers to alert students to the particulars of a learning task and the thinking needed. We must make the needed thinking visible rather than simply assuming all students will approach the tasks with effective strategies. This is perhaps why "cognitive task analysis," as discussed in Mindset 5, was the instructional intervention having the greatest effect on student achievement of all those Hattie studied (Hattie and Zierer 2017). When we provide the structures and tools that routinely demystify the complexity of thinking, we make meaningful strides toward achieving the larger goal of nurturing learners who see

Figure 10.1 Four practices of making thinking visible.

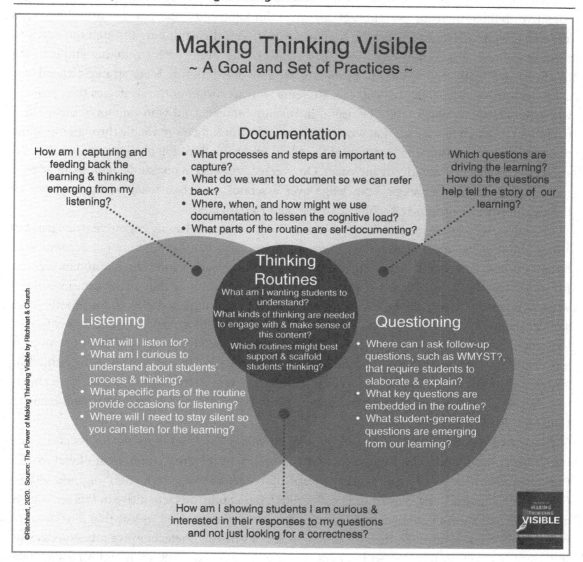

themselves as thinkers ready to take on new ideas and information. That said, "Learning that is more investigative, participatory, and personal, can affect students' approaches to learning regardless of their conceptions of learning" (Dart et al. 2000). It seems such tasks, the very ones being advocated throughout this book, help to break the cycle of "school learning" and unleash new potential.

Helping students better recognize when and *how* thinking is happening can improve meta-cognitive abilities, increase awareness of one's own thinking, and foster positive attitudes toward learning (Dajani 2016). Learners then have more control of their thinking through the development of meta-strategic knowledge—one's awareness of the strategies for thinking and learning one possesses. With awareness of our thinking, we gain more control. Meta-strategic knowledge is key to learner independence. We want students who are aware of the strategies they possess, who can determine which might be useful in various contexts, and who can apply them effectively. Our research has shown that when teachers make thinking more visible through modeling their own thinking, using the language of thinking, and using thinking routines, students' meta-strategic knowledge dramatically increases. On average, students in our study demonstrated 60% more growth in meta-strategic knowledge over a school year than what would be expected through normal maturation (Ritchhart, Turner, and Hadar 2009).

Of course, we want students who are not only able to select and apply cognitive strategies, but also to monitor the implementation of those strategies. If students' actions are not accompanied by appropriate metacognitive monitoring, their actions may lead to unproductive and unsuccessful efforts (Kuzle 2013). "Students should be able to articulate how they make decisions about what is important in a given context and how those decisions enhance their overall comprehension," learning, and progress (Keene 2002, p. 1). Students' thinking must be visible to themselves. One very effective way students do this is through self-verbalizing the steps needed to complete a task and self-questioning through the process (Hattie 2009). This externalizes their thinking and makes it visible to both themselves and to their teachers. These strategies have been shown to be a particularly powerful boost to learning for lower-ability and special education students (Huang 1991; Rock 1985).

These two processes, that is, the selection of strategies based on one's awareness and active monitoring throughout their implementation, complement the third component of metacognition, which is the more summative process of reflection and evaluation of one's efforts (Papleontiou-Louca 2003; Wilson and Clarke 2004). Being fully metacognitive in this sense gives students active and full control over the cognitive processes involved in learning. For decades, research has consistently identified the development of students' metacognitive processes as having a strong effect on learning with an effect size of 0.69 (Chiu 1998; Finn and Metcalfe 2008; Haller et al. 1988; Hattie 2009; Weil et al. 2013). Readers, listeners, and viewers must actively monitor their comprehension. Problem solvers, designers, and inventors must monitor their ongoing efforts toward solutions. Furthermore, one's metacognitive ability plays a role in improving and advancing one's learning by enabling us to focus more efficiently on what we still need to learn (Finn and Metcalfe 2008) by knowing what we don't know.

Enhancing Expertise and Deeper Learning

Expertise in any field is not merely acquiring the knowledge base of that field, but of mastering the way people in that field think through problems, make decisions, and create new knowledge. Thus, learning to think like an expert is a central part of developing disciplinary understanding and deep learning (Gardner and Boix-Mansilla 1994). And yet, too often, we hide these processes from students and continue teaching "about" the subject, robbing students of the opportunity to develop real expertise. Teaching for understanding requires that students not only access and delve deeply into the knowledge base of a discipline, but also the methods, forms, and purposes of that discipline (Boix Mansilla and Gardner 1998). These "methods" constitute the way experts build new knowledge, deepen their understanding, assess the validity of information, and go about the authentic work of the discipline. Recall Nick Collins's mathematics classroom from Case Two in Mindset 5. When students walked into the room, there was a sign reading, "Math is an activity: questioning, noticing, calculating, exploring, organizing, persevering, making sense, understanding, applying connections." By specifically naming the thinking of mathematicians, Nick made these sometimes invisible and even untaught processes visible to students, which then came to life in the way he taught mathematics.

Picking up the almost intuitive ways of acting, processing, and approaching problems in any field or area can seem daunting. Experts just seem to know what to do in ways that seem mysterious to novices. This unarticulated, tacit knowledge can be difficult to acquire. Typically, "Learning tacit knowledge and skills requires continuous day-to-day contact with the person, team, or organization possessing such knowledge," which can be extremely time consuming (Chennamaneni and Teng 2011). This process can be sped up and made more effective if, instead of relying on some mysterious tacit knowledge transfer, experts made their thinking visible to novices through a "cognitive apprenticeship." Collins, Brown, and Holum, in their seminal article on "Cognitive Apprenticeship: Making Thinking Visible," stress that it is "the interplay among observation, scaffolding, and increasingly independent practice [that] aids apprentices both in developing self-monitoring and correction skills and in integrating the skills and conceptual knowledge needed to advance toward expertise" (Collins et al. 1991, p. 2).

Reciprocal teaching is a well-researched reading intervention developed by Annemarie Palinscar and Ann Brown. It uses the cognitive apprenticeship model to develop students' metacognitive abilities as readers (Palinscar and Brown 1984). In reciprocal teaching, the teacher models expert strategies. Students know they will soon undertake the same task independently and attention is placed on the thinking that individuals are doing within the group learning context. Four key thinking processes are highlighted and made visible through modeling: 1) making predictions, 2) raising questions, 3) clarifying any misunderstandings or confusions, and

4) summarizing (Oczkus 2018). Reciprocal teaching is extremely effective. In a pilot study with individual students who were poor readers, the method raised their reading comprehension test scores from 15% to 85% accuracy after about 20 training sessions (Palinscar and Brown 1984). Similar results have been attained in subsequent studies (Reutzel, Smith, and Fawson 2005; Rosenshine and Meister 1994). These are very dramatic effects for any instructional intervention. For over 40 years, the highly effective Public Education and Business Coalition (PEBC) in Denver, Colorado, has fostered students' reading comprehension through a similar strategy of cognitive apprenticeship to share and demystify the comprehension strategies employed by effective readers (Keene and Zimmermann 1997).

Academic Achievement

Data from individual teachers and schools who have embraced making thinking visible have seen substantial gains for students on a variety of standardized tests. In 2010, the English department at Washington International School (WIS) saw average student subject scores on the International Baccalaureate (IB) Diploma, both Higher Level (HL) and Standard Level (SL), increase significantly year to year. These gains were especially dramatic for students in the SL English classes where average scores went from 5.2 (on the IB Diploma's 7-point scale) in 2009 to 6.07 in 2010. Furthermore, 79.3% of SL students received a top score of a 7 or 6 on their English subject area exams in 2010 compared with 30% in the previous year. In 2011, scores held steady for students in the HL classes but continued to climb for SL English students, reaching an average score of 6.23 with 87.1% scoring a 6 or 7, and no student scoring below 5. This was not only a strong uptick in performance, but also one that was surprising due to the larger number of learning support students in 2011. The benefit of making thinking and learning processes visible for more marginalized or lower-ability students has been a consistent finding across various research studies (Hattie 2009).

St. Leonard's College, in Melbourne, Australia, has worked to build a culture of thinking by employing visible thinking practices for over four years. Principal Stuart Davis believed the best way to assess the impact this was making was to look at median scores (the point at which half the students score above and half below) and at the scores of students in the bottom quartile of the school as opposed to just top-performing students. In other words, do MTV practices help lower and middle performing students? St. Leonard's median ATAR (Australian Tertiary Admission Rank) scores, representing a percentile ranking of all Grade 12 students in Australia, have climbed steadily each year: 2015 = 81.55, 2016 = 85.58, 2017 = 87.4, and 2018 = 90.5. Those for the lower quartile of students also increased: 2015 = 68.92, 2016 = 73.06, 2017 = 76.97, and 2018 = 78.24.

The Mandela International Magnet School (MIMS) in Santa Fe, New Mexico, was founded in 2014 as a nonselective middle school magnet using the IB Middle Years Program. The school would eventually grow to include students in grades 7–12. We have worked with this school since its inception under a grant from the Hankins Foundation. During the three years that New Mexico administered the PARCC exam consistently (there was an interruption with COVID); MIMS scores steadily rose in 8th grade English with proficiency rates of 46% in 2016 (27% for Hispanic students), 60% in 2017 (41% for Hispanic), and 67% in 2018 (59% for Hispanic). It is also instructive to look at a cohort progressing through the school to see what happens to their proficiency levels over time. The English level proficiency rates of students went from 46% in 2016, to 67% in 2017, to 77% in 2018. Considering just Hispanic students in this cohort, scores went from 24% in 2016, to 41% in 2017, to 56% in 2018.

PRINCIPLES AND PRACTICES: *HOW* MIGHT IT LOOK?

With a better understanding of the various mechanisms educators can use to make learners' thinking visible and why they are important, we want to now explore what it might look like in schools and classrooms where teachers are making full use of these techniques. How might such a classroom look, sound, and feel? What might be different or unexpected? What might constitute a subtle yet powerful shift? In our exploration, we first work to construct a vision of such a place. Next, we explore two case studies. The first is adapted from an account in *Visible Learners: Promoting Reggio-Inspired Approaches in All Schools* (Krechevsky, Mardell, Rivard, and Wilson 2013) and through discussion with my colleagues in this project. The second is from a secondary history class I observed in Melbourne, Australia.

Constructing Our Vision

Imagine you are going on a study tour with a few colleagues to visit schools that have made visibility of thinking and learning a chief goal and worked to successfully embed the four practices for making thinking visible (see Figure 10.1) in their day-to-day operation. You have a chance to visit teachers teaching your subject and grade level and watch several lessons. In addition, your group walks the halls and visits classroom spaces throughout the school. In advance of your visit, you consider the following with your team:

- What might be the first signal a visitor gets that this school values thinking and making it visible?
- What do you expect to see as you roam the halls of the school?

- How do you think the classroom walls might be different than your own or that of other schools? How do you expect the teachers will use their physical environment to make thinking visible?

- What do you expect the teaching to be like? What might teachers be doing differently?

- What might the students' role be in making their own thinking and learning visible?

- Are there things or practices you expect *not* to see? Which common teaching practices might be jettisoned in favor of others that better focus on making thinking and learning visible?

- How do you think having a visibility mindset will affect not just a teacher's teaching practices but their whole approach in the classroom?

Contemplating Pictures of Practice

Case One: The Amazing Circus Act. Secondary mathematics teacher Doug McGlathery at Cambridge Rindge and Latin School, a large public school in Cambridge, Massachusetts, uses the Interactive Mathematics Program as his teaching guide (Fendel, Resek, Alper, and Fraser 1997). Rather than a standard math textbook laid out in a series of discrete topics, IMP is a four-year, problem-based series that integrates algebra, geometry, and statistics topics in a set of complex problems. It is designed to be taught in heterogeneous rather than tracked groups and aims to increase equity in the learning of mathematics. In the program, students are introduced to a problem, play around with it, develop conjectures, and then spend about three weeks investigating and learning the mathematics needed to solve the problem. This process concludes in a culminating project that captures students' learning and thinking throughout the process (Alper, Fendel, Fraser, and Resek 1997).

In year three of the IMP series (typically done in 10th grade), students encounter the "High Dive" problem, which involves trigonometry, polar coordinates, and the physics of falling objects. The task is to model the problem: "When should a diver on a Ferris wheel aiming for a moving tub of water be released to create a splash instead of a splat?" As students conclude the unit and enter the write-up phase, Doug provides them with a long, rolled sheet of paper on which to record their final equation. The paper is purposely large to celebrate not only the enormity of the problem students have solved, but also to provide space for careful examination and reflection. Students can add to their scroll of paper as needed. As Nora and Joan's recorded equation expands (it eventually reached 25 feet), they ask if they can work in the hall. Doug agrees. Working in the hallway creates additional opportunities for learning. As Nora and Joan's work becomes visible to students, friends, and teachers walking by, they frequently find themselves entertaining questions and giving verbal explanations of their learning.

Because the process of solving the equation had been done in segments of learning that focused on aspects of the equation, Nora and Joan struggle with what they initially thought was a simple step: writing down the equation. They recognize that they had forgotten the meaning behind the various parts of the equation. The pieces were all there, but they no longer recalled which phrase of the equation corresponds to which part of the problem. Consequently, they decide it would be useful to color code the various parts and to create a key that observers could use to make sense of it themselves. As Joan explains, "Math isn't as sticky in your head as some of the other subjects. When we color coded it, we relearned it. Having it that way made it easier to see and easier to remember." The visibility was not just a feature of the product, but a process that facilitated their learning and allowed them to link the concrete with the abstract symbolic notation.

Doug periodically goes into the hallway to watch and listen. Sometimes Doug digitally records the girls. In doing so, he captures one spirited discussion between them and a passerby in which a question is asked, "Is eight feet of water really deep enough to survive?" Until this moment, Joan and Nora had just taken this information for granted as it was part of the stated problem. Now they are curious about the physics of high diving. Doug suggests they walk down the hall to talk to the physics teacher and find out more.

As the girls work, they realize they are not just doing work for the teacher to fulfill their assignment, but creating an opportunity to teach others. Consequently, they find themselves constantly thinking about their potential audience, students not in their class. Joan explains the issue, "The thing about having stuff in the hallway is that people never really look at stuff in the hallway. I want to think that people will stop and look at [it], but Nora is more realistic about things. . . . I think sometimes I [take the] complicated route and Nora is, like, 'People aren't really going to look at this' and suggests ways to make it simpler."

After the girls' display has been up a few days, the pre-calculus teacher next door invites Joan and Nora to present to her class. She feels it would help her students to see some of the relevance of the math they are learning. The girls develop a plan to engage their audience in thinking about the problem, what was known and unknown, and identify significant relationships and their influence so that they can better engage with the equation. Afterward, Joan remarks, "Once we made the presentation, I felt like we really know it all the way through." You can view an animated video of Joan and Nora's learning by scanning the QR code.

QR Code for Amazing Circus Act video.

SCAN ME

Case Two: Australian Popular Culture. Cameron Paterson's Year 10 history class at Sydney's Shore school is completely quiet. They have been studying Australian popular culture from 1945 to 2000, and Cameron has just set a five-minute free write, a familiar practice in his class. "Remember, you must keep your pen moving. The only mistake you can make is to pause in your writing and thinking." The ungraded, free write is a chance for students to take the ideas floating around in their heads and express them in words. This externalization on paper serves several functions: 1) the act of retrieving ideas from memory increases their storage strength and helps to embed them in long-term memory (Karpicke 2012), 2) expression of ideas in writing prepares all students to participate actively in the upcoming discussion, and 3) the facts that students retrieve will become the basis for the larger lesson of cause and effect, underlying forces, and deeper analysis of events.

At five minutes, Cameron calls time. "Thanks, everyone," he announces. "Today we are going to begin synthesizing and organizing our thinking about popular culture in the latter half of the 20th century. So, we're going to move now into an activity that you have done before, the Micro Lab. We're doing two rounds. First, we're just going to look at your general thoughts about Australian popular culture in this period. Then there's going to be a second follow-up where we're going to start exploring: What were the key turning points?" Cameron reviews the guidelines for the Micro Lab: students form groups of three, each student has one minute of uninterrupted talk time, and this is followed by 30 seconds of whole-class silence. The second speaker then adds on, elaborates, and connects to the previous speaker as best he can. This process ensures that every student in the class speaks, further solidifying their memory of ideas as they move their writing into verbalization.

As the Micro Lab begins, Cameron has three roles: timekeeper, listener, and documenter. Cameron moves around the room, gathering ideas students are sharing and recording them on the whiteboard. Students mention the influence of Britain and America, changes in fashion and music, environmental issues, and multiculturalism among others. By writing these ideas on the whiteboard, they become visible for the ensuing discussion. This documentation lessens students' cognitive load and makes the possibility of seeing connections easier. As the second Micro Lab shifts to "turning points," the conversation deepens. Students begin to talk about the influence of technology, greater sensitivity to indigenous rights, and immigration policy.

At the end of the second Micro Lab, Cameron brings the class together. "So, you'll notice what I've been doing as you guys have been having those triad discussions. I've been listening to what you've been saying. Just grabbing some snippets from conversations, trying to pick up the flow of words and phrases coming up. If you glance down this list, you'll notice the change in conversation. Particularly how things shifted toward the end as we were really focusing on key turning points. I have an open question for you: What do you think is fairly central to Australian popular culture and the turning points in this period?" This question asks students to synthesize their discussions and identify not just events but the underlying forces at work.

After a rich discussion in which students take different positions and defend them with evidence, Cameron again pushes students' thinking forward. "We're starting to move beyond that detail and evidence that I talk about in history to now dig a little bit deeper. You're starting to give me some analysis. You're starting to throw some insights out. So, here's a big question I'd like you to think about. When we look at this period, what do you think is really going on under the surface? What's key to understanding all of this?" To help students answer this question, Cameron informs them they will be creating a group concept map using the Generate-Sort-Connect-Elaborate routine. He explains, "Now we have some fun. These three front tables, your job is to be observers for the next three or four minutes. To watch closely and think about what's going up. The back three tables, your job is to come up and put your ideas on the whiteboard, sorting your ideas according to how important they are, with most important ideas toward the center of the board."

After four minutes of somewhat frantic writing, Cameron asks those at the board to sit, and he addresses the class, "Now everybody take a step back and let's just pause for a moment and look what's up on the board. I'm seeing technology, I'm seeing sport, I'm seeing multiculturalism, youth culture, the emergence of teenagers, U.S. influence, Australia's developing identity, the emergence of the internet, Beatles, Walkman. Now those of you that haven't been up to the board, you get to do the really fun stuff! Here's the new instructions: I want you to see what's on the board and I want you to look for connections. I want you to draw connecting lines between the ideas that have something in common. And perhaps a very brief comment explaining the connection. Also, you can elaborate on any of the thoughts by adding any new ideas or expanding anything there. So, if there's anything you think is missing, or if there's anything you think that needs a little bit more explanation. Go for it."

Once this second group completes its additions, Cameron asks them to explain some of the connections they have made but not written anything about. He frequently asks, "What makes you say these two ideas are connected?" The giant concept map on the board has now made "Australian Pop Culture" visible for the students in a way it wasn't at the beginning of the lesson. Individual knowledge has become collective understanding. The map provides a memory of the group's process of building understanding from discrete bits of knowledge. There is much here to discuss and build on, and Cameron takes photographs for use in the next lesson and encourages his students to do the same. He leaves them to ponder one last question that the class will take up tomorrow: "How would other people view what's just gone up on your board? What would your grandparents say? Given that you've been interviewing your grandparents about their perspectives of popular culture, what would they notice if they saw what was on the board now? What might they think was missing or important?" Scan the QR code to view a video of this lesson.

Choosing Questions and Recording Responses

Different questions serve us at different times in our learning. Therefore, I suggest you read through the questions and identify:

➤ One or two that speak to you now. Questions that might challenge you or take your thinking in new directions.
➤ One or two you would most like to discuss with your colleagues.
➤ Circle and date the questions you select now so you can identify how your focus shifts with time and experience.
➤ Use the blank pages at the end of this chapter or your note-taking device to record your reflections.

• At the end of today's lesson, what insights did I gain into my students as learners and thinkers?

• What are the "go-to" routines for learning and thinking in my class? Why these routines? What do I learn from them? What do my students learn?

• Where, when, and how am I *planning* for students to look closely, make connections, uncover complexity, or other thinking moves (see Figure 5.1)?

• How do I recognize thinking as it unfolds in real time in front of me? What do I *prime* myself to look for and notice? How do I avoid overly focusing on correctness and right answers?

• How do I interact with my students around the thinking they are making visible both in and beyond the current moment?

• How do/might I *press* for thinking in a way that communicates the value and importance I place on thinking?

• When, where, and how am I returning documentation to my students to examine, reflect, and learn from?

- When using thinking routines, how do I frame their use? Do I position them as tools and a series of moves that I want students to grow into and develop expertise in or are they just activities?

- Where and when am I making my own thinking visible?

- What do I document as a teacher? What do I wish I were doing a better job of capturing in terms of students' learning? How might I begin to do just a bit more in this area?

- Where, when, and how might I engage students in self-documentation?

- How am I capturing the story of learning happening across a unit of study in such a way that it is more than just a series of activities?

DATA, PRINCIPLES, AND PRACTICES: *WHAT* ACTIONS CAN WE TAKE?

With a clear understanding of both why and how we should be making students' learning and thinking visible as a central element of our instruction, we are ready to move toward action. First, though, we want to explore the current state of things in our classrooms. Most teachers will already be engaged in making thinking and learning visible in some way. We collect street data to help us better understand the reach and effect of these practices so that we can build upon them.

Collecting Street Data

Street Data

➤ Helps us understand our own context as well as students' perspectives.
➤ Is relatively easy and quick to collect.
➤ Can be immediately analyzed and acted upon straightaway.
➤ Is meant to inform and suggest action.
➤ Is NOT an evaluation or measure of success but a snapshot of practice.
➤ Can take many forms: observations, interviews, surveys, exit tickets, recordings, and so on.

Street Data Action One: MYST. In thinking classrooms, teachers ensure that thinking is regularly modeled, discussed, shared, displayed, and challenged so that students are immersed in thinking, and it is no longer invisible and mysterious. Use the MYST tool (Me, You, Space, Time) to take stock of how thinking is being made visible in your classrooms across these four domains.

Me = How am I modeling *my* own thinking? How does *my* use of language highlight thinking?

You = What are you noticing about *your* students' language, questions, contributions, and/or attitudes in relation to thinking?

Space = In what ways are you using the physical *space* to record, process, and interact with the group's thinking and learning?

Time = How are you allocating *time* differently to create opportunities for thinking? What effect is that having on students?

Use this framework at the end of a class or the conclusion of a day so that you reflect on very concrete examples rather than generally. Do this over several days so that you become accustomed to noticing, paying attention to, and leveraging these occasions. At the end of your data collection period, look at your data and consider the following questions:

- What questions, surprises, or reflections does the data evoke?
- Which questions were the hardest for you to answer and provide specific evidence for? Why were these challenging?
- What additional data might you collect to help you better answer these questions with more concrete evidence?
- What implications do your responses have for you going forward? What might need more attention or refinement?
- If you asked a colleague or your students to fill out MYST on your classroom, what do you think their responses would be?

Street Data Action Two: Ghost Walk. As you may recall from the Street Data Action in Mindset 2, the Ghost Walk is a structured process for a collaborative walk through a school when classes are not in session. It can be done by pairs or by a larger group. It also may be done by critical friends from outside the school who can look at the physical environment objectively. If done within a school, it is often advised that teachers do not visit their own team, department, or grade level so that they might have an easier time seeing things with fresh eyes. This format has been adapted from the "Collaborative Ghost Walk" protocol developed by Debbie Bambino (2021). This time, you will focus on the visibility of thinking and learning (see Appendix I).

Stating the Mindset as Principles for Action

In the expression of this mindset, we have an overarching goal, "to make thinking and learning visible" accompanied by a rationale, "to demystify, inform, and illuminate these processes." To move into action, we need to get specific about what we will do to facilitate making the somewhat invisible processes of learning and thinking visible while avoiding the trap of relying only on products and outcomes as evidence. This brings us back to the four practices of making thinking and learning visible presented in Figure 10.1. Restated here with a bit more specificity to provide an even clearer direction for our actions:

- *Document* and share diverse representations of learning throughout the learning process to allow students both to demonstrate and deepen their learning.
- Use protocols, *routines*, and structures to support and prompt students' thinking as a vehicle for externalizing their thoughts.
- *Listen* for learning with your ears, your eyes, and your heart by being curious about your students' emergent thinking and learning.
- *Question* in a way that probes students' thinking and pushes them to go deeper and explain more.

Possible Actions

The preceding four principles are not necessarily discrete practices. They are highly integrated and overlapping. Consequently, I have not used them to identify specific actions. Instead, you will see these principles referenced as appropriate in the actions below. In addition, you will notice that I have not included much in the way of developing students' metacognition and meta-strategic knowledge in the following actions. Refer to Mindset 2 for specific actions you might take in those specific areas. As many readers will recognize, the use of thinking routines has been a core practice of building a culture of thinking about which much has been written. Here, I present practices that might both build off of, connect to, and go beyond the use of routines.

Making thinking and learning visible is both a goal and a set of practices. The following actions described are tied to some top-level goals that can motivate actions. These are:

➤ Drawn from our work in schools as part of the Worldwide Cultures of Thinking Project.
➤ Connected to the principles for action as appropriate though all four of these practices are highly integrated in our teaching.
➤ Modifiable to fit your local context.
➤ Connected to the most relevant cultural forces to which each specific action is associated. Both frameworks, the 8 cultural forces and the 10 mindsets, are synergistic and you can begin your journey either place.

Plan for Thinking. The biggest misconception about thinking *routines* is that they are merely activities rolled out to move a lesson along. To make them work as tools for facilitating thinking and making thinking visible, we must first *plan* for thinking. With any piece of content, what is the thinking that students will need to do to make meaning of it? What is the thinking they will need to do to move beyond a superficial understanding to a deeper one? Your responses to these questions will allow you to choose a thinking routine that best prompts and scaffolds student thinking. The books *Making Thinking Visible* (Ritchhart et al. 2011) and *The Power of Making Thinking Visible* (Ritchhart and Church 2020), as well as *Protocols in the Classroom* (Allen, Blythe, Dichter, and Lynch 2018) provide extensive resources on routines and protocols along with guidelines for how to use them and gather useful information from their enactment. Being primed for thinking connects to your *expectations* for learners and facilitates more effective listening. Ready yourself to listen for and spot thinking occasions for the types of thinking you are trying to encourage. If you want to promote "reasoning with evidence," look for where, when, and how you see that emerging. Notice, name, and support it.

Structure Discussions. Thinking *routines* and protocols can be excellent ways to structure students' discussion and exploration of ideas because they carefully guide students through a process designed to help them reach higher levels of understanding. By its very nature, a discussion protocol changes the free-flowing nature of conversation. We accept this trade-off because the added structure helps to guide our thinking, ensures more voices are heard, makes the overall conversation more productive, completes the discussion in the time allotted, and facilitates positive *interactions*. In the previous Case Two of Cameron Paterson, he made strategic use of the Micro Lab to make sure all students uncovered, expressed, and formulated ideas.

Of course, a student-led discussion provides an excellent opportunity for our listening and documentation. Note how Cameron was strategic in his listening and documenting to provide a shared compilation of ideas, which the class used to advance its conversation. His listening fit his instructional goals. Sometimes teachers think the goal of discussion is just to share, to get ideas out, expressing the belief that everyone's ideas are valid or there are no right answers. Although this might come from a good-hearted place, it can keep the learning at a surface level. There is a role for teachers in a discussion that is distinct from delivery. The role is to capture, highlight, and cue up opportunities to press for even deeper thinking.

Develop a Formative Assessment Practice. One of the goals of making thinking and learning visible is to inform. We want to use students' responses to thinking *routines* as ongoing, integrated, and formative information to guide lesson planning. Similarly, as we document students' learning and thinking, we are not merely doing so to create displays or more work for ourselves, but to gather information, details, and insights that might inform our instruction and students' learning. In both cases, it is important not to think of formative assessment as a task one gives students, but rather as a practice in which we engage as teachers. This means we have to prime ourselves to look for evidence of learning and thinking happening so that we will be alert to it when it happens. If one is primed only to look for examples of correctness and right answers, as most teachers have been trained to do, then this is what one will be most inclined to notice. However, when thinking is an *expectation*, then we become curious and accustomed to looking for thinking and learning. Consequently, it seems that more thinking is surfacing. You can prime your own looking by identifying certain aspects of thinking and learning to which you want to attend. This might be the connections students are making, the questions that get raised, the misconceptions they might have, and so on.

Share Documentation. A key distinction between documentation and display is that documentation is always returned to learners and used to help advance and propel learning. Thus, we must ask ourselves, what is it that I want to document or capture so that we as a class can refer back to it? As my colleagues in the Making Learning Visible project at Harvard Project Zero state, "Sharing concrete documentation with students and teachers anchors the social process of learning and invites multiple perspectives, interpretation, and theory building. The selection of what to share often entails emotional considerations; for example, whether one wants viewers to experience wonder, surprise, or other feelings. Finally, the act of collecting documentation can heighten teachers' and students' sense of directing their own learning" (Krechevsky et al. 2013, p. 59). Sharing documentation isn't merely an act of presenting, but an invitation to analyze, interpret, and evaluate both individual as well as the group's learning, as we saw in Mindset 6 in Case One: The City of Reggio. It is a key means of substantively *interacting* with our students that may also get represented in the physical *environment* either in the short or long term. Here, once again, the documentation becomes formative in shaping the design of future learning.

Use Documentation as Collective Memory. One way in which documentation can be used is to help to download or distribute our intelligence (Pea 1993) within the physical *environment* of the classroom. This is useful because it lessens the cognitive load for learners (Seufert and Brünken 2006). In Cameron Paterson's case, both students' free writing and the group's communal concept map served this purpose. Students' talk with peers during the Micro Lab was facilitated by having notes to which they could refer. The concept map allowed students to see and make connections more easily because they did not have to hold all the information in their heads. In Cameron's case, documentation was planned and strategic. He knew that there were a lot of ideas floating around, many facts, and that making connections between events was a key goal of the lesson. Documentation facilitated this. In other instances, documentation may be emergent. We might recognize that there is just too much information in play and some students are struggling to track it all. Consequently, we might start documenting.

Documentation can also serve as the "memory of the group" with respect to the bigger learning journey of the class (Krechevsky et al. 2013, p. 81). Students will often forget their original questions, confusions, or nascent ideas from the start of a unit as these are replaced with more sophisticated ones as the study progresses. Therefore, capturing these provides opportunities to revisit and celebrate the collective learning. In addition, such memories can be shared to invite others into the learning. This kind of documentation is helpful as we seek to tell a broader, more inclusive, and robust story of learning to families, colleagues, and the community. Documentation of this sort often becomes a part of the physical *environment* of the class or school, the way Nora and Joan's equation did in Case One.

Look for Learning. As stated at the beginning of this chapter, as a society, we have become very accustomed to looking for learning in the outcomes, tests, and products students produce. Learning is seen as an outcome rather than as a continual process of formation. To change this, we must retune our attention beyond products. Where, then, might we see the learning happening? Figure 10.2 identifies five potential areas: 1) in the "Why" of the learning, what is propelling it? 2) in the connections students are making between the new learning, themselves, and their prior knowledge; 3) in the ongoing actions of individuals and the group, 4) in the final works that are produced, and 5) in the students' collective and individual reflections on the learning journey. You will find that when you are not merely monitoring the work but are looking for the learning, the way you *interact* with students will shift.

Get Curious. It will be hard to listen, to question, to make learning and thinking visible if we are not genuinely curious about our students and their learning. Real listening emerges when we take a vigorous interest in the other as poet Alice Duer Miller proclaims. When we have such curiosity, it is easier for us to direct our listening. Where and when will we listen?

Figure 10.2 Looking for learning.

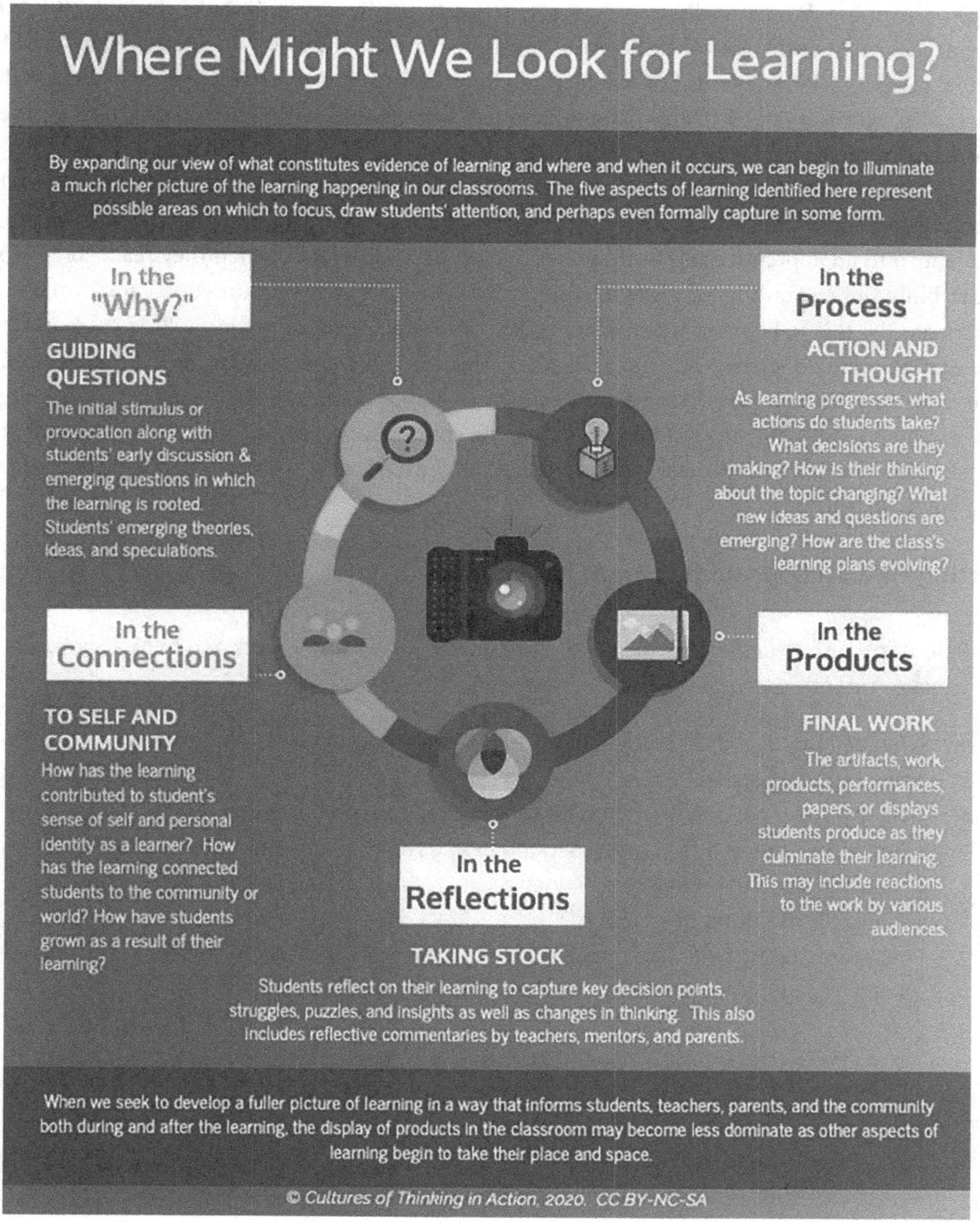

Where Might We Look for Learning?

By expanding our view of what constitutes evidence of learning and where and when it occurs, we can begin to illuminate a much richer picture of the learning happening in our classrooms. The five aspects of learning identified here represent possible areas on which to focus, draw students' attention, and perhaps even formally capture in some form.

In the "Why?"

GUIDING QUESTIONS

The initial stimulus or provocation along with students' early discussion & emerging questions in which the learning is rooted. Students' emerging theories, ideas, and speculations.

In the Process

ACTION AND THOUGHT

As learning progresses, what actions do students take? What decisions are they making? How is their thinking about the topic changing? What new ideas and questions are emerging? How are the class's learning plans evolving?

In the Connections

TO SELF AND COMMUNITY

How has the learning contributed to student's sense of self and personal identity as a learner? How has the learning connected students to the community or world? How have students grown as a result of their learning?

In the Products

FINAL WORK

The artifacts, work products, performances, papers, or displays students produce as they culminate their learning. This may include reactions to the work by various audiences.

In the Reflections

TAKING STOCK

Students reflect on their learning to capture key decision points, struggles, puzzles, and insights as well as changes in thinking. This also includes reflective commentaries by teachers, mentors, and parents.

When we seek to develop a fuller picture of learning in a way that informs students, teachers, parents, and the community both during and after the learning, the display of products in the classroom may become less dominate as other aspects of learning begin to take their place and space.

What are we listening for and trying to understand? Responsive questioning flows from this type of listening. We naturally want to know more, to dig deeper, and make students' thinking visible. Consequently, we ask follow-up questions to probe, push, and further uncover students' thinking. We make use of the facilitative questions and the reflective toss that are discussed in Mindset 8. All of this strengthens our *interactions* with students by making them more substantive and connected.

Model Thinking. I've discussed the importance of *modeling* thinking at several points in this book already (see Mindsets 2 and 5). When we model our thinking through think alouds, we invite students into an apprenticeship in thinking to learn what experts do when they read, solve problems, build understanding, or make decisions. Thus, we demystify thinking in context, which can be messy. For this to be most effective, it needs to be authentic. If we are just telling students what we want them to do it isn't really modeling; it is direction. Modeling requires us to be authentically metacognitive. As my good friend Ellin Keene states in her book *Mosaic of Thought*, "Modeling is an essential, inestimably important step in helping children observe and then use the mental processes used by proficient readers" (Keene 2002, p. 39). I would add that this not only applies to reading but to all learning.

Fitting New Actions with Current Realities

Before you rush to implement the actions you are eager to try, step back and think about what you are currently doing at your school (see Figure 10.3):

➤ What actions, already in place, can be *amplified* and grown by applying some of the principles identified above?
➤ What practices need to be rethought or *modified* considering this mindset?
➤ What do you need to stop doing altogether and *remove* from our repertoire? Why? Does it run counter to this mindset? Is it ineffective? What "moveable barriers" are standing in the way of truly living this mindset?
➤ Finally, are there things that you need to *create*, totally new processes, structures, or actions to begin to put in place?

Figure 10.3 Amplify-Modify-Remove-Create.

Review of Current Practice: What do we need to...

AMPLIFY	MODIFY	REMOVE	CREATE

——— Conclusion: Our Theory of Action ———

What might we expect to see if we operate from the mindset that we need to make learning and thinking visible to tell a broader and richer story of learning? As we have seen, visibility can act as a demystifying practice that invites students, families, and the community into the process. It is an informative practice that enriches our instruction and students' learning. Finally, it is a culture builder in that it facilitates our learning in, from, and with groups more effectively as we become aware of both our own and other's thinking. I offer the following as a theory of action we might use to propel our actions and take stock of our progress:

> *If* **we regularly make our students' thinking and learning visible,** *then* **we will demonstrate the value of learning, gain useful formative assessment data, build community, and engage students as active agents in their own learning.**

Notes

I began this book with an apology to those who might have expected a how-to manual that would walk them step-by-step through how to create a culture of thinking in their schools and classrooms. As I explained, that was never the intent of this book, nor would it have been in keeping with my work on developing cultures of thinking over the last two decades. Nonetheless, I hope I have lived up to the "in action" portion of the title. Looking back chapter by chapter, I count over 50 specific actions that could be useful in advancing a culture of thinking. In addition, there are 20 cases and 20 video links to help you better understand and bring these actions to life. Furthermore, to facilitate your choice of actions best fitting your context, I shared over 20 ways of gathering data to help you reveal the status of these mindsets in your classroom and school. Indeed, an early reader of this book, Julie Landvogt, who is also a good friend and long-time colleague, shared, "The suggestions in each chapter are one of the book's great strengths. They illuminate and make doable the exceedingly valuable theory and research presented to support each mindset. This will be useful both to those who are new to the field and those who are not, but it will be of particular value to those who are leading professional learning in schools."

I agree. Having concrete actions to employ is valuable. In fact, taking action can be an important way to develop new mindsets. We can act ourselves into new ways of being. When chosen wisely, our actions can help us enter a new space of possibility—a space where we can develop new perspectives, greater understanding, and re-create ourselves as teachers. However, to do this we must accompany those actions with reflection. We must interrogate our assumptions and challenge the grammar of schools that too often keep us trapped in the status quo and locked in a pattern of merely adding on a few things here and there, but never actually making substantive change. Only through action coupled with deep reflection is one likely to realize the full power of the actions presented here.

Therefore, my hope is that another great strength you have taken from this book is the importance of dialogue. As you have read, my wish is that two types of dialogue were sparked: an internal dialogue with yourself as well as a dialogue with colleagues. As readers, we often engage in that metacognitive internal dialogue (recall Mindsets 2 and 10) to help us make sense as we read. We think about how ideas might look in our own classrooms, or how a practice extends or builds on to what we are currently doing. We try to make sense of the research findings that may surprise us and perhaps challenge our assumptions about learning and teaching. Think about the research presented on the outside influence of curiosity (Mindset 2), desirable difficulties (Mindset 5), student questioning as a study practice (Mindset 8), and the fact that engagement trumped achievement in the long run (Mindset 9), among others. I've tried to spark additional internal dialogue through the numerous reflective questions offered in each chapter. The idea is that you might start with one or two questions that meet you where you are, but that you will return to the list to continue your reflections as you allow your thoughts to percolate and your actions to take hold.

As important as our internal dialogue is to our transformation and development of mindsets, it is extended and enriched through dialogue with our colleagues. It is here that one will find support for change, growth, and development. To drive this point home, I want to return to a passage from Mindset 6: "Learning and Thinking Are as Much a Collective Enterprise as They Are an Individual Endeavor." Here, I've edited it slightly to help us better see ourselves.

> *Through the process of explaining, defending and discussing with one another, ~~children~~ **teachers** make use of their ~~peers'~~ **colleague's** ideas as "thinking devices" which enable them to reflect on and transform their own thinking (N. M. Webb and Palincsar 1996). When ~~students~~ **educators** learn alongside their ~~more~~ experienced peers, opportunities to "work together, brainstorm possibilities, pool knowledge and insights, conduct collective analyses, critique each other, and draw energy from a common goal" allow for deep learning to take place (Halpern et al. 2013). Through talking to one another, ~~students~~ **educators** co-construct new knowledge and the "cognitive conflicts" that arise serve as the "power driving intellectual development" (Perret-Clermont 1980). Therefore, learning as a collective enterprise builds on or extends, rather than replaces, the work of individuals.*

If you take this passage to heart, it will be important to your long-term learning to seek out and find time to sit beside colleagues in extended, regular dialogue around growing these 10 Mindsets and making them the guiding force of your teaching. Here, once again, the reflective questions provide an opportunity to extend your internal dialogue. So, too, all the Street Data Actions would benefit from a collective analysis of that data to bring in different perspectives and encourage other interpretations. Use the "theory of action" that closes each chapter as a touchstone to which you constantly return. Are you seeing the expected effects? Does the theory of action need modification to better match your actions and expectations?

Such conversations with our colleagues have the potential to move us beyond the simple "How do we implement these new practices?" or the bag-of-tricks approach to professional learning that seeks to seed a few new practices in the short term. We are all way too familiar with this kind of superficial learning typical of traditional professional development. True dialogue with colleagues helps to move us beyond "informational learning" into the deeper and more productive realm of "transformational learning." It is only here that we can begin to challenge the grammar of schools and explore new possibilities. "Transformational learning occurs when people collaborate and learn to think and learn together in relationship. This is not about sharing practice and solving problems (informational learning). It's about finding problems and collective new meanings through dialogue" (Interlead 2019). What we seek, then, in the truest sense, is the creation of a culture of thinking for ourselves (Mindset 1). In such a culture we can explore complex issues from multiple points of view. To do so openly, we must each suspend or at least be willing to confront our assumptions. When we do that, true dialogue opens, and ideas are explored freely in the context of everyone's experience. Consequently, it may be easier to let go of engrained practices and explore new possibilities.

One approach I have been using with schools to spark such dialogue is to engage teachers in a Design Cycle focused on inquiry and action around a chosen mindset (see Figure E.1). Since individuals will gravitate toward, be provoked by, or be poised to begin with different mindsets, I have teachers form like-minded groups to explore a mindset of their choosing. Even though individuals may have a different focus, we all work through the Design Cycle together. We begin by *immersing* ourselves in the mindset through reading and collecting street data. We then progress to the *ideation* phase in which we think broadly about possibilities for action before winnowing those down using the Action Sorts routine to identify our best bets for action. Next begins a long *development* phase not of implementation but trial, experimentation, and prototyping. We don't wait for perfectly planned actions. We jump in and do and learn from the doing. We collect more street data to inform, refine, and polish our actions. Finally, we share and *reflect* on what we have tried, discuss the artifacts from our experimentation, identify key learnings, raise questions, and begin to think about next steps.

Figure E.1 Design Cycle for exploring culture *of* thinking *in* action mindsets.

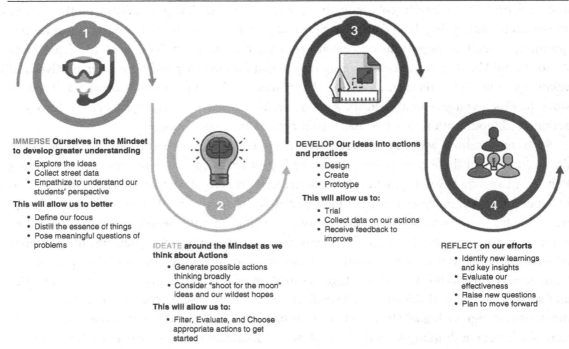

IMMERSE Ourselves in the Mindset to develop greater understanding

- Explore the ideas
- Collect street data
- Empathize to understand our students' perspective

This will allow us to better

- Define our focus
- Distill the essence of things
- Pose meaningful questions of problems

IDEATE around the Mindset as we think about Actions

- Generate possible actions thinking broadly
- Consider "shoot for the moon" ideas and our wildest hopes

This will allow us to:

- Filter, Evaluate, and Choose appropriate actions to get started

DEVELOP Our ideas into actions and practices

- Design
- Create
- Prototype

This will allow us to:

- Trial
- Collect data on our actions
- Receive feedback to improve

REFLECT on our efforts

- Identify new learnings and key insights
- Evaluate our effectiveness
- Raise new questions
- Plan to move forward

Design Cycle for Exploring Culture *of* Thinking *in* Action Mindsets

Whether you choose to engage with others in this way or not, it is often helpful to choose one mindset that really intrigues you or seems just made for you to address at this moment in your teaching career and focus on that as your starting place. You could then use the design cycle individually, with a teammate, or with a larger group of colleagues to the extent it helps to frame your exploration.

Finally, I want to invite you to engage in one final type of dialogue and that is a dialogue with the broader community that is the Worldwide Culture of Thinking Project. As I work with teachers around the world in exploring these mindsets, I am inviting educators to share their stories of learning, promising insights, tales of transformation, and emerging questions with the broader community. You can access some educator stories from the Cultures of Teaching (CoT) Fellows program now being conducted in various cities by scanning the QR code. You will find a "Share Your Learning" button at the bottom of the page that you can use to share with me the story of your learning for possible inclusion on the website. The form provides the options of sharing documents and websites if you have a short story to tell through either video or print.

You also can join the conversation and share your learning and activities on Twitter, Instagram, or TikTok by using the #CoTiAInquiry and tagging @RonRitchhart.

I hope you are as excited as I am about this process of transformation through action and deep reflection. I see it as an opportunity to reclaim and bolster our professionalism and agency as educators, and to make deep and powerful change in our schools and classrooms. It is a process that can take us into the heart of teaching as we examine our beliefs and values. It's a process that helps us uncover our "Why," and from that vantage point we can teach both authentically and powerfully. This process allows us to take a stance as agents of transformation rather than deliverers of information, providing us with a renewed sense of purpose as educators.

Ron Ritchhart

APPENDIX A: SNAPSHOT OBSERVATION PROTOCOL

Goals: A Snapshot Observation is first and foremost an opportunity to reflect on one's teaching practice. It is not an assessment, evaluation, or appraisal of a lesson or a teacher. In a Snapshot Observation, the learning is for the observers (usually a team of 3-6) and occurs primarily through the follow-up discussion immediately after the Snapshot Observation. From observing others, we find ourselves reflecting on our own practice and effectiveness in our own classrooms. The entire Snapshot Observation Protocol is designed to be completed in a single class period so that scheduling and release time are minimized while learning is maximized. Ideally, schools will establish a professional learning culture in which observation is the norm and not seen as threatening.

Protocol:

- *Setup*: One does not need a lot of time to get a feel for the culture of a classroom, and in fact staying too long can put the focus more on the lesson than the culture. A visit of 10 minutes is sufficient. The observed teacher is one who merely opens up their classroom; they are not putting on a specially planned lesson.

- *Focus.* The observing team will focus their observations on the three prompts below around expectations, opportunities, and thinking. Reacquaint yourself with the three prompts before going into the classroom.

- *Observe.* Take nothing with you as you enter the classroom. Paper and note-taking can some-times suggest evaluation. Be as close to a fly on the wall as possible. Enter quietly. Do not make eye contact. Do not greet the class as this will disrupt the lesson. We want students to recog-nize that teachers routinely visit each other's classrooms to learn.

- *Make Notes.* Upon leaving the observation take at least five minutes to gather notes related to the three prompts before discussing. Include anything else that might have caught your attention.

- *Reflect in Dialogue.* The reflective dialogue that follows is loosely centered on the prompts but will include other elements as well. To keep the focus on analysis rather than judgment, it is useful to use the language of "I noticed. . . ." rather than "I liked. . . ." Keep the conversation reflective in nature by focusing on each teacher clarifying for themselves how they are making sense of the teaching. For instance, it is fine to raise an issue, concern, or a positive from the lesson, but conversation should then turn back to oneself: Do I do that? Is that something I struggle with? How might that look in my classroom?

- *Close.* The Snapshot Observation closes by having each observer write a brief (sticky-note sized) thank-you note to the observed teacher, sharing how the observation and subsequent discussion is causing them to think differently about their own teaching. It is important NOT to give feedback and NOT to use "I liked how you . . ." statements. Focus only on your own learning. The group then reads its thank-you notes aloud by way of closing.

Prompts for observation:

1. *Expectations for Work or Learning:* Are the students working, avoiding working, or learning? How do I know? What do I see and notice that tells me this? What other messages about learning/school/teaching are being sent?

2. *Opportunities for Learning:* What are the opportunities for learning here? Are they deep and rich or surface? What am I basing that on? What would take these opportunities to the next level?

3. *Presence of and Support for Thinking:* What's the thinking students are required to do? How is it being promoted and encouraged . . . or being left untapped and unsupported? If routines are being used, how are they facilitating students' deep thinking and rich exploration of content? How might this be enhanced even more? How else was students' thinking made visible?

A note about privacy: To build a culture of thinking for teachers, we need to develop trust and respect while honoring the complexity of teaching and learning. That means we should not gossip or share stories about others' teaching or individual learners that might be disrespectful. When talking with colleagues not participating in a Snapshot Observation, the best approach is to focus only on one's own learning and the discussion. For example, "Our discussion got me thinking more about. . . ."

APPENDIX B: THINKING-ROUTINES–BASED LEARNING LABS

Learning Labs are based off the Japanese Lesson Study. Labs provide an opportunity for teachers to plan a lesson together around the use of a new thinking routine, carry out the co-constructed lesson immediately in a classroom, and discuss their observations of how the planned lesson could be improved, extended, and modified to fit different ages and subjects. As opposed to a "model lesson" in which teachers are observing an expert model a pre-planned lesson, the Learning Lab is focused on the planning aspect of the lesson. This helps teachers understand how to choose a routine, fit it to appropriate content, and make decisions around grouping, documentation, and scaffolding. The process encourages piloting, prototyping, and learning from action. A Lab can vary in size from as small as 3–4 or as large as 10 if the space permits. Lab participants may consist of a small group of teachers from within the school or include teachers from visiting schools. A thinking-routines–based Lab experience generally is conducted in a half day (3 class periods), though the three phases may be scheduled across multiple days.

PLANNING. The host teacher brings with them a couple of options of content their class is ready to explore along with an idea of what learnings, understandings, and thinking they are trying to encourage. If they have an idea of a few thinking routines that might be useful, that can be part of the discussion. Selecting a thinking routine is a big part of the planning session. With the support of a coach or facilitator, the group explores possible thinking routines that might fit the content and understanding goals, exploring the pros and cons of each. Once a routine is selected, the group co-plans the lesson, thinking through how the routine will be introduced, documented, and supported. Issues around grouping students and possible scaffolding are discussed. This is not meant to be a perfect lesson, but a pilot lesson. As such, difficulties, questions, and issues may be identified that the group is curious to find out if they will arise. This helps set a focus for observation

LESSON OBSERVATION. As the host teacher, with the support of the coach/facilitator, carries out the planned lesson, the observing teachers are focused on the lesson itself, paying particular attention to the decisions they made as co-constructors of the lesson and the students' thinking and engagement. Observers are not focused on the teacher's performance. Everyone is trying to understand the new thinking routine being used with a focus on how they might apply the same routine in their classrooms. The facilitator of the Lab may also act as a coach during the lesson as needed. Observers act as documenters of the learning, collecting data that can then be discussed later. They are not evaluators but co-learners with the teacher trying to better understand students' thinking and learning.

DISCUSSION. Observing teachers take five minutes to silently develop their notes from the observation. The host teacher joins the group after handing off classroom responsibilities. Observers share their documentation and discuss its implications. The focus is on understanding the routine and how it helped to promote students' thinking as well as looking at how it might be adapted to other situations or used more effectively in the future. Particular attention is given to the various planning decisions the group made and how they played out. Was the grouping effective? Were the set up and directions effective? Were the decisions around documentation appropriate? Did we correctly anticipate struggles? What did we miss? All participants seek to draw implications for their own teaching from the observation. The group also discusses how the host teacher might build on the observed thinking and learning in subsequent lessons.

APPENDIX C: 4 TYPES OF TEACHER DIALOGUE IN PROFESSIONAL LEARNING CONTEXTS*

DISCONNECTED AND DISTRACTED TALK:

- Teachers' comments are disconnected from each other and the group's collaborative purpose.

- Teachers tell stories and give each other advice: "Here's what I think/do. . . ."

- Comments are authoritative statements or personal stories: "What I do for that is. . . ."

- Talk about teaching is general and there's frequent use of labels and generalizations: "We've got to get those low kids up."

- Claims are asserted as fact with only anecdotal evidence: "That's not developmentally appropriate."

- Teachers are very sure of what they say: "That's not going to work."

- When questions are asked, they are technical, procedural, or personal: "What is it you want us to do?"

- Knowledge and beliefs are fixed: "We've got the curriculum to get through, so we can't. . . ."

- Teachers are congenial with each other, but some don't contribute. Many tune in and out.

- The take-away from these conversations is superficial, informational, or just sound bites.

CONNECTED TALK:

- Comments connect to an immediate task but don't build on other teachers' ideas. Lots of talking about and around. Talk rambling and unfocused at times: "We need to get back on task."

- Ideas are shared as factual or authoritative: "This is a really effective way to do it."

- The dialogue is descriptive or evaluative with frequent use of labels and generalizations: "That's really good, it will keep the boys engaged."

- Anecdotal evidence is used to justify claims. "Well in my classroom. . . ."

*Adapted from Nelson, T.M., Slavit, D., and Deuel, A. (2012, August). Two dimensions of an inquiry stance toward student-learning data. *Teachers College Record* 114(8): 1–42.

- Teachers occasionally express uncertainty or curiosity: "Why might that be happening?"
- Questions are procedural, technical, or for clarification: "So what is our plan?"
- Focus on activities and actions rather than outcomes and effects: "Great, so we have all our activities for that unit."
- Teachers are more or less congenial, with some members contributing only occasionally.
- The take-away is ideas and activities.

EXPLORATORY TALK:

- Teachers build on each others' ideas and pursue common meaning-making and alternatives: "Exploring Julie's idea a bit further. . . ."
- Teachers reach out to each other for genuine dialogue asking probing questions: "I think a lot of their misconceptions are quite revealing."
- Evidence is shared, but it may be weak or unclear; questions are raised: "I'm not sure what to make of these responses."
- There's a noticeable element of wondering and uncertainty: "Why do you think the students reacted that way?"
- Authentic questions emerge; meanings, assumptions, beliefs, values are raised but not always pursued: "How can we get them to go more deeply in their responses?"
- Links to instruction are made: "If we activate their prior knowledge, I think we can then identify potential areas to be developed further."
- Knowledge and beliefs are occasionally questioned and reexamined: "I'm really finding that when I step back and talk less, students have much more to say that I expected."
- Teachers are congenial, and most contribute in discussions.
- The take-away is understanding and new questions.

INQUIRY-BASED TALK:

- Teachers' comments build on each other and dialogue spans meetings.
- Teachers critique each other; alternatives are posed and examined: "Our conversations last meeting really inspired me to reexamine how I was presenting information."
- Teachers' comments are tentative and invite dialogue: "I tried it as we discussed, but I wasn't sure how to push to the next level—what did other people find?"

- Descriptions support analysis: "What I am noticing is lots of connecting language that I think shows students really beginning to synthesize."

- Evidence is sought, provided, and critically analyzed by the group, and new questions are raised: "I think we need to start documenting the conversations the small groups are having to better understand. . . ."

- Teachers hypothesize; group members often use open or conditional statements like, "I wonder," "Maybe," and "Do you think?"

- Authentic questions emerge from artifacts; meanings, assumptions, beliefs, and values are examined: "I think my meaning of 'rigor' is really beginning to shift."

- Links to instructional practices are critically examined.

- Knowledge and beliefs are regularly questioned and examined: "I'm rethinking some of my ideas about what it means to teach inquiry."

- Teachers are collegial with each other, and, over time, all participants contribute.

- The take-away is emerging theories, deep understanding, appreciation of complexity.

APPENDIX D: CULTURE MESSAGING GHOST WALK*

The Ghost Walk is a structured process for a collaborative walk-through of a school when classes are not in session. It can be done by pairs or by a larger group. It is often done by critical friends from outside a school who can look at the physical environment with fresh eyes. If done within a school, it is often advised that teachers do not visit their own team, department, or grade level so that they might have an easier time seeing things more objectively.

1. The group brainstorms evidence that it would expect to see in a school or classroom where creating a culture of thinking is the focus. Chart these expectations. (10 minutes)

2. The group walks through the building silently in pairs or triads, making note of evidence they observe that supports *or* doesn't support the focus on a culture of thinking. For instance, there may be messages being sent about work and compliance as opposed to learning and thinking. (20–30 minutes)

3. The group returns to the meeting room and shares its observations, which are charted next to its expectations. In sharing observations, names of teachers, departments, and classrooms should be avoided. The goal is to get a broad sense of messaging across the school and not single out individuals. The group discusses their findings, looking for any patterns or surprises. Much of the discussion will be to try to uncover what message is being sent to students from what was visible in the school. (10 minutes)

4. The group turns its attention to what surprised, challenged, pushed, and/or added to their thinking about creating a culture of thinking. (5 minutes)

5. Debrief the process and make plans to do again if appropriate.

---

*Adapted by Ron Ritchhart from the "Collaborative Ghost Walk" protocol developed by Debbie Bambinon.

APPENDIX E

In this class period we spent **_MOST_** of our time. . . .

Date: _____ Class Period: _____ Subject: _____

	Select the three actions the class spent the most time doing. Rank your choices 1, 2, and 3. #1 is what the class spent the most time doing, then #2 for the next most, and then #3.
	Looking closely at things, describing them, noticing details, or detecting patterns.
	Building our own explanations, theories, hypotheses, or interpretations.
	Reasoning with evidence and supporting our ideas with facts and reasons.
	Wondering, raising issues, and showing curiosity about what we are studying.
	Making connections between different things, to the world, or to our own lives.
	Looking at things from different perspectives and points of view to see things in a new way.
	Identifying the central or core ideas, forming conclusions, or capturing the essence of things.
	Digging deeply into a topic to uncover mysteries, complexities, and challenges.
	Organizing and pulling together ideas, information, and notes to make sense of them.
	Reflecting on where we are in our learning and understanding to determine where to go next.
	Using and applying our learning to solve new problems or create something original.
	Reviewing and going over information from the readings or previous class work.
	Reading, listening, or getting new information about the topic we are studying.
	Practicing the skills and procedures the class has already learned.

In this class, I was really pushed to think *(CIRCLE ONE)*

(NOT AT ALL)   *(A LITTLE)*   *(SOME)*   *(A LOT)*

As a learner, it would have helped me if *I* had . . .

_____

_____

As a learner, it would have helped me if the ***teacher*** had . . .

_____

_____

APPENDIX F: FUNCTIONING IN GROUPS*

As you listen in on and observe groups, note where and when any group member is engaged in any of the following actions. Record the group member's initials in the appropriate box. You might also want to record the time at which the action took place. Note: The bottom row is unproductive behaviors that sometimes occur in groups.

Initiating—convening the group, suggesting procedures, changing direction, providing new energy and ideas.	**Seeking information or opinions**—requesting facts, preferences, suggestions, or ideas.	**Giving information or opinions**—providing facts, data, information from research or experience.	**Questioning**—stepping back and challenging the group or asking questions about the task.
Clarifying—interpreting ideas or suggestions, clearing up confusions, defining terms or asking others to clarify.	**Connecting**—drawing connections among contributions or linking up ideas.	**Recording**—helping to track the group's ideas and conversation in some concrete way.	**Summarizing**—putting contributions into a pattern, while adding no new information.

---

*Ron Ritchhart 2021 / https://www.cultures-of-thinking.org/6-collective-learning / last accessed Feb 14, 2023.

Supporting—being encouraging & responsive to others through gestures, smiles, or making eye contact.	**Revising**—revising or modifying one's initial statements based on new information or increased understanding.	**Observing Process**—noticing & commenting on the dynamics of the group.	**Mediating**—recognizing disagreements & figuring out what is behind them. Accommodating other values, views & approaches.
Reconciling—reconciling disagreements. Emphasizing shared views among members can reduce tension.	**Compromising**—yielding a position or modifying opinions. This can help move the group forward.	**Making a personal comment**—occasional personal comments as they relate to the work may strengthen a group.	**Humor**—good-natured comments to relieve tension, deal with dominating participants, or provide a break from concentration.
Dominating or reluctant participants—talking too often, asserting superiority, or not letting others finish.	**Digressions and tangents**—too many interesting side stories can be obstacles to group progress.	**Rush to work**—a lack of pertinence, pressuring the group to move on before others are ready.	**Feuds**—conflicts carried over into the group that impede its work.

APPENDIX G: SUCCESS ANALYSIS PROTOCOL: POWERFUL LEARNING OPPORTUNITIES*

1. **Identify a success.** (1 minute)

   Do a mental review of the lessons you have taught over the last year. Identify an example of a Powerful Learning Opportunity from your own teaching. This should be an instance where _students were highly engaged, actively involved in thinking, and building a robust understanding_ of the topic at hand. Most likely, this was a teaching occasion where you walked away wishing every class could be just like that.

2. **Reflect in writing.** (4 minutes)

   Describe the Powerful Learning Opportunity you identified in writing. Be as specific as you can about what was planned, what happened, how you and students responded, and so on. How was this experience different from other episodes of teaching you have had? Name those qualities, actions, or elements.

Steps 3–6 are repeated until all members of the group have had a turn. Each round of sharing should not exceed 15 minutes.

3. **Share the success.** (3–4 minutes)

   The first person shares the story of the Powerful Learning Opportunity they identified.

4. **Clarifying questions.** (1–2 minutes)

   The listeners ask clarifying questions about the event. Clarifying questions are short, focused questions designed to elicit missing details and background information about the event. Generally, they can be answered in a sentence or less. Clarifying questions benefit the question asker.

5. **Probing questions.** (3–4 minutes)

   The listeners ask probing questions about the event. Probing questions are designed to get the presenter to reflect on, elaborate on, and build a greater understanding of the event. Good probing questions require introspection and lead to insights. Probing questions benefit the responder.

---

*Adapted from a series of protocols by the School Reform Initiative.

6. **Recording of criteria.** (2–3 minutes)

The group reflects together on the vignette just shared and collectively extrapolates, from the story and questioning, to identify the criteria or qualities of the event that seemed most important to its success. What were the ingredients of success? These are recorded on a whiteboard or piece of chart paper. As each group member shares, new criteria are added to the list.

The group holds a final reflection after all group members have shared.

7. **Group reflection.** (5 minutes)

After all group members have shared, the group reflects on all the criteria/qualities of Powerful Learning Opportunities that the group identified. Are the criteria/qualities clear? Can they be made more specific and action oriented so as to be more helpful in planning future opportunities for learning? The group then discusses how each criteria/quality might be applied to their teaching. Finally, the group identifies their top, best-bets-for-success criteria.

APPENDIX H: THE SLICE PROTOCOL

Step 1. Determine the Slice focus. The focus identifies the particular set of opportunities you wish to examine and identifies a time period. For instance, your Slice might focus on all the homework assignments students were given at a grade level over a week, all the tasks/activities done by students during second period at your school, all the summative assessments given first term in your department, all the long-term projects students in 7th grade experience, the student work produced from a task, or other targeted area you would like to understand better. In whatever manner it is focused, you will be gathering data within that single domain.

Step 2. Identify an analytical frame. This can be general: What do these assignment/tasks reveal about the kinds of opportunities we are providing students? Or more focused: To what extent are our students asked to give "reproductive versus original" responses to our assignments? A bit more fine grained, one might look at a task's cognitive demand using Webb's Depth of Knowledge levels (Webb 2002):

1. Recall and Reproductive
2. Basic Application of Skills/Concepts
3. Strategic Thinking—involving reasoning, planning, and decision making
4. Extended Thinking—involving investigation, application, problem solving, or research

Your question then might be, "What does this work reveal about the cognitive demands and level of challenge we are providing students?" The four design elements presented in Figure 9.1 could also be used as a frame for analysis. Your question then might be, "What does this sample of work reveal about how we are incorporating the four elements of powerful learning opportunities?"

Step 3. Analyze the work. The number of tasks being examined and the complexity of the analytic frame will determine the time needed. Focusing on just homework assignments from your class over a week, and looking at the response required (original or reproductive), might only take 30 minutes. However, focusing on all the summative assessments for a term across a school analyzing for cognitive demand may require a full day. Doing the analysis with a partner often yields greater insight.

Step 4. Noticings, questions, and insights. Whether done individually or with a partner, you will want to quantify your findings (e.g., researchers typically have found 80% of tasks call for only reproductive responses). Name and then step back from your findings:

- Is this what you expected?
- What questions does the analysis raise?
- What might it look like to move forward?

If you are doing this as a whole school, it is likely people saw different things or have different interpretations about what they saw. Consequently, you may want to start the discussion with sharing broad noticings, and then move into discussing the guiding question (see Step 2) along with supporting evidence before discussing next steps.

APPENDIX I: VISIBILITY GHOST WALK*

The Ghost Walk is a structured process for a collaborative walk-through of a school when classes are not in session. It can be done by pairs or by a larger group. It is often done by critical friends from outside a school who can look at the physical environment with fresh eyes. If done within a school, it is often advised that teachers do not visit their own team, department, or grade level so that they might have an easier time seeing things objectively.

1. Review what you would expect to see in a school or classroom focused on making thinking and learning visible. You may want to return to your responses from the "Constructing our Vision" section in Mindset 10. It is sometimes useful to list these from the group on one-half of a whiteboard. (10 minutes)

2. The group walks through the building silently in pairs or triads, making note of evidence that supports *or* doesn't support the focus on making learning and thinking visible. This might include evidence of the process of thinking and learning over just products, the extent walls are filled with display or documentation, products or process focus, current and ongoing learning versus past or static displays, or student voice/choice or teacher's voice. (20–30 minutes)

3. The group returns to the meeting room and shares observations, charting them next to what group members expected to see. Names of teachers, departments, and classrooms are avoided. The goal is to get a broad sense of what is noticeable across the school and not to single out individuals. The group discusses the findings, looking for patterns. (10 minutes)

4. The group turns its attention to what surprised, challenged, pushed, and/or added to its thinking about making learning and thinking visible. (5 minutes)

5. Debrief the process and make plans to repeat if appropriate. (5 minutes)

---

*Adapted by Ron Ritchhart from the "Collaborative Ghost Walk" protocol developed by Debbie Bambino.

MINDSET 2

1. For an explanation of the contributions of these various perspectives, see Ritchhart 2002.
2. Throughout this book, I cite Hattie and his meta-analysis. In doing so, I report the effect sizes he has identified for particular interventions. For readers unfamiliar with effect sizes, the idea is to create a common metric so that effects of various interventions can be easily compared. Thus, an effect of 0.69 is larger than an effect of 0.42. Hattie considers effect sizes above 0.4 to be worth consideration. Effect sizes are calculated comparing the mean outcome of one group over that of another (or pre-test over post-test) and then dividing by the standard deviation (the spread or distribution) of the group.

MINDSET 3

1. This case draws on Trevor's account as reported in his book *Inquiry Mindset: Assessment Edition* (MacKenzie 2021) as well as from personal correspondence.

MINDSET 5

1. One area that might not require thinking in the traditional sense is motor learning. Physical skills tend to accumulate without much thought and are even hard to identify how we learned them after the fact. Furthermore, such learning doesn't reside in the hippocampus, an area of the brain associated with building memory. The second area is perceptual intuition, learning to discriminate between different sets of things such as art movements, types of skin rashes, different types of mushrooms, dinosaurs, and so on. We see this exhibited in any expert that

just instantly can look at something and know what is going on. While such learning can be done thoughtfully by using pattern recognition, close observation, pattern detection, and so on, studies have shown that the same learning can be done through "Perceptual Learning or Training Modules." See the book *How We Learn: The Surprising Truth about When, Where, and Why It Happens* by Benedict Carey (2015) for more information on this type of learning.

2. Hattie continually updates his effect sizes based on new studies and data, so these change over time with new data.

3. This case is excerpted, in part, from the account provided in the book *In Search of Deeper Learning: The Quest to Remake the American High School* (Mehta and Fine 2019).

MINDSET 7

1. This case was drawn from a blog series on teaching 21st-century skills by The Brookings Institute (Mills 2017). Direct quotes are taken from the blog post, though the write-up presented here is my own words and with my own commentary. Another version of this blog can be found here and served as a secondary source: https://taraandkate.wordpress.com/2016/12/27/when-met-with-struggle-focus-on-strategies/#more-2139. Readers are directed there for more information.

2. This case was constructed through personal conversation with Mark Church over years of our working together. Specifics and details were added through personal communication (Church 2022).

MINDSET 8

1. This case comes from research I did while writing the book *Intellectual Character* (Ritchhart 2002), during which I spent extensive time in Heather's classroom both observing and interviewing her.

2. This case is adapted from an article written by co-directors of the Right Question Institute that appeared in Educational Leadership (Rothstein 2015) as well as other writings about the QFT itself (Rothstein 2011). The wording and commentary are my own, though the quotes from students and teachers come from the original article.

MINDSET 9

1. This case comes from the article "Children Are Citizens: The Everyday and the Razzle-Dazzle" (Krechevsky, Mardell, Filippini, and Tedeschi 2016) and personal correspondence with Mara Krechevsky.

2. The following list of "opportunities" is adapted from the American Institute for Research's evaluation of Deeper Learning Network Schools (Zeiser, Taylor, Rickles, Garet, and Segeritz 2014).

MINDSET 10

1. Some readers will be familiar with John Hattie's book *Visible Learning* (2009), a book I have referenced in almost every chapter to identify the effects of various teaching practices on student performance. This is valuable and useful research. However, in my opinion, Hattie is not actually making learning visible. Too often, he is engaging in the same trope of equating learning with test scores that I have called out as narrow and a "single story." Hattie's goal was to create a "continuum of achievement effects," which are almost always measured by outcomes on tests (p. 7). Thus, what he really has done is make the effects of teaching practices on students' measured outcomes visible. This is a huge contribution to the field to be sure, but quite different from illuminating the processes of learning and thinking we are exploring in this chapter.

REFERENCES

Abernathy, D.J. (1999). A chat with Chris Argyris. *Training & Development* 53(5): 80–85.

Adichie, C.N. (2009). The danger of a single story. TED Talk.

Aguiar, O.G., Mortimer, E.F., and Scott, P. (2010). Learning from and responding to students' questions: The authoritative and dialogic tension. *Journal of Research in Science Teaching: The Official Journal of the National Association for Research in Science Teaching* 47(2): 174–193.

Allen, D., and Blythe, T. (2015). *Facilitating for Learning: Tools for Teacher Groups of All Kinds*. Teachers College Press.

Allen, D., Blythe, T., Dichter, A., and Lynch, T. (2018). *Protocols in the Classroom: Tools to Help Students Read, Write, Think, & Collaborate*. Teachers College Press.

Alper, L., Fendel, D., Fraser, S., and Resek, D. (1997). Designing a high school mathematics curriculum for all students. *American Journal of Education* 106(1): 148–178.

Anderson, M. (2022). *How social-emotional learning became a frontline in the battle against CRT*. Retrieved from https://www.npr.org/2022/09/26/1124082878/how-social-emotional-learning-became-a-frontline-in-the-battle-against-crt.

Anfara Jr., V.A., Evans, K.R., and Lester, J.N. (2013). Restorative justice in education: What we know so far. *Middle School Journal* 44(5): 57–63.

Angus, M., McDonald, T., Ormond, C., Rybarcyk, R., Taylor, A., and Winterton, A. (2009). The Pipeline Project: trajectories of classroom behaviour and academic progress: A study of engagement with learning.

Archer, L. (2012). Between authenticity and pretension: parents', pupils' and young professionals' negotiations of minority ethnic middle-class identity. *The Sociological Review* 60(1): 129–148.

Arnstine, D. (1995). *Democracy and the Arts of Schooling*. Albany: State University of New York Press.

Ashby, F.G., and Isen, A.M. (1999). A neuropsychological theory of positive affect and its influence on cognition. *Psychological Review* 106(3): 529.

Atkin, J. (2019). Teaching in contemporary learning spaces. Retrieved from https://www.teachermagazine.com/au_en/articles/teaching-in-contemporary-learning-spaces.

Baehr, J. (2011). *The Inquiring Mind: On Intellectual Virtues and Virtue Epistemology.* OUP Oxford.

Baehr, J. (2013). Educating for intellectual virtues: From theory to practice. *Journal of Philosophy of Education* 47(2): 248–262.

Bambino, D. (2021). Collaborative Ghost Walk. Retrieved from https://www.schoolreforminitiative.org/download/collaborative-ghost-walk/.

Banilower, E.R., Boyd, S.E., Pasley, J.D., and Weiss, I.R. (2006). Lessons from a decade of mathematics and science reform: A capstone report for the local systemic change through Teacher Enhancement Initiative. Horizon Research, Inc. (NJ1).

Barnett, T., Lawless, B., Kim, H., and Vista, A. (2017). Complementary strategies for teaching collaboration and critical thinking skills. *Education Plus Development: Skills for a Changing World.* Retrieved from https://www.brookings.edu/blog/education-plus-development/2017/12/12/complementary-strategies-for-teaching-collaboration-and-critical-thinking-skills/.

Barron, B. (2003). When smart groups fail. *The Journal of the Learning Sciences* 12(3): 307–359.

Battistich, V., Schaps, E., and Wilson, N. (2004). Effects of an elementary school intervention on students' "connectedness" to school and social adjustment during middle school. *Journal of Primary Prevention* 24(3): 243–262.

Baumeister, R.F., and Leary, M.R. (2017). The need to belong: Desire for interpersonal attachments as a fundamental human motivation. *Interpersonal Development*, 57–89.

Baumeister, R.F., Twenge, J.M., and Nuss, C.K. (2002). Effects of social exclusion on cognitive processes: anticipated aloneness reduces intelligent thought. *Journal of Personality and Social Psychology* 83(4):817.

Beier, Y. (2019). *Conscious Collaboration.* A Conversation with Dr. Paul Zak—The Neuroscience of Trust. Retrieved from https://collaborative-coaching.com.

Bereiter, C., and Scardamalia, M. (1989). Intentional learning as a goal of instruction. *Knowing, Learning, and Instruction: Essays in Honor of Robert Glaser*, 361–392.

Berger, G. (2016). Data reveals the most in-demand soft skills among candidates. Retrieved from https://www.linkedin.com/business/talent/blog/talent-strategy/most-indemand-soft-skills.

Berger, R., Gardner, H., Meier, D., Sizer, T.R., and Lieberman, A. (2003). *An Ethic of Excellence: Building a Culture of Craftsmanship with Students.* Heinemann: Portsmouth, NH.

Berger, W. (2014). *A More Beautiful Question: The Power of Inquiry to Spark Breakthrough Ideas*. Bloomsbury Publishing USA.

Berkowitz, M.W., and Bier, M.C. (2005). What works in character education: A research-driven guide for educators. Washington, D.C.: Character Education Partnership.

Berkowitz, M.W., Bier, M.C., and McCauley, B. (2016). Effective features and practices that support character development. In National Academies of Sciences, Engineering, and Medicine Workshop on Defining and Measuring Character and Character Education, July.

Bjork, R.A. (1975). Retrieval as a memory modifier: An interpretation of negative recency and related phenomena. *Information Processing and Cognition: The Loyola Symposium*. R.L. Solso (ed.). Lawrence Erlbaum: 123–144.

Bjork, R.A. (2013). Desirable difficulties perspective on learning. *Encyclopedia of the Mind* 4: 134–146.

Bjork, R. (2015). The critical distinction between learning and performance. YouTube.com, LastingLearning.com. Retrieved from https://www.youtube.com/watch?v=K0ZxGGN4R90.

Bjork, R.A., and Bjork, E.L. (2020). Desirable difficulties in theory and practice. *Journal of Applied Research in Memory and Cognition* 9(4): 475.

Blazar, D., and Pollard, C. (2022). Challenges and tradeoffs of "good" teaching: The pursuit of multiple educational outcomes.

Bloom, P. (2001). Précis of how children learn the meanings of words. *Behavioral and Brain Sciences* 24(6): 1095–1103.

Blythe, T., and Associates. (1998). *The Teaching for Understanding Guide*. San Francisco: Jossey-Bass.

Boaler, J. (2006). Promoting respectful learning. *Educational Leadership* 63(5): 74.

Boaler, J. (2008). Promoting "relational equity" and high mathematics achievement through an innovative mixed-ability approach. *British Educational Research Journal* 34(2): 167–194.

Boaler, J. (2019). Why struggle is essential for the brain—and our lives. *Voices: Learning Research*. Retrieved from https://www.edsurge.com/news/2019-10-28-why-struggle-is-essential-for-the-brain-and-our-lives.

Boix Mansilla, V., and Gardner, H. (1998). What are the qualities of understanding. *Teaching for Understanding*, 161–196.

Borko, H. (2004). Professional development and teacher learning: Mapping the terrain. *Educational Researcher* 33(8): 3–15.

Brenneman, R. (2016). Gallup student poll finds engagement in school dropping by grade level. *Education Week* 35(25): 6.

Briggs, S. (2017). Why curiosity is essential to motivation. Retrieved from https://www.opencolleges.edu.au/informed/features/curiosity-essential-motivation/.

Brookfield, S.D. (2006). *The Skillful Teacher: On Technique, Trust, and Responsiveness in the Classroom*. Jossey-Bass.

Broom, C. (2015). Empowering students: Pedagogy that benefits educators and learners. *Citizenship, Social and Economics Education* 14(2): 79–86.

Brown, G. (2002). Student beliefs about learning: New Zealand students in year 11. *Academic Exchange Quarterly* 6(1): 110–114.

Bruner, J. (1996). *The Culture of Education*. Cambridge, MA: Harvard University Press.

Bruner, J.S. (1973). *Beyond the Information Given: Studies in the Psychology of Knowing*. WW Norton.

Bullock, K. (2011). International Baccalaureate learner profile: Literature review. Retrieved from https://www.ibo.org/globalassets/new-structure/research/pdfs/iblearnerprofileeng.pdf.

Burgess, S., Rawal, S., and Taylor, E.S. (2021). Teacher peer observation and student test scores: Evidence from a field experiment in English secondary schools. *Journal of Labor Economics* 39(4): 1155–1186.

Busching, B.A., and Slesinger, B.A. (1995). Authentic questions: What do they look like? Where do they lead? *Language Arts* 72(5): 341–351.

Buschkuehl, M. (2018). What are schemas? Retrieved from https://blog.mindresearch.org/blog/schema-in-education.

Butler, J. (1999). *Gender Trouble: Feminism and the Subversion of Identity*. Routledge.

Calderhead, J. (1996). Teachers: Beliefs and knowledge. In: *Handbook of Educational Psychology* (Eds. D.C. Berliner and R.C. Calfee), 709–725. New York: Macmillan.

Campbell, C. (2018). Developing teacher leadership and collaborative professionalism to flip the system: Reflections from Canada. In: *Flip the System Australia*, 74–84. Routledge.

Caram, C.A., and Davis, P.B. (2005). Inviting student engagement with questioning. *Kappa Delta Pi Record* 42(1): 19–23.

Carey, B. (2015). *How We Learn: The Surprising Truth about When, Where, and Why It Happens*. Random House Trade Paperbacks.

Carlone, H.B., Huffling, L.D., Tomasek, T., Hegedus, T.A., Matthews, C.E., Allen, M.H., and Ash, M.C. (2015). "Unthinkable" Selves: Identity boundary work in a summer field ecology enrichment program for diverse youth. *International Journal of Science Education* 37(10): 1524–1546.

Carlsen, W.S. (1991). Questioning in classrooms: A sociolinguistic perspective. *Review of Educational Research* 61(2): 157–178.

Carpenter, S.M., Peters, E., Västfjäll, D., and Isen, A.M. (2013). Positive feelings facilitate working memory and complex decision making among older adults. *Cognition & Emotion* 27(1): 184–192.

Carr, P.B., and Walton, G.M. (2014). Cues of working together fuel intrinsic motivation. *Journal of Experimental Social Psychology* 53: 169–184.

Carter, C.J. (1997). Why reciprocal teaching? *Educational Leadership* 54: 64–69.

Casner-Lotto, J., and Barrington, L. (2006). Are they really ready to work? Partnership for 21st Century Skills, Retrieved from https://files.eric.ed.gov/fulltext/ED519465.pdf.

Cheeseman, J., Clarke, D., Roche, A., and Walker, N. (2016). Introducing challenging tasks: Inviting and clarifying without explaining and demonstrating. *Australian Primary Mathematics Classroom* 21(3): 3–6.

Chen, C.-H., and Yang, Y.-C. (2019). Revisiting the effects of project-based learning on students' academic achievement: A meta-analysis investigating moderators. *Educational Research Review* 26: 71–81.

Chennamaneni, A., and Teng, J.T. (2011). An integrated framework for effective tacit knowledge transfer. AISeL. AMCIS 2011 Proceedings.

Chiu, C.W. (1998). Synthesizing metacognitive interventions: What training characteristics can improve reading performance? Paper presented at the Annual Meeting of the American Educational Research Association. San Diego.

Choppin, J. (2011). The impact of professional noticing on teachers' adaptations of challenging tasks. *Mathematical Thinking and Learning* 13(3): 175–197.

Chouinard, M.M., Harris, P.L., and Maratsos, M.P. (2007). Children's questions: A mechanism for cognitive development. *Monographs of the Society for Research in Child Development*, i–129.

Christenson, S., Reschly, A.L., and Wylie, C. (2012). *Handbook of Research on Student Engagement* (Vol. 840). Springer.

Christoph, J.N., and Nystrand, M. (2001). Taking risks, negotiating relationships: One teacher's transition toward a dialogic classroom. *Research in the Teaching of English*, 249–286.

City, E.A., Elmore, R.F., Fiarman, S.E., and Teitel, L. (2009). *Instructional Rounds in Education: A Network Approach to Improving Teaching and Learning*. Cambridge, MA: Harvard Educational Publishing Group.

Claxton, G., Chambers, M., Powell, G., and Lucas, B. (2011). *The Learning Powered School: Pioneering 21st Century Education*. Bristol: TLO Limited.

Cobb, P., and Jackson, K. (2011). Towards an empirically grounded theory of action for improving the quality of mathematics teaching at scale. *Mathematics Teacher Education and Development* 13(1): 6–33.

Cochran-Smith, M., and Lytle, S. (1999). Relationships of knowledge and practice: Teacher learning in communities. *Review of Research in Education* 24: 249–305. Retrieved from http://www.jstor.org/stable/1167272.

Cochran-Smith, M., and Lytle, S.L. (2015). *Inquiry as Stance: Practitioner Research for the Next Generation*: Teachers College Press.

Coe, R., Rauch, C., Kime, S., and Singleton, D. (2020). *Great Teaching Toolkit: Evidence Review*. Cambridge Assessment International Education. Retrieved from https://bibliotecadigital.mineduc.cl/bitstream/handle/20.500.12365/17347/33%20Great%20teaching%20toolkit%20evidence%20review.pdf?sequence=1.

Coggshall, J.G., Rasmussen, C., Colton, A., Milton, J., and Jacques, C. (2012). Generating teaching effectiveness: The role of job-embedded professional learning in teacher evaluation. Research & Policy Brief. *National Comprehensive Center for Teacher Quality*.

Cohen, D.K., and Ball, D.L. (2000). Instructional innovation: Reconsidering the story. In *Annual Meeting of the American Educational Research Association*, New Orleans.

Cohen, D.K., and Mehta, J.D. (2017). Why reform sometimes succeeds: Understanding the conditions that produce reforms that last. *American Educational Research Journal* 54(4): 644–690.

Collins, A., Brown, J.S., and Holum, A. (1991). Cognitive apprenticeship: Making thinking visible. *American Educator,* Winter.

Comer, J.P. (1993). *School Power: Implications of an Intervention Project*. Free Press.

Cook, C.R., Fiat, A., Larson, M., Daikos, C., Slemrod, T., Holland, E.A., Thayer, A.J., Renshaw, T. (2018). Positive greetings at the door: Evaluation of a low-cost, high-yield proactive classroom management strategy. *Journal of Positive Behavior Interventions* 20(3): 149–159.

Cornelius-White, J. (2007). Learner-centered teacher-student relationships are effective: A meta-analysis. *Review of Educational Research* 77(1): 113–143. doi:10.2307/4624889.

Costa, A.L., and Kallick, B. (2002). *Habits of Mind* (Vol. I–IV). Alexandria, VA: Association for Supervision and Curriculum Development.

Covey, S. (1989). *The Seven Habits of Highly Effective People*. New York: Simon and Schuster.

Cox, A. (2020). Why you shouldn't always just "Google it." Retrieved from https://www.linkedin.com/pulse/why-you-shouldnt-always-just-google-alistair-cox.

Croft, A., Coggshall, J.G., Dolan, M., and Powers, E. (2010). Job-embedded professional development: What it is, who is responsible, and how to get it done well. Issue Brief. *National Comprehensive Center for Teacher Quality*.

Crosswhite, F.J., J.A. Dossey, and S.M. Frye (1989). NCTM standards for school mathematics: Visions for implementation. *The Arithmetic Teacher* 37(3): 55–60.

Crouch, C.H., and Mazur, E. (2001). Peer instruction: Ten years of experience and results. *American Journal of Physics* 69(9): 970–977.

Cuban, L. (2019). Challenging the grammar of schooling. Retrieved from https://larrycuban .wordpress.com/2019/05/06/challenging-the-grammar-of-schooling-part-2/.

Cuban, L. (2022). Two teaching traditions: Which is most effective in getting students to learn? (Part 1). Retrieved from https://larrycuban.wordpress.com/2022/02/03/two-teaching-traditions-which-is-most-effective-in-getting-students-to-learn/.

Cushman, K. (1997). A "vertical slice" of student work. *Horace* 13(2). Retrieved from http://essentialschools.org/horace-issues/sampling-a-vertical-slice-of-student-work/.

Cushman, K. (2005). *Fires in the Bathroom: Advice for Teachers from High School Students*. The New Press.

Cushman, K. (2014). Conditions for motivated learning. *Phi Delta Kappan* 95(8): 18–22.

Cushman, K., and Rogers, L. (2009). *Fires in the Middle School Bathroom: Advice for Teachers from Middle Schoolers*. The New Press.

Dajani, M. (2016). Using thinking routines as a pedagogy for teaching English as a second language in Palestine. *Journal of Educational Research and Practice* 6(1): 1–18.

Damon, W. (2008). *The Path to Purpose: Helping Our Children Find Their Calling in Life*. Simon and Schuster.

Damon, W., and Malin, H. (2020). The development of purpose. *The Oxford Handbook of Moral Development: An Interdisciplinary Perspective*, 110.

Dana-Center. (2020). Culture of learning. *Learning and the Adolescent Mind*. Retrieved from http://learningandtheadolescentmind.org/ideas_community.html.

Darling-Hammond, L., Burns, D., Campbell, C., Goodwin, A.L., Hammerness, K., Low, E.-L., . . . Zeichner, K. (2017). *Empowered Educators: How High-Performing Systems Shape Teaching Quality around the World*. John Wiley & Sons.

Dart, B.C., Burnett, P.C., Purdie, N., Boulton-Lewis, G., Campbell, J., and Smith, D. (2000). Students' conceptions of learning, the classroom environment, and approaches to learning. *The Journal of Educational Research* 93(4): 262–270.

Davey, C.G., Allen, N.B., Harrison, B.J., Dwyer, D.B., and Yücel, M. (2010). Being liked activates primary reward and midline self-related brain regions. *Human Brain Mapping* 31(4): 660–668.

Deci, E.L. (1995). *Why We Do What We Do: Understanding Self-Motivation.* New York: G. P. Putnam's Sons.

Department of Education and Training (2017). State of Victoria, Australia High Impact Teaching Strategies Excellence in Teaching and Learning. Retrieved from: https://www.education.vic.gov.au/Documents/school/teachers/management/highimpactteachingstrat.pdf.

Deresiewicz, W. (2015). *Excellent Sheep: The Miseducation of the American Elite and the Way to a Meaningful Life.* Simon and Schuster.

Derman-Sparks, L., and Moore, E., (2016). Two teachers look back: The Ypsilanti Perry Preschool, Part I. *YC Young Children* 71(4), 82.

Deslauriers, L., McCarty, L.S., Miller, K., Callaghan, K., and Kestin, G. (2019). Measuring actual learning versus feeling of learning in response to being actively engaged in the classroom. *Proceedings of the National Academy of Sciences,* September 2019. https://doi.org/10.1073/pnas.1821936116.

Dewey, J. (1933). *How We Think: A Restatement of the Relation of Reflective Thinking to the Educative Process.* DC Heath.

DeWitt, P. (2017). Why does teacher talk still dominate high school classrooms? Retrieved from https://blogs-edweek-org.ezp-prod1.hul.harvard.edu/edweek/finding_common_ground/2017/05.

Dillon, J.T. (1994). *Using Discussion in Classrooms.* Oxford: Open University Press.

Dochy, F., Segers, M., Van den Bossche, P., and Gijbels, D. (2003). Effects of problem-based learning: A meta-analysis. *Learning and Instruction* 13(5): 533–568.

Donker, A.S., De Boer, H., Kostons, D., Van Ewijk, C.D., and van der Werf, M.P. (2014). Effectiveness of learning strategy instruction on academic performance: A meta-analysis. *Educational Research Review* 11: 1–26.

Doyle, W. (1983). Academic work. *Review of Educational Research* 53(2): 159–199.

Drulak, J.A., Domitrovitch, C.E., Weissberg, R.P., and Gullotta, T.P. (Eds.). (2015). *Handbook of Social and Emotional Learning: Research and Practice.* New York: The Guilford Press.

Dunster, G.P., de la Iglesia, L., Ben-Hamo, M., Nave, C., Fleischer, J.G., Panda, S., and de la Iglesia, H.O. (2018). Sleepmore in Seattle: Later school start times are associated with more sleep and better performance in high school students. *Science Advances* 4(12). doi: 10.1126/sciadv.aau6200.

Dweck, C. (2006). *Mindset: The New Psychology of Success.* New York: Ballantine Books.

Dweck, C. (2015). Carol Dweck revisits the growth mindset. *Education Week* 35(5): 20–24.

Ebersbach, M., Feierabend, M., and Nazari, K.B.B. (2020). Comparing the effects of generating questions, testing, and restudying on students' long-term recall in university learning. *Applied Cognitive Psychology* 34(3): 724–736. Retrieved from https://doi.org/10.1002/acp.3639.

Education, M.D.O. (2015). Spotlight on . . . Formative assessment: Learning intentions & success criteria. *Literacy Links: The Monthly Literacy Newsletter from the Maine Department of Education* 12(2): 1–4.

Edutopia. (2015). Having students lead parent conferences. Retrieved from https://www.edutopia.org/practice/student-led-conferences-empowerment-and-ownership.

Eells, R.J. (2011). *Meta-Analysis of the Relationship between Collective Teacher Efficacy and Student Achievement*. Loyola University Chicago.

Eisner, E.W. (2001). What does it mean to say a school is doing well? *Phi Delta Kappan* 82(5): 367–372.

Elmore, R.F. (2019). The future of learning and the future of assessment. *ECNU Review of Education* 2(3): 328–341.

Engel, S. (2011). Children's need to know: Curiosity in schools. *Harvard Educational Review* 81(4): 625–645.

Engel, S. (2016). But why? Children's curiosity in the classroom. Paper presented at the Grit + Imagination: An educator's summit, Philadelphia. Retrieved from https://cpb-us-w2.wpmucdn.com/web.sas.upenn.edu/dist/8/471/files/2018/06/Susan_Engel-1l0il50.pdf.

Engel, S.L. (2015a). *The End of the Rainbow: How Educating for Happiness Not Money Would Transform Our Schools*. New York: The New Press.

Engel, S.L. (2015b). *The Hungry Mind: The Origins of Curiosity in Childhood*. Cambridge, MA: Harvard University Press.

Engel, S.L. (2021). *The Intellectual Lives of Children*. Cambridge, MA: Harvard University Press.

Eppley, K., and Dudley-Marling, C. (2019). Does direct instruction work? A critical assessment of direct instruction research and its theoretical perspective. *Journal of Curriculum and Pedagogy,* 16(1): 35–54.

Erickson, H.L. (2006). *Concept-Based Curriculum and Instruction for the Thinking Classroom*. Corwin Press.

Facione, P.A., Facione, N.C., and Sanchez, C.A. (1992). *The California Critical Thinking Dispositions Inventory*. Millbrae, CA: The California Academic Press.

Fendel, D., Resek, D., Alper, L., and Fraser, S. (1997). *Interactive Mathematics Program: Year 3*. Emeryville, CA: Key Curriculum Press.

Ferlazzo, L. (2019). To maximize group work, make it metacognitive. Retrieved from http://blogs.edweek.org.ezp-prod1.hul.harvard.edu/teachers/classroom_qa_with_larry_ferlazzo/2019/05/response_to_maximize_group_work_make_it_metacognitive.html.

Finn, B., and Metcalfe, J. (2008). Judgments of learning are influenced by memory for past test. *Journal of Memory and Language* 58(1): 19–34.

Fiori, N., Boaler, J., Cleare, N., DiBrienza, J., and Sengupta, T. (2004). What discussions teach us about mathematical understanding: Exploring and assessing students' mathematical work in classrooms. *Psychology of Mathematics Education NA*. Toronto, Ontario.

Fisher, D., and Frey, N. (2014). Speaking volumes. *Educational Leadership* 72(3): 18–23.

Flynn, L., and Colby, S.R. (2017). Cultivating classroom spaces as homes for learning. *Middle Grades Review* 3(3): 3.

Frazier, B.N., Gelman, S.A., and Wellman, H.M. (2009). Preschoolers' search for explanatory information within adult–child conversation. *Child Development* 80(6): 1592–1611.

Fredricks, J.A., Blumenfeld, P.C., and Paris, A.H. (2004). School engagement: Potential of the concept, state of the evidence. *Review of Educational Research* 74(1): 59–109.

Freire, P. (1996). *Pedagogy of the Oppressed*. Bloomsbury Publishing.

Freire, P. (2021). *Education for Critical Consciousness*. Bloomsbury Publishing.

Friday Pulse. (2022). An introduction to fairness and respect. *Be Fair*. Retrieved from https://app.fridaypulse.com/en/cultures-of-thinking-foundation/help-center/be-fair/about-fairness-and-respect.

Fronius, T., Persson, H., Guckenburg, S., Hurley, N., and Petrosino, A. (2016). Restorative justice in US schools: A research review. *WestEd*.

Fry, E., Kress, J., and Fountoukidis, D. (2000). *The Reading Teacher's Book of Lists*. Somerset, NJ: Jossey-Bass/Wiley.

Fryer Jr., R.G. (2018). The "pupil" factory: Specialization and the production of human capital in schools. *American Economic Review* 108(3): 616–656.

Fullan, M., and Hargreaves, A. (1996). *What's Worth Fighting for in Your School? Revised Edition*. ERIC.

Furtak, E.M., and Kunter, M. (2012). Effects of autonomy-supportive teaching on student learning and motivation. *The Journal of Experimental Education* 80(3): 284–316.

Gadge, U. (2018). *Effects of Cognitively Guided Instruction on Teacher Created Opportunities to Engage Students in Problem-Solving*. University of Miami.

Garcia, G.C. (2003). *English Learners: Reaching the Highest Level of English Literacy*. ERIC.

Gardner, H., and Boix-Mansilla, V. (1994, February). Teaching for understanding—within and across the disciplines. *Educational Leadership*, 14–18.

Gillies, R.M. (2014). Developments in classroom-based talk. *International Journal of Educational Research* 63: 63–68.

Gino, F. (2018). The business case for curiosity. *Harvard Business Review* 96(5): 48–57.

Gladwell, M. (2008). *Outliers: The Story of Success*. Little, Brown.

GMAC Research Team. (2020). Employers still seek communication skills in new hires. Retrieved from https://www.mba.com/information-and-news/research-and-data/employers-seek-communications-skills.

Goddard, Y., Goddard, R., and Tschannen-Moran, M. (2007). A theoretical and empirical investigation of teacher collaboration for school improvement and student achievement in public elementary schools. *Teachers College Record* 109(4): 877–896.

Goddard, Y.L., Miller, R., Larsen, R., Goddard, R., Madsen, J., and Schroeder, P. (2010). Connecting principal leadership, teacher collaboration, and student achievement. Online Submission. Retrieved from https://files.eric.ed.gov/fulltext/ED528704.pdf.

Godinho, S., and Wilson, J. (2006). *How to Succeed with Questioning*. Curriculum Corporation.

Goldenberg, S. (2022). *Radical Curiosity: Questioning Commonly Held Beliefs to Imagine Flourishing Futures*. New York: Crown.

Goss, P., Sonnemann, J., and Griffiths, K. (2017). Engaging students: Creating classrooms that improve learning. Grattan Institute.

Graff, G. (2008). *Clueless in Academe: How Schooling Obscures the Life of the Mind*. Yale University Press.

Graves, D.H. (1983). *Writing: Teachers and Children at Work*. ERIC.

Greene, M. (2000). *Releasing the Imagination: Essays on Education, the Arts, and Social Change*. John Wiley & Sons.

Greenleaf, C.L., Litman, C., Hanson, T.L., Rosen, R., Boscardin, C.K., Herman, J., . . . Jones, B. (2011). Integrating literacy and science in biology: Teaching and learning impacts of reading apprenticeship professional development. *American Educational Research Journal* 48(3): 647–717.

Gruber, M.J., and Ranganath, C. (2019). How curiosity enhances hippocampus-dependent memory: The prediction, appraisal, curiosity, and exploration (PACE) framework. *Trends in Cognitive Sciences* 23(12): 1014–1025.

Haller, E.P., Child, D.A., and Walberg, H.J. (1988). Can comprehension be taught? A quantitative synthesis of "metacognitive" studies. *Educational Researcher* 17(9): 5–8.

Halpern, R., Heckman, P., and Larson, R. (2013). *Realizing the Potential of Learning in Middle Adolescence*. West Hills, CA: The Sally and Dick Roberts Coyote Foundation.

Hamari, J., Shernoff, D.J., Rowe, E., Coller, B., Asbell-Clarke, J., and Edwards, T. (2016). Challenging games help students learn: An empirical study on engagement, flow and immersion in game-based learning. *Computers in Human Behavior* 54: 170–179.

Hamre, B.K., and Pianta, R.C. (2001). Early teacher–child relationships and the trajectory of children's school outcomes through eighth grade. *Child Development* 72(2): 625–638.

Hargreaves, A., and O'Connor, M.T. (2018). *Collaborative Professionalism: When Teaching Together Means Learning for All*. Corwin Press.

Harvey, S., and Goudvis, A. (2013). Comprehension at the core. *The Reading Teacher* 66(6): 432–439.

Hattie, J. (2009). *Visible Learning: A Synthesis of Over 800 Meta-Analyses Relating to Achievement*. New York: Routledge.

Hattie, J. (2015). The applicability of visible learning to higher education. *Scholarship of Teaching and Learning in Psychology* 1(1): 79.

Hattie, J., and Timperley, H. (2007). The power of feedback. *Review of Educational Research* 77(1): 81–112.

Hattie, J., and Zierer, K. (2017). *10 Mindframes for Visible Learning: Teaching for Success*. Routledge.

Hazra, R. (2022, July 31). Student Voices: Why the educational system is flawed, and what to do about it. Student Voices guest columnist. *The Seattle Times*. Retrieved from https://www.seattletimes.com/education-lab/student-voices-why-the-educational-system-is-flawed-and-what-to-do-about-it/.

Hennessey, M.G. (1999). Probing the dimensions of metacognition: Implications for conceptual change teaching-learning. Paper presented at the *Annual Meeting of the National Association for Research in Science Teaching* (Boston, MA, March 28–31, 1999). Retrieved from https://files.eric.ed.gov/fulltext/ED446921.pdf.

Hiebert, J., Stigler, J., Jacobs, J., Givvin, K., Garnier, H., and Smith, M. (2005). Mathematics teaching in the United States today (and tomorrow): Results from the TIMSS 1999 video study. *Educational Evaluation and Policy Analysis* 27: 111–132.

Hill, A.J., and Jones, D.B. (2018). A teacher who knows me: The academic benefits of repeat student-teacher matches. *Economics of Education Review* 64, 1–12.

Hill, H.C., Litke, E., and Lynch, K. (2018). Learning lessons from instruction: Descriptive results from an observational study of urban elementary classrooms. *Teachers College Record* 120(12): 1–46.

Hofstadter, R. (1963). *Anti-Intellectualism in American Life.* (3. Print.) (Vol. 713). Vintage.

Howard, J.R., Milner-McCall, T., and Howard, T.C. (2020). *No More Teaching without Positive Relationships.* Heinemann.

Hsee, C., Ruan, B., and Y Lu, Z. (2015). Creating happiness by first inducing and then satisfying a desire: The case of curiosity. *ACR North American Advances.*

Huang, Z. (1991). *A Meta-Analysis of Student Self-Questioning Strategies.* Hofstra University.

Humes, W. (2007). The meaning of collegiality. Retrieved from https://www.tes.com/magazine/archive/meaning-collegiality.

Imbertson, D. (2017). The importance of student talk and strategies for promoting classroom conversations. Retrieved from Sophia, the St. Catherine University repository website: https://sophia.stkate.edu/maed/204.

Interlead. (2019). Developing a Dialogue Driven School: The Key to Unlocking Your School as a Professional Learning Community Explained. Retrieved from https://www.interlead.co.nz/wp-content/uploads/2019/09/DevelopingaDialogueDrivenSchoolSept2019.pdf.

Irving, S.E. (2004). *The Development and Validation of a Student Evaluation Instrument to Identify Highly Accomplished Mathematics Teachers.* University of Auckland, Auckland, New Zealand.

Izuma, K., Saito, D.N., and Sadato, N. (2010). Processing of the incentive for social approval in the ventral striatum during charitable donation. *Journal of Cognitive Neuroscience* 22(4): 621–631.

Johnston, P.H. (2004). *Choice Words: How Our Language Affects Children's Learning.* Stenhouse Publishers.

Jones, B., Valdez, G., Nowakowski, J., and Rasmussen, C. (1994). Meaningful, engaged learning. *Designing Learning and Technology for Educational Reform.* Oak Brook, IL: North Central Regional Educational Laboratory.

Jones, S.M., and Kahn, J. (2017). The evidence base for how we learn: Supporting students' social, emotional, and academic development. Consensus Statements of Evidence from the Council of Distinguished Scientists. Aspen Institute.

Kane, T.J., and Staiger, D.O. (2012). Gathering feedback for teaching: Combining high-quality observations with student surveys and achievement gains. Research Paper. MET Project. Bill & Melinda Gates Foundation.

Kang, H. (2017). Preservice teachers' learning to plan intellectually challenging tasks. *Journal of Teacher Education* 68(1): 55–68.

Karpicke, J.D. (2012). Retrieval-based learning: Active retrieval promotes meaningful learning. *Current Directions in Psychological Science* 21(3): 157–163.

Katz, L., and Raths, J.D. (1985). Dispositions as goals for teacher education. *Teaching and Teacher Education* 1(4): 301–307.

Katz, L.B., and Leirer, V.O. (1980). Cognitive representation of personality impressions: Organizational processes in first impression formation. *Journal of Personality and Social Psychology* 39(6): 1050–1063.

Kaufman, S.B. (2017). Schools are missing what matters about learning. Retrieved from https://amp.theatlantic.com/amp/article/534573/.

Keay, J.K., Carse, N., and Jess, M. (2019). Understanding teachers as complex professional learners. *Professional Development in Education* 45(1): 125–137.

Keene, E. (2002). Comprehension strategies. Retrieved from https://murdock10.typepad.com/files/comprehension-strategiesforparents.pdf.

Keene, E., and Zimmermann, S. (1997). *Mosaic of Thought*. Portsmouth, NH: Heinemann.

Keep, B. (2021). The power of worked examples for learning. Retrieved from https://medium.com/age-of-awareness/the-power-of-worked-examples-for-learning-48be6ac90ec4.

Ketsman, O. (2013). The creative process entailed in the co-construction of classroom curriculum. *Critical Questions in Education* 4(1): 21–29.

Kilcher, A., and Arends, R. (2010). *Teaching for Student Learning: Becoming an Accomplished Teacher*. Routledge.

King, N. (2020). *The Excellent Mind: Intellectual Virtues for Everyday Life*. Oxford University Press.

Kittle, P., and Gallagher, K. (2020). The curse of "helicopter teaching." *Educational Leadership* 77(6): 14–19.

Knight, J. (2007). *Instructional Coaching: A Partnership Approach to Improving Instruction*. Corwin Press.

Kohn, A. (1997). How not to teach values: A critical look at character education. Retrieved from https://www.alfiekohn.org/article/teach-values/.

Koretz, D. (2017). *The Testing Charade*. University of Chicago Press.

Kort, B., Reilly, R., and Picard, R.W. (2001). An affective model of interplay between emotions and learning: Reengineering educational pedagogy-building a learning companion. Paper presented at the *Proceedings IEEE International Conference on Advanced Learning Technologies*.

Kramarski, B., and Mevarech, Z.R. (2003). Enhancing mathematical reasoning in the classroom: The effects of cooperative learning and metacognitive training. *American Educational Research Journal*, 40(1), 281–310.

Krechevsky, M., Mardell, B., Filippini, T., and Tedeschi, M. (2016). Children are citizens: The everyday and the razzle-dazzle. *Innovations in Early Education: The International Reggio Emilia Exchange* 23(4): 4–15.

Krechevsky, M., Mardell, B., Rivard, M., and Wilson, D. (2013). *Visible Learners: Promoting Reggio-Inspired Approaches in All Schools.* John Wiley & Sons.

Krechevsky, M., and Stork, J. (2000). Challenging educational assumptions: Lessons from an Italian-American collaboration. *Cambridge Journal of Education* 30(1): 57–74.

Kuhn, D., and Siegler, R. (2006). Cognition, perception, and language (Vol. 2). W. Damon and R. Lerner (series eds.). *Handbook of Child Psychology.*

Kuzle, A. (2013). Patterns of metacognitive behavior during mathematics problem-solving in a dynamic geometry environment. *International Electronic Journal of Mathematics Education* 8(1): 20–40.

Labaree, D.F. (2021). The dynamic tension at the core of the grammar of schooling. *Phi Delta Kappan* 103(2): 28–32.

Lacey, A., and Cornell, D. (2013). The impact of teasing and bullying on schoolwide academic performance. *Journal of Applied School Psychology* 29(3): 262–283.

Lamborn, S., Newmann, F., and Wehlage, G. (1992). The significance and sources of student engagement. *Student Engagement and Achievement in American Secondary Schools*, 11–39.

Lamnina, M., and Chase, C.C. (2019). Developing a thirst for knowledge: How uncertainty in the classroom influences curiosity, affect, learning, and transfer. *Contemporary Educational Psychology* Oct 1, 59. Retrieved from https://doi.org/10.1016/j.cedpsych.2019.101785.

Lampert, M. (2015). *Deeper Teaching.* Boston, MA: Jobs for the Future.

Langer, E. (1997). *The Power of Mindful Learning.* Reading, MA: Addison-Wesley.

Lappan, G., Fey, J., Fitzgerald, W., Friel, S., and Phillips, E. (1997). *Connected Mathematics* (Grade 6, Vols. 1–8). Palo Alto, CA: Dale Seymour.

Lara-Alecio, R., Tong, F., Irby, B.J., Guerrero, C., Huerta, M., and Fan, Y. (2012). The effect of an instructional intervention on middle school English learners' science and English reading achievement. *Journal of Research in Science Teaching* 49(8): 987–1011.

Larkin, I. (2011). Paying $30,000 for a gold star: An empirical investigation into the value of peer recognition to software salespeople. Unpublished working paper.

Lave, J., and Wenger, E. (1991). *Situated Learning: Legitimate Peripheral Participation.* Cambridge, UK: Cambridge University Press.

Lawrence-Lightfoot, S. (1999). *Respect: An Exploration*. Perseus Books.

Le Fevre, D.M. (2014). Barriers to implementing pedagogical change: The role of teachers' perceptions of risk. *Teaching and Teacher Education* 38: 56–64.

Lenz, B., Wells, J., and Kingston, S. (2015). *Transforming Schools Using Project-Based Learning, Performance Assessment, and Common Core Standards*. John Wiley & Sons.

Leonard, J.A., Martinez, D.N., Dashineau, S.C., Park, A.T., and Mackey, A.P. (2021). Children persist less when adults take over. *Child Development*, 92(4), pp. 1325–1336.

Lepper, M.R., and Henderlong, J. (2000). Turning "play" into "work" and "work" into "play": 25 years of research on intrinsic versus extrinsic motivation. *Intrinsic and Extrinsic Motivation*, 257–307.

Levine, M. (2005). *Ready or Not, Here Life Comes*. Simon and Schuster.

Lieberman, M.D. (2013). *Social: Why Our Brains Are Wired to Connect*. OUP Oxford.

Liljedahl, P. (2020). *Building Thinking Classrooms in Mathematics, Grades K–12: 14 Teaching Practices for Enhancing Learning*. Corwin Press.

Little, J.W. (1990). The persistence of privacy: Autonomy and initiative in teachers' professional relations. *Teachers College Record* 91(4): 509–536.

Lukehart, W. (2019). Engaging young citizens. *News & Features*. Retrieved from https://www.slj.com/story/engaging-young-citizen-activists.

Lukianoff, G., and Haidt, J. (2019). *The Coddling of the American Mind: How Good Intentions and Bad Ideas Are Setting Up a Generation for Failure*. Penguin.

Luntley, M. (2008). Learning, empowerment and judgement. *Critical Thinking and Learning*, 79–92.

MacKenzie, T. (2021). *Inquiry Mindset: Assessment Edition*. Columbia, SC: Elevate Books Edu.

MacKenzie, T., and Bathurst-Hunt, R. (2019). *Inquiry Mindset*. Elevate Books Edu.

Magner, T., Soule, H., and Wesolowski, K. (2011). The partnership for 21st century skills-framework for 21st century learning. gov.ezproxy.bethel.edu/fulltext/ED543030.pdf.

Malaguzzi, L. (1994). Your image of the child: Where teaching begins. *Child Care Information Exchange*, 3: 1–5.

Martínez, M., McGrath, D., and Foster, E. (2016). *How Deeper Learning Can Create a New Vision for Teaching*. Arlington, Virginia: Consulted Strategists.

May, W.T. (1993). Teaching as a work of art in the medium of curriculum. *Theory into Practice* 32(4): 210–218.

Mayer, R.E. (2003). *Learning and Instruction*. Prentice Hall.

McGrath, S. (2019). Talk less so students learn more. Retrieved from https://www.edutopia.org/article/talk-less-so-students-learn-more.

McGregor, J. (2004a). Space, power and the classroom. Paper presented at the Forum for Promoting 3–19 Comprehensive Education.

McGregor, J. (2004b). Spatiality and the place of the material in schools. *Pedagogy, Culture and Society* 12(3): 347–372.

McKinney, G., and Rondot, Z. (2021). *The Expert Effect*. Alexandria, VA: EduMatch.

McLeod, S. (2012). What is the zone of proximal development? Retrieved from https://www.simplypsychology.org/Zone-of-Proximal-Development.html.

McTighe, J., and Silver, H.F. (2020). *Teaching for Deeper Learning: Tools to Engage Students in Meaning Making*. ASCD.

Mehta, J. (2015). The problem with grit. *Opinion*. Retrieved from https://www.edweek.org/education/opinion-the-problem-with-grit/2015/04.

Mehta, J., and Fine, S. (2019). *In Search of Deeper Learning: The Quest to Remake the American High School*. Cambridge, MA: Harvard University Press.

Mercer, N. (2003). Helping children to talk and think together more effectively. *Polifonia* 7(07).

Meyer, D. (2010). Math class needs a makeover. TED Talk.

Meyer, D. (2011). The three acts of a mathematical story. Retrieved from https://blog.mrmeyer.com/2011/the-three-acts-of-a-mathematical-story/.

Meyer, D. (2016). Beyond relevance & real world: Stronger strategies for student engagement. Paper presented at the NCTM Annual Meeting, Phoenix, AZ.

Meyer, M.L., Davachi, L., Ochsner, K.N., and Lieberman, M.D. (2019). Evidence that default network connectivity during rest consolidates social information. *Cerebral Cortex* 29(5): 1910–1920.

Mezirow, J. (2000). Learning to think like an adult. *Learning as Transformation: Critical Perspectives on a Theory in Progress*, 3–33.

Michaels, S., O'Connor, M.C., Hall, M.W., and Resnick, L.B. (2010). *Accountable talk sourcebook: For classroom conversation that works*. Pittsburgh, PA: University of Pittsburgh Institute for Learning.

Mitra, S. (2003). Minimally invasive education: A progress report on the "hole-in-the-wall" experiments. *British Journal of Educational Technology* 34(3): 367–371.

Mitra, S., Kulkarni, S., and Stanfield, J. (2016). Learning at the edge of chaos: Self-organising systems in education. In: *The Palgrave International Handbook of Alternative Education*, 227–239. Springer.

Mizell, H. (2010). *Why Professional Development Matters*. ERIC.

Mongeau, L. (2019). Sending your boy to preschool is great for your grandson, new research shows. Retrieved from https://hechingerreport.org/sending-your-boy-to-preschool-is-great-for-your-grandson-new-research-shows/.

Moore, S.G., and Bulbulian, K.N. (1976). The effects of contrasting styles of adult-child interaction on children's curiosity. *Developmental Psychology* 12(2): 171.

Muis, K.R., and Duffy, M.C. (2013). Epistemic climate and epistemic change: Instruction designed to change students' beliefs and learning strategies and improve achievement. *Journal of Educational Psychology* 105(1): 213.

Murdoch, K. (2015). *The Power of Inquiry*. Seastar Education.

Murdoch, K. (2022). *Getting Personal with Inquiry Learning*. Melbourne, Australia: Seastar Education.

Murphy, S. (2008). Back to the Future protocol. Retrieved from https://www.schoolreforminitiative.org/download/future-protocol-a-k-a-back-to-the-future/.

Murray, K. (1999). Collective Intelligence: Mankind's Emerging World in Cyberspace by Pierre Lévy. *Leonardo* 32(1): 70–71.

Myers, C.G. (2018). Coactive vicarious learning: Toward a relational theory of vicarious learning in organizations. *Academy of Management Review* 43(4): 610–634.

Neill, A.S., and Lamb, A. (1992). *Summerhill School: A New View of Childhood*. New York: St. Martin's Press.

Nelson, T., Deuel, A., Slavit, D., Kennedy, A. (2010). Leading deep conversations in collaborative inquiry groups. *The Clearing House*, 83(5), pp. 175–179.

Nelson, T.H., Slavit, D., and Deuel, A. (2012). Two dimensions of an inquiry stance toward student-learning data. *Teachers College Record* 114(8): 1–42.

Newmann, F.M. (1992). *Student Engagement and Achievement in American Secondary Schools*. ERIC.

Newmann, F.M. (1996). *Authentic Achievement: Restructuring Schools for Intellectual Quality*. Jossey-Bass.

Newmann, F.M., Bryk, A.S., and Nagaoka, J.K. (2001). Authentic intellectual work and standardized tests: conflict or coexistence. Retrieved from https://files.eric.ed.gov/fulltext/ED470299.pdf.

Newmann, F.M., Marks, H.M., and Gamoran, A. (1996). Authentic pedagogy and student performance. *American Journal of Education* 104(4): 280–312.

Nias, J., Southworth, G., and Yeomans, R. (2002). The culture of collaboration. In: *Teaching and Learning in the Primary School*, 268–282. Routledge.

NIFDI.org. (2018). Basic Philosophy of Direct Instruction. Retrieved from https://www.nifdi .org/what-is-di/basic-philosophy.html.

Nottingham, J. (2017). *The Learning Challenge: How to Guide Your Students through the Learning Pit to Achieve Deeper Understanding*. Corwin Press.

Nuthall, G. (2007). *The Hidden Lives of Learners*. NZCER Press.

Nystrand, M., Gamoran, A., Kachur, R., and Prendergast, C. (1997). *Opening Dialogue*. New York: Teachers College Press.

Nystrand, M., Wu, L.L., Gamoran, A., Zeiser, S., and Long, D.A. (2003). Questions in time: Investigating the structure and dynamics of unfolding classroom discourse. *Discourse Processes* 35(2): 135–198.

O'Hara, L.A., and Sternberg, R.J. (2001). It doesn't hurt to ask: Effects of instructions to be creative, practical, or analytical on essay-writing performance and their interaction with students' thinking styles. *Creativity Research Journal* 13(2): 197–210.

Oakeshott, M. (1959). *The Voice of Poetry in the Conversation of Mankind: An Essay*. Bowes and Bowes.

Oczkus, L.D. (2018). *Reciprocal Teaching at Work: Powerful Strategies and Lessons for Improving Reading Comprehension*. ASCD.

Okada, T., and Simon, H.A. (1997). Collaborative discovery in a scientific domain. *Cognitive Science* 21(2): 109–146.

Opfer, V.D., and Pedder, D. (2011). Conceptualizing teacher professional learning. *Review of Educational Research* 81(3): 376–407.

Ostroff, W.L. (2020). Empowering children through dialogue and discussion. *Educational Leadership* 77(7): 14–20.

Ott, E. (2018). The take care of me list. Retrieved from https://www.edutopia.org/article/ take-care-me-list.

Ouchi, Y., Okada, H., Yoshikawa, E., Nobezawa, S., and Futatsubashi, M. (1999). Brain activation during maintenance of standing postures in humans. *Brain* 122(2): 329–338.

Owen, L. (2014). 7. Continuing professional development: Can it ever be creative? *Ten Essays on Improving Teacher Quality*, 60.

Owen, S.M. (2015). Teacher professional learning communities in innovative contexts: "ah hah moments," "passion" and "making a difference" for student learning. *Professional Development in Education* 41(1): 57–74.

Pacchiano, D.M., Whalen, S.P., Horsley, H.L., and Parkinson, K. (2016). Efficacy study of a professional development intervention to strengthen organizational conditions and effective teaching in early education settings. *Society for Research on Educational Effectiveness Spring Conference*. Retrieved from https://files.eric.ed.gov/fulltext/ED567221.pdf.

Paley, V.G. (1986). On listening to what the children say. *Harvard Educational Review*, 56(2), pp. 122–132.

Palinscar, A.S., and Brown, A.L. (1984). Reciprocal teaching of comprehension-fostering and comprehension-monitoring activities. *Cognition and Instruction* 1: 117–125.

Pandolpho, B. (2018). Listening is a teacher's most powerful tool. *Education Weekly*. Retrieved from https://www.edweek.org/teaching-learning/opinion-listening-is-a-teachers-most-powerful-tool/2018/03.

Papleontiou-Louca, E. (2003). The concept and instruction of metacognition. *Teacher Development* 7(1): 9–30.

Parrish, S. (2021). The Feynman learning technique. Retrieved from https://fs.blog/feynman-learning-technique/.

Patall, E.A., Cooper, H., and Wynn, S.R. (2010). The effectiveness and relative importance of choice in the classroom. *Journal of Educational Psychology* 102(4): 896.

Patchin, J.W., and Hinduja, P.D.S. (2020). Tween cyberbullying. Retrieved from http://www.infocop.es/pdf/CN_Stop_Bullying_Cyber_Bullying_Report_9.30.20.pdf.

Patton, A. (2012). *Work That Matters: The Teacher's Guide to Project-Based Learning*. Paul Hamlyn Foundation.

Pea, R.D. (1993). Practices of distributed intelligence and designs for education. In: *Distributed Cognitions* (ed. G. Salomon), 47–87. New York: Cambridge University Press.

Perkins, D.N. (1992). *Smart Schools: From Training Memories to Educating Minds*. New York: The Free Press.

Perkins, D.N. (1993). Teaching for understanding. *American Educator: The Professional Journal of the American Federation of Teachers* 17(3): 8–35.

Perkins, D.N. (2002). *King Arthur's Round Table: How Collaborative Conversations Create Smart Organizations*. Hoboken, NJ: John Wiley & Sons, Inc.

Perkins, D.N. (2010). Forward in Swartz, R.J., Costa, A.L., Beyer, B.K., Reagan, R., and Kallick, B. (2010). *Thinking-Based Learning: Promoting Quality Student Achievement in the 21st Century*. ERIC.

Perkins, D.N., Jay, E., and Tishman, S. (1993). Beyond abilities: A dispositional theory of thinking. *Merrill-Palmer Quarterly* 39(1): 1–21.

Perkins, D.N., and Ritchhart, R. (2004). When is good thinking? In: *Motivation, Emotion, and Cognition: Integrative Perspectives on Intellectual Functioning and Development* (eds. D.Y. Dai and R.J. Sternberg). Mawah, NJ: Erlbaum.

Perkins, D.N., and Salomon, G. (1988, September). Teaching for transfer. *Educational Leadership*, 22–32.

Perkins, D.N., Tishman, S., Ritchhart, R., Donis, K., and Andrade, A. (2000). Intelligence in the wild: A dispositional view of intellectual traits. *Educational Psychology Review* 12(3): 269–293.

Perret-Clermont, A.-N. (1980). *Social Interaction and Cognitive Development in Children*. Academic Press.

Peters, T.J., and Austin, N. (1985). *A Passion for Excellence: The Leadership Difference*. New York: Warner Books.

Peterson, R. (1992). *Life in a Crowded Place: Making a Learning Community*. Heinemann Educational Books.

Petty, G. (2020). Professor John Hattie's Table of Effect Sizes. *The Teachers Toolbox—Documents*. Retrieved from https://www.teacherstoolbox.co.uk/effect-sizes/.

Piaget, J. (2003). *The Psychology of Intelligence*. Routledge.

Piggot-Irvine, E. (2012). Creating authentic collaboration: A central feature of effectiveness. *Action Research for Sustainable Development in a Turbulent World*, 89–106.

Pluck, G., and Johnson, H. (2011). Stimulating curiosity to enhance learning. *GESJ: Education Sciences and Psychology*, 2.

Pope, D.C. (2008). *Doing School: How We Are Creating a Generation of Stressed Out, Materialistic, and Miseducated Students*. Yale University Press.

Pozuelos, J.P., Combita, L.M., Abundis, A., Paz-Alonso, P.M., Conejero, Á., Guerra, S., and Rueda, M.R. (2019). Metacognitive scaffolding boosts cognitive and neural benefits following executive attention training in children. *Developmental Science* 22(2): e12756.

Price, C. (2022). *The Power of Fun: Why Fun Is the Key to a Happy and Healthy Life*. Random House.

Project Zero. (2006a). The boy's city. Retrieved from http://www.mlvpz.org/documentation/paged978.html.

Project Zero. (2006b). What is documentation? Making learning visible. Retrieved from http://www.mlvpz.org/indexfd69.html.

Protocols (n.d.) Retrieved from https://www.schoolreforminitiative.org/protocols/.

Ramachandran, V. (2021). Stanford researchers identify four causes for "Zoom fatigue" and their simple fixes. Retrieved from https://news.stanford.edu/2021/02/23/four-causes-zoom-fatigue-solutions/.

Rebora, A. (2020). Better listening, better teaching. *Educational Leadership*, 77(7), p. 9.

Reeves, P.M., Pun, W.H., and Chung, K.S. (2017). Influence of teacher collaboration on job satisfaction and student achievement. *Teaching and Teacher Education* 67: 227–236.

Rendas, A.B., Fonseca, M., and Pinto, P.R. (2006). Toward meaningful learning in undergraduate medical education using concept maps in a PBL pathophysiology course. *Advances in Physiology Education* 30(1): 23–29.

Renton, M. (2020). *Challenging Learning through Questioning: Facilitating the Process of Effective Learning*. Corwin Press.

Resnick, L.B., Asterhan, C.S., and Clarke, S.N. (2018). Accountable talk: Instructional dialogue that builds the mind. Geneva, Switzerland: The International Academy of Education (IAE) and the International Bureau of Education (IBE) of the United Nations Educational, Scientific and Cultural Organization (UNESCO).

Reutzel, D.R., Smith, J.A., and Fawson, P.C. (2005). An evaluation of two approaches for teaching reading comprehension strategies in the primary years using science information texts. *Early Childhood Research Quarterly* 20(3): 276–305.

Ritchhart, R. (2002). *Intellectual Character: What It Is, Why It Matters, and How To Get It*. San Francisco: Jossey-Bass.

Ritchhart, R. (2015). *Creating Cultures of Thinking: The 8 Forces We Must Master to Truly Transform Our Schools*. San Francisco: Jossey-Bass.

Ritchhart, R. (2022). Cultures of thinking. Retrieved from http://www.pz.harvard.edu/projects/cultures-of-thinking

Ritchhart, R., and Church, M. (2020). *The Power of Making Thinking Visible*. San Francisco: Jossey-Bass.

Ritchhart, R., Church, M., and Morrison, K. (2011). *Making Thinking Visible: How to Promote Engagement, Understanding, and Independence for All Learners*. San Francisco, CA: Jossey-Bass.

Ritchhart, R., Turner, T., and Hadar, L. (2009). Uncovering students' thinking about thinking using concept maps. *Metacognition and Learning*, 3.

Roberts, C. (2001). Teachers—and students—love to loop. Retrieved from https://www.edutopia.org/best-kind-deja-vu.

Roble, D.B. (2017). Communicating and valuing students' productive struggle and creativity in calculus. *Turkish Online Journal of Design Art and Communication* 7(2): 255–263.

Rock, D. (2009). Managing with the brain in mind. *Strategy+Business*.

Rock, S.L. (1985). *A Meta-Analysis of Self-Instructional Training Research*. University of Illinois at Urbana-Champaign.

Roediger III, H.L., and Karpicke, J.D. (2006). The power of testing memory: Basic research and implications for educational practice. *Perspectives on Psychological Science* 1(3): 181–210.

Roehlkepartain, E., Pekel, K., Syvertsen, A., Sethi, J., Sullivan, T., and Scales, P. (2017). *Relationships First: Creating Connections that Help Young People Thrive*. Minneapolis, MN: Search Institute, 1–20.

Rogoff, B. (1990). *Apprenticeship in Thinking*. New York: Oxford University Press.

Rohrer, D., and Taylor, K. (2007). The shuffling of mathematics problems improves learning. *Instructional Science* 35(6): 481–498.

Romero, C. (2015). What we know about growth mindset from scientific research. *Mindset Scholars Network*, 1–4.

Rosenholtz, S.J. (1989). Workplace conditions that affect teacher quality and commitment: Implications for teacher induction programs. *The Elementary School Journal* 89(4): 421–439.

Rosenshine, B., and Meister, C. (1994). Reciprocal teaching: A review of the research. *Review of Educational Research* 64(4): 479–530.

Ross, D.D., Bondy, E., Bondy, E., and Hambacher, E. (2008). Promoting academic engagement through insistence: Being a warm demander. *Childhood Education* 84(3): 142–146.

Rothstein, D., and Santana, L. (2011). *Make Just One Change: Teach Students to Ask Their Own Questions*. Harvard Education Press.

Rowe, M. (2008). Micro-affirmations and micro-inequities. *Journal of the International Ombudsman Association* 1(1): 45–48.

Ryan, R.M., and Deci, E.L. (2000). Self-determination theory and the facilitation of intrinsic motivation, social development, and well-being. *American Psychologist* 55(1): 68.

Saaris, N. (2017). Mastering metacognition: The what, why, and how. Retrieved from https://www.activelylearn.com/post/metacognition.

Sadowski, M. (2013). There's always that one teacher. *Educational Leadership* 71(1): 28–32.

Safir, S., and Dugan, J. (2021). *Street Data: A Next-Generation Model for Equity, Pedagogy, and School Transformation*. Corwin.

Santelises, S.B., and Dabrowski, J. (2015). *Checking In: Do Classroom Assignments Reflect Today's Higher Standards? K–12 Practice. Equity in Motion Series.* Education Trust.

Sarisohn, H. (2018). Study reveals teachers don't have enough time for peer collaboration. Retrieved from http://blogs.edweek.org/teachers/teaching_now/2018/04/teachers-dont-have-enough-time-for-peer-collaboration.html.

Sarrasin, J.B., Nenciovici, L., Foisy, L.-M.B., Allaire-Duquette, G., Riopel, M., and Masson, S. (2018). Effects of teaching the concept of neuroplasticity to induce a growth mindset on motivation, achievement, and brain activity: A meta-analysis. *Trends in Neuroscience and Education* 12: 22–31.

Scales, P.C., Van Boekel, M., Pekel, K., Syvertsen, A.K., and Roehlkepartain, E.C. (2020). Effects of developmental relationships with teachers on middle-school students' motivation and performance. *Psychology in the Schools* 57(4): 646–677.

Scheffler, I. (1991). *In Praise of Cognitive Emotions.* New York: Routledge.

Schoenfeld, A.H. (1983). Beyond the purely cognitive: Belief systems, social cognitions, and meta-cognitions as driving forces in intellectual performance. *Cognitive Science* 7(4): 329–363.

Schoenfeld, A.H. (2010). *How we think: A theory of goal-oriented decision making and its educational applications.* Routledge.

Schon, D.A. (2010). Educating the reflective practitioner: Toward a new design for teaching and learning in the professions. *Australian Journal of Adult Learning* 50(2): 448–451.

Schulz, B. (2008). The Importance of Soft Skills: Education beyond Academic Knowledge. *NAWA Journal of Language and Communication:* 146–154. Retrieved from https://ir.nust.na/jspui/bitstream/10628/39/1/The%20Importance%20of%20Soft%20%20Skills-Education%20beyond%20academic%20knowledge.pdf.

Schwartz, K. (2016). 7 qualities that promote teacher leadership in schools. Retrieved from https://www.kqed.org/mindshift/44295/7-qualities-that-promote-teacher-leadership-in-schools.

Schwartz, K. (2018). How debate structures allow English learners' brilliance to shine. Retrieved from https://www.kqed.org/mindshift/50983/how-debate-structures-allow-english-learners-brilliance-to-shine.

Schwartz, K. (2020). Why focusing on adult learning builds a school culture where students thrive. Retrieved from https://www.kqed.org/mindshift/54750/why-focusing-on-adult-learning-builds-a-school-culture-where-students-thrive.

Scott, B.M., and Levy, M.G. (2013). Metacognition: Examining the components of a fuzzy concept. *Educational Research eJournal* 2(2): 120–131.

Seifert, T. (2004). Understanding student motivation. *Educational Research* 46(2): 137–149.

Seldin, M., and Yanez, C. (2019). Student Reports of Bullying: Results from the 2017 School Crime Supplement to the National Crime Victimization Survey. Web Tables. NCES 2019-054. National Center for Education Statistics.

Senge, P.M. (2006). *The Fifth Discipline: The Art and Practice of the Learning Organization.* Broadway Business.

Sepulveda, Y., and Venegas-Muggli, J.I. (2020). Effects of using thinking routines on the academic results of business students at a Chilean tertiary education institution. *Decision Sciences Journal of Innovative Education.*

Seton, H. (2021). A daily ritual that builds trust and community among students. Retrieved from https://www.edutopia.org/article/daily-ritual-builds-trust-and-community-among-students.

Seufert, T., and Brünken, R. (2006). Cognitive load and the format of instructional aids for coherence formation. *Applied Cognitive Psychology: The Official Journal of the Society for Applied Research in Memory and Cognition* 20(3): 321–331.

Sevigny, P. (2012). Extreme discussion circles: Preparing ESL students for "the Harkness method." *Polyglossia* 23: 181–191.

Sfard, A. (1998). On two metaphors for learning and the dangers of choosing just one. *Educational Researcher* 27(2): 4–13.

Shabani, K., Khatib, M., and Ebadi, S. (2010). Vygotsky's zone of proximal development: Instructional implications and teachers' professional development. *English Language Teaching* 3(4): 237–248.

Shah, P.E., Weeks, H.M., Richards, B., and Kaciroti, N. (2018). Early childhood curiosity and kindergarten reading and math academic achievement. *Pediatric Research* 84(3): 380–386. doi:10.1038/s41390-018-0039-3.

Shalaby, C. (2017). *Troublemakers: Lessons in Freedom from Young Children at School.* The New Press.

Shernoff, D.J. (2010). *The Experience of Student Engagement in High School Classrooms: Influences and Effects on Long-Term Outcomes.* Saarbruken: Lambert

Shernoff, D. J. (2013). Optimal learning environments to promote student engagement. Springer.

Shin, M.-H. (2018). Effects of project-based learning on students' motivation and self-efficacy. *English Teaching* 73(1): 95–114.

Sinek, S. (2009). *Start with Why: How Great Leaders Inspire Everyone to Take Action.* Penguin.

Sinha, T., and Kapur, M. (2021). When problem solving followed by instruction works: Evidence for productive failure. *Review of Educational Research* 91(5): 761–798.

Smith, T.W., Baker, W.K., Hattie, J., and Bond, L. (2008). Chapter 12: A validity study of the certification system of the National Board for Professional Teaching Standards. In: *Assessing Teachers for Professional Certification: The First Decade of the National Board for Professional Teaching Standards,* Vol. 11 (eds. R.E. Stake, S. Kushner, L. Ingvarson, and J. Hattie), 345–378. Emerald Group Publishing Limited.

Sparks, S.D. (2010). Character education found to fall short in federal study. Retrieved from https://www.edweek.org/leadership/character-education-found-to-fall-short-in-federal-study/2010/10.

Staff, T. (2013). Mothers asked nearly 300 questions a day, study finds. Retrieved from https://www.telegraph.co.uk/news/uknews/9959026/Mothers-asked-nearly-300-questions-a-day-study-finds.html.

Steen, M. (2017). When teachers become better listeners, students become better learners—here's why. Retrieved from https://resilienteducator.com/classroom-resources/teachers-listening-skills/.

Stefanou, C.R., Perencevich, K.C., DiCintio, M., and Turner, J.C. (2004). Supporting autonomy in the classroom: Ways teachers encourage student decision making and ownership. *Educational Psychologist* 39(2): 97–110.

Stein, M.K., and Lane, S. (1996). Instructional tasks and the development of student capacity to think and reason: An analysis of the relationship between teaching and learning in a reform mathematics project. *Educational Research and Evaluation* 2(1): 50–80.

Stigler, J.W., and Perry, M. (1988). Mathematics learning in Japanese, Chinese, and American classrooms. *New Directions for Child and Adolescent Development* 41: 27–54.

Stixrud, W., and Johnson, N. (2019). *The Self-Driven Child: The Science and Sense of Giving Your Kids More Control over Their Lives.* Penguin.

Stoll, L., Bolam, R., McMahon, A., Wallace, M., and Thomas, S. (2006). Professional learning communities: A review of the literature. *Journal of Educational Change* 7(4): 221–258.

Swanson, K. (2014). Edcamp: Teachers take back professional development. *Educational Leadership* 71(8): 36–40.

Tabibnia, G., Satpute, A.B., and Lieberman, M.D. (2008). The sunny side of fairness: Preference for fairness activates reward circuitry (and disregarding unfairness activates self-control circuitry). *Psychological Science* 19(4): 339–347.

Taylor, C. (2005). *Walking the Talk.* London: Random House Business.

Terenzini, P.T. (2020). Rethinking effective student learning experiences. *Inside Higher Education*. Retrieved from https://www.insidehighered.com/advice/2020/07/29/six-characteristics-promote-student-learning-opinion.

Thomas, D., and Brown, J.S. (2011). A new culture of learning. *Issue Eleven* September 2014, 10(11).

Thomas, K., and Velthouse, B.A. (1990). Cognitive elements of empowerment: An "interpretive" model of intrinsic task motivation. *Academy of Management Review* 15(4): 666–681.

Thompson, A.G. (1992). Teachers' beliefs and conceptions: A synthesis of research. In: *Handbook of Research on Mathematics Teaching and Learning* (ed. D.A. Grouws), 127–146. New York: MacMillan Publishing Company.

Thompson, T. (2010). Are you scaffolding or rescuing? Retrieved February, 12, 2016.

Thoreau, H.D. (1862). Autumnal tints. *The Atlantic Monthly* October, 385–402.

Tiersma, J. (2021). The value of mailing encouraging notes to students. Retrieved from https://www.edutopia.org/article/value-mailing-encouraging-notes-students.

Tishman, S. (1994). What makes a good thinker? A look at thinking dispositions. *Education Alumni Bulletin* 39(1): 7–9.

Tishman, S., Perkins, D.N., and Jay, E. (1995). *The Thinking Classroom: Learning and Teaching in a Culture of Thinking*. Needham Heights: Allyn and Bacon.

Tomlinson, C.A. (2001). *How to Differentiate Instruction in Mixed-Ability Classrooms*. ASCD.

Tough, P. (2012). *How Children Succeed: Grit, Curiosity, and the Hidden Power of Character*. Boston: Houghton Mifflin Harcourt.

Toyani, C. (2015). Let's Switch Questioning Around. *Educational Leadership* 73(1): 30–35.

Tyack, D., and Cuban, L. (1995). Why the grammar of schooling persists. *Tinkering toward Utopia*, 85–109.

UQx. (2017). LEARNx deep learning through transformative pedagogy. *LEARNx*. Retrieved from https://granite.pressbooks.pub/teachingdiverselearners/chapter/surface-and-deep-learning-2/.

Van Boxtel, C., van der Linden, J., Roelofs, E., and Erkens, G. (2002). Collaborative concept mapping: Provoking and supporting meaningful discourse. *Theory into Practice* 41(1): 40–46.

Van Rossum, E.J., and Schenk, S.M. (1984). The relationship between learning conception, study strategy and learning outcome. *British Journal of Educational Psychology* 54(1): 73–83.

Van Zee, E., and Minstrell, J. (1997). Using questioning to guide student thinking. *The Journal of the Learning Sciences* 6(2): 227–269.

Vedantam, S., Cohen, R., Boyle, T. (2019). What's not on the test: The overlooked factors that determine success. Retrieved from https://www.npr.org/2019/05/09/721733303/whats-not-on-the-test-the-overlooked-factors-that-determine-success.

Vermunt, J.D., and Verloop, N. (1999). Congruence and friction between learning and teaching. *Learning and Instruction* 9(3): 257–280.

Vescio, V., Ross, D., and Adams, A. (2008). A review of research on the impact of professional learning communities on teaching practice and student learning. *Teaching and Teacher Education* 24(1): 80–91.

Visible-Learning. (2019). Visible Learning 250+ influence on student achievement. In: visible-learningplus.com. Corwin.

Vogler, K.E. (2008). Asking good questions. *Educational Leadership* 65(9).

Vrugt, A., and Oort, F.J. (2008). Metacognition, achievement goals, study strategies and academic achievement: Pathways to achievement. *Metacognition and Learning* 3(2): 123–146.

Vygotsky, L.S. (1978). *Mind in Society*. Cambridge, MA: Harvard University Press.

Waack, S. (2014). Hattie Ranking: 252 influences and effect sizes related to student achievement. Retrieved from https://visible-learning.org/hattie-ranking-influences-effect-sizes-learning-achievement/.

Walton, G.M., and Cohen, G.L. (2007). A question of belonging: Race, social fit, and achievement. *Journal of Personality and Social Psychology* 92(1): 82.

Webb, N.L. (2002). Depth-of-knowledge levels for four content areas. *Language Arts* 28, March.

Webb, N.M., and Palincsar, A.S. (1996). *Group Processes in the Classroom*. Prentice Hall International.

Webb, R.B., and Ashton, P.T. (1986). Teacher motivation and the conditions of teaching: A call for ecological reform. *Journal of Thought*, 43–60.

Wei, R.C., Darling-Hammond, L., Andree, A., Richardson, N., and Orphanos, S. (2009). Professional learning in the learning profession: A status report on teacher development in the US and abroad. *Technical Report*. National Staff Development Council.

Weikart, D.P., and Schweinhart, L.J. (1997). *High/Scope Perry Preschool Program*.

Weil, L.G., Fleming, S.M., Dumontheil, I., Kilford, E.J., Weil, R.S., Rees, G., . . . Blakemore, S.-J. (2013). The development of metacognitive ability in adolescence. *Consciousness and Cognition* 22(1): 264–271.

Wentzel, K.R., and Caldwell, K. (1997). Friendships, peer acceptance, and group membership: Relations to academic achievement in middle school. *Child Development*, 1198–1209.

Wiliam, D. (2009). *Dylan Wiliam, Content Then Process: Teacher learning communities in the service of formative assessment.* Solution Tree.

Wiliam, D. (2014). Is the feedback you're giving students helping or hindering? Retrieved from https://www.dylanwiliamcenter.com/is-the-feedback-you-are-giving-students-helping-or-hindering/.

Wilson, J., and Clarke, D. (2004). Towards the modelling of mathematical metacognition. *Mathematics Education Research Journal* 16(2): 25–48.

Wilson, T. (2021). What to say instead of "I'm proud of you." Retrieved from https://www.edutopia.org/article/what-say-instead-im-proud-you.

Wing, E.A., Burles, F., Ryan, J.D., and Gilboa, A. (2022). The structure of prior knowledge enhances memory in experts by reducing interference. *Proceedings of the National Academy of Sciences* 119(26): e2204172119.

Wirebring, L.K., Lithner, J., Jonsson, B., Liljekvist, Y., Norqvist, M., and Nyberg, L. (2015). Learning mathematics without a suggested solution method: Durable effects on performance and brain activity. *Trends in Neuroscience and Education* 4(1–2): 6–14.

Wise, W., and Littlefield, C. (2017). *Ask Powerful Questions: Create Conversations That Matter.* We and Me, Inc.

Wiske, M.S. (Ed.) (1997). *Teaching for Understanding.* San Francisco: Jossey-Bass.

Wolf, D. (1987). The art of questioning. *Academic Connections*, 1–7.

Wolpert-Gawron, H. (2018). What giving students choice looks like in the classroom. *KQED Mindshift Blog.*

World Economic Forum (2020). *Schools of the Future: Defining New Models of Education for the Fourth Industrial Revolution* (Ref 09012020). Retrieved from https://www3.weforum.org/docs/WEF_Schools_of_the_Future_Report_2019.pdf.

Yazzie-Mintz, E. (2007). Voices of students on engagement: A report on the 2006 high school survey of student engagement. Center for Evaluation and Education Policy, Indiana University.

Yu, S., and Zhao, X. (2021). The negative impact of bullying victimization on academic literacy and social integration: Evidence from 51 countries in PISA. *Social Sciences & Humanities Open* 4(1). Retrieved from https://doi.org/10.1016/j.ssaho.2021.100151.

Yuan, K., and Le, V. (2012). Estimating the percentage of students who were exposed to deeper learning on the state achievement tests. Santa Monica, CA: Rand. Retrieved from https://hewlett.org/wp-content/uploads/2016/08/Estimating_Percentage_Students_Tested_on_Cognitively_Demanding_Items_Through_the_State_Achievement_Tests_RAND_3_2012.pdf.

Yuan, K., and Le, V.-N. (2014). Measuring deeper learning through cognitively demanding test items: Results from the analysis of six national and international exams. Research Report. *RAND Corporation.*

Zak, P.J. (2014). Why your brain loves good storytelling. *Harvard Business Review*, 28: 1–5.

Zak, P. (2017). *Trust Factor: The Science of Creating High-Performance Companies.* Amacom.

Zeiser, K., Taylor, J., Rickles, J., Garet, M., and Segeritz, M. (2014). Findings from the study of deeper learning: Opportunities and outcomes. *American Institutes for Research.* Retrieved December 16, 2014.

Zeiser, K.L., Taylor, J., Rickles, J., Garet, M.S., and Segeritz, M. (2014). Evidence of deeper learning outcomes. Findings from the study of deeper learning opportunities and outcomes: Report 3. *American Institutes for Research.*

Zenger, J., and Folkman, J. (2016). What great listeners actually do. *Harvard Business Review,* 14.

Zhao, Y. (2012). *World Class Learners: Educating Creative and Entrepreneurial Students.* Corwin Press.

INDEX

Dispositions
    assessing, 36–37
    definition of, 31
    development, 34–35
    as an entitlement, 43
    four-part nature, 42, 46
    lists of, 32
    as routine behavior, 48
    success dispositions, 41–42
Documentation
    as collective memory, 240
    and community building, 47
    an making thinking visible, 224, 225, 254
    and messaging, 269
    and metacognition, 44
    sharing, 138, 239
    usage, 130, 207, 232, 240
Duke's Center for Cognitive Neuroscience, 32

E

Efficacy
    assessing, 136
    developing, 59, 63, 128, 163, 170, 215
    and relationships, 80
Effective communication, as a quality of opportunities, 202, 203f, 216–216
Eisner, Eliot, 193, 199, 201
Elmore, Richard, 199
Empowered learners, 57
    constructing a vision of, 61, 62
Empowerment
    components of, 205
    cultivating in first grade, 63
    as an emergent characteristics, 203
    and thinking, 204
Enculturation
    explained, 35
    process of, 34–35, 38
    role of in dispositional development, 32, 40
Engaged learners, 57t
    constructing a vision of, 61, 62
    and demanding tasks, 155
    and discussion, 139
    invest in learning, 203
    in joyful purpose, 129

    naming and noticing of, 72
    promoting, 116, 191
    rarity of, 200, 204
Engel, Susan, 178
Environment, cultures force of, xxix, 12, 24, 44, 48, 53, 70, 91, 138, 166, 193, 230, 236, 239, 240, 259
Equity Maps, usage, 67
Evaluation
    of Chicago Public Schools, 202
    of Deeper Learning Network of schools, 201
    in the Design Cycle, 11f, 248f
    done too soon, 38
    of group learning, 239
    and metacognition, 226
    and Satellite data, xxvii
    in science, 156
    and Snapshot Observations, 21, 251
    of successful teaching practices, 137
    teachers' fear of, 21
Exit ticket (prompt), 41, 112, 162
Expectations
    around visibility, 259
    cultural force of, xxix, 21, 24, 43, 53, 70–72, 138, 238, 251, 252
    warm demander and, 80
Experience Struggles-Puzzles-Insights (ESP+1) routine, 169
Expertise
    distributed, 126
    enhancement, 224, 227–228
    and practice, 102
    in teaching, 153, 199
    that students bring, 77, 143
Exploratory talk, 6, 23, 256
Explicit
    attention to thinking, 101, 114, 116–117
    goals, 41
    modeling, 141
    teaching, 69
Externalization
    of dispositions, 42, 43
    of ideas through writing, 231
    and sociocultural perspective, 125
    of thinking through talk, 102, 168, 226, 237

I

IB Learner Profile, 32
Ice cream cone conversations, 141
Ideal student, constructions, 60
Identity
    development, 69, 72, 205
    gender, 91
In the Lake of the Woods (O'Brien), 131–132
In This Class survey, 112–113
Incidental learning, 101
Independence, student/learner, 63, 69, 70, 116,
    193, 223, 226
Informational conversations, shift, 19
Informational learning, xxi, 3, 4, 247, 255
    transformational learning, contrast, xxi, 3,
    4, 247
Initiative,
    developing, 59, 161
    noticing and naming, 157
Innovation
    encouragement, 20, 23, 24
    importance, 7
Inquirers
    becoming, 193
    teachers as, 10, 13
Inquiry
    case study, 208–209
    communities of, 4–6, 13, 22
    curiosity as basis for, 32, 33
    design cycle, 10, 11f, 247
    learning, xxiv
    listening, 59
    meaningful, 202, 215, 216
    questions, 109, 176, 179, 187, 189, 193
    transformative power, 6–7
Inquiry-based talk, 6, 22–24, 194, 256–257
Insights and Questions (IQ) routine, 208
Institutional mirroring, 3, 5, 7–8
"Instructional Rounds," 199
Intelligence, distributed, 240
Intellectual development, 127, 246
Intellectual Virtues, 32
Intention
    learning, 218
    questioning and, 176, 180, 190, 195

teaching with, 37
Interaction analysis, 88–89
Interactions, cultural force of, xxix, 23, 44, 45, 53, 70–72,
    89, 90, 92, 139–141, 143, 163, 168, 188,
    190, 238, 242
International Academy, 22
Irving, Stephen, 199

K

Keene, Ellin, 242
Keep, Benjamin, 166
Keep-thinking questions, 187, 193
Knollwood School, 157
Knowledge gap, leading to questions, 178
Kohn, Alfie, 32
Koretz, Daniel, 223
Kullberg, Kristen, 83–84, 117

L

Ladder of Feedback, 23, 141, 143, 144f, 217
Lampert, Magdalene, 200
Landvogt, Julie, xvi, 245
Language, 47
    absolute versus conditional, 6, 47, 167, 190
    analysis, 89, 236
    body, 88
    common professional, 11, 13, 21, 22, 24, 251
    cultural force of, xxix, 22–24, 44, 45, 47, 48, 53, 71,
    72, 89, 93–95, 116, 140, 142, 166, 169
    development, 19, 37, 38, 59, 102, 127, 142, 166
    disciplinary, 201, 202, 214
    of feedback, 140
    home, 85
    of learning and thinking, 116, 117, 157, 226, 236
    of listening, 140
    of praise, 165
    usage, 22
Latin School, 230
Lawless, Ben, 117
Leaderless Discussion routine, 143, 192
Leaders
    assumptions, 3, 33
    Golden Circle, and xxii
    as learners, 5, 11
    reflections for, 14–15, 38